PREVIOUSLY PUBLISHED IN THIS SERIES

Educational Foundations of the Jesuits in Sixteenth-Century New Spain
By Jerome V. Jacobsen, S.J., Ph.D.

Pioneer Black Robes on the West Coast
By Peter Masten Dunne, S.J., Ph.D.

PIONEER JESUITS IN NORTHERN MEXICO

A RELIC OF EARLY DAYS AT PARRAS

Pioneer Jesuits
in Northern Mexico

✠

By Peter Masten Dunne, S.J.

University of California Press
Berkeley and Los Angeles · 1944

UNIVERSITY OF CALIFORNIA PRESS
BERKELEY AND LOS ANGELES
CALIFORNIA

CAMBRIDGE UNIVERSITY PRESS
LONDON, ENGLAND

COPYRIGHT, 1944, BY
THE REGENTS OF THE UNIVERSITY OF CALIFORNIA

TO
HERBERT EUGENE BOLTON
INSPIRER OF
THIS SERIES OF STUDIES
HISTORIAN AND ASSIDUOUS COLLECTOR OF
HISTORICAL DOCUMENTS

EDITOR'S PREFACE

THE THIRD VOLUME *in a series devoted to the activities of the Jesuits in Spanish North America, this work is the logical successor of Jacobsen's* Educational Foundations of the Jesuits in Sixteenth-Century New Spain *and Dunne's* Pioneer Black Robes on the West Coast, *two books which have met a flattering reception and have done much toward enlarging the perspective of Western Hemisphere history in one of its important phases. Other volumes in the same series are already prepared and, it is hoped, will be published without undue delay.*

Some books are called "scholarly" because they are unfinished. The staging and debris accumulated in the process of constructing the edifice have not been cleared away. This volume meets a higher test of scholarship. The result of the author's assiduous research in manuscripts, printed documents, and monographs; of his personal reconnaissance of the terrain concerned; and of his sound knowledge of Jesuit history and institutions which it exemplifies—the finished product is freed from a parade of apparatus and is presented in a form acceptable to the general reader as well as to the specialist.

The editor of a series of volumes should blush to find one of them dedicated to himself, and this I appropriately do; yet I have no disposition to remedy the impropriety. On the contrary, I gratefully accept the generous tribute from a friend and fellow worker, and let it stand where, without consulting me, it was put by the author.

HERBERT E. BOLTON

Berkeley, July 20, 1944.

AUTHOR'S PREFACE

THIS VOLUME *continues the historical narrative told in the author's Pioneer Black Robes on the West Coast, a detailed account of the mission system along the Pacific shore of North America, a story of hardship endured and adventures hazarded by Jesuit padres for the Christianization of the native Indian. In its full content that story had not yet been made available in English. The missions became famous in the colonial history of North America and ultimately extended from Sinaloa in western Mexico to San Francisco Bay in California. Begun in 1591, the mission chain was carried on up the coast for a century and three-quarters. The Jesuits were then expelled and their place was taken by Franciscans, who, beginning in 1769, began the forging of new links of the chain and carried the missions up into Alta California.*

The present volume deals with the same mission chain, narrating the early adventures and hardships of another group, those who founded missions a little farther east, in and beyond the great mountain system called the Sierra Madre Occidental. What Fathers Tapia and Pérez accomplished on the coast in the 1590's, Ramírez and Espinosa effected, during the same decade, to the eastward, in the present Mexican states of Durango and Coahuila. This part of the mission story has not before been delivered in its detail to English-speaking readers; yet it contributed its own influence to the march of civilization north toward what is now the United States. And this, too, is a tale of adventure, its pages reddened with the blood of martyrdom. There was attempted, on the scene of this history, in 1616, an Indian rebellion which threatened ruin to the entire Jesuit undertaking; the detailed account of it comprises the central chapters of this book. The story is carried on to the 1630's, when stability and prosperity had long been restored, and when the missionary fathers were beginning to reach again farther north into the Tarahumar country.

The author owes gratitude to many persons. Old Jesuit letter writers, God bless them, reporting to their superiors, have supplied to history the indispensable documents. Old Jesuit historians and publicists have bequeathed books of which all praisers of good and brave men will always be proud. Among friends, confreres, and colleagues many could be singled out for thanks, Dr. Herbert E. Bolton most of all; for it was he who conceived this series in the beginning and who has since been its faithful promoter as well as its historical editor. Besides, the great collection of copies of Jesuit documents which he has procured has contributed vastly to whatever value this volume may possess and has put all future historians of this field in his debt. Jesuit superiors have been encouraging and appreciative. The staffs of the Bancroft Library at the University of California and of the Archivo Nacional in Mexico City have been, as is their wont, most courteous and helpful. Confreres in Mexico have delightfully contributed to the author's travels over the regions of old-time missionary endeavor. And finally the author wishes to thank those who at the expense of much time and labor have gone over and over the manuscript and who have so carefully prepared the index.

P. M. D.

Department of History,
University of San Francisco
July 1, 1944.

CONTENTS

CHAPTER	PAGE
I. The Coming of the Black Robe	1
II. The Permanent Missions	7
III. East of the Mountains	14
IV. The Missions of the Lagoon	20
V. The Tepehuanes	32
VI. The Heart of the Sierra	45
VII. A Mountain Revolt	56
VIII. Success amid Hardships	65
IX. The Laguneros Won Over	74
X. North into the Mountains	87
XI. Urdiñola Subdues the Xiximes	97
XII. Floods, Plagues, and Devils	109
XIII. Distant Rumblings	118
XIV. The Storm Breaks	126
XV. The Nations Stir	135
XVI. The Governor Rides Forth	143
XVII. The Death of Cogoxito	153
XVIII. Reconciliation and Reconstruction	166
XIX. New Nations	176
Epilogue	185
Appendix	187
Essay on Sources	189
Bibliography	193
Notes	201
Index	219

ILLUSTRATIONS

	PAGE
A Relic of Early Days at Parras	*Frontispiece*
Hernando de Santarén	*Facing* 114
Hernando de Tovar	" 114
Gerónimo de Moranta	" 115
Juan Fonte	" 115
Luis de Alabez	" 130
Juan del Valle	" 130
Diego de Orozco	" 131
Bernardo de Cisneros	" 131

[The portraits are from the Jesuit gallery of portraits in Rome. The originals were sent from Mexico to Rome, and were contemporaneous with the martyrdoms.]

MAP

Jesuit Missions in Mountain and Plain, 1593–1640 . . . . *Following* 228

Chapter I

THE COMING OF THE BLACK ROBE

URING THE YEARS when Ignatius Loyola was maturing plans for the organization and spirit of his religious order, a thought uppermost in his mind was the preaching of Catholicism to the heathen in far-off lands. And from 1534, when his first companions pronounced their vows, to 1540, when the society was officially recognized in Rome, the same intention prevailed.

Francis Xavier sailed from Lisbon in April, 1541, bound for the Indies of the East, where the Portuguese had flung a thriving empire over the coasts and islands of the Indian Ocean. Xavier's success in baptizing thousands of souls resounded over the nations of Europe and he became the prototype of the apostle of modern times. By 1552, the year of his death, he had begun the Christianization of Japan and had gazed from the Isle of Sancian upon the coasts of China. Before that decade was over the Jesuits Méndez and Vállez were martyred on the coasts of southern India, Baretto and two companions had been sent to Abyssinia, and John Bayra was laboring in Ceylon. Islands farther east were reached as speedily; the coast of Celebes heard the preaching of Magallanes, and the soil of Amboyna received Ribiera's blood. The Congo was penetrated in 1553 and China in 1556.

Portugal's great rival, Spain, was spreading a still vaster empire over the Indies of the West, and by the time the Jesuit Order was founded she had performed and was still performing fabulous feats of exploration and was becoming a colossus of colonization. The islands of the Caribbean; Mexico, Peru, Chile, and La Plata; the Tierra Firme of the Spanish Main—these were already on their way to power and wealth.

One would not expect, in view of the Jesuit missionary activities in the East, that the new lands of the West, the recently discovered Americas, would long remain without invasion by this new missionary force born within the Church. The first Jesuits to set foot on American soil were Portuguese. They made part of Portugal's first large and successful effort to place the settlement of Brazil upon a permanent and organized basis. The royal colonies of Portugal were called *capitaneas*, and the first was founded in 1549 by Thomé de Sousa, "one of the great men of colonial Brazil," who sailed from Lisbon with approximately a thousand souls. Some of these venturers were criminals under sentence of deportation, others were judges, still others were Jesuits; most of them were soldiers and other settlers. The Jesuits, seven in number, were headed by a really great man, Father Manoel de Nóbrega. In 1553 came Father José de Anchieta, Nóbrega's most famous subject. Missions were begun north of Bahia, the settlement organized by Sousa. These two Jesuits carved their names deep in the history of the beginnings of Brazil and inaugurated in the Americas a missionary system that still stands unrivaled in the story of modern civilization.[1]

A decade before Portugal's successful efforts in the east of South America the Pizarro brothers in the west were conquering Peru for Spain. By the year the Jesuits landed in Brazil, Peru already had a history that rang with arms and was dyed in blood. The leaders had quarreled, Francisco Pizarro had been assassinated, Gonzalo had rebelled against the authority of Charles V, and La Gasca had sailed from Spain to stamp out the revolt. It was not until almost two decades after all this and after the death of the Emperor Charles, first of the name as King of Spain, that his son Philip II asked Francis Borgia, General of the Jesuits, for men for Peru. Eight were granted, four fathers and four brothers, led by Gerónimo Ruiz del Portillo as Provincial of the Province of Peru. They sailed from Spain in November, 1567, and arrived in Lima the following spring.[2]

North America received its first Jesuits the year before the Peruvian venture, and Florida became the first stage—and a tragic one—upon which their drama was enacted. The French Huguenot, Laudonnière, in 1564 had settled with a colony on the St. Johns River in Florida, and had built a blockhouse which he called Fort Caroline in honor of the boy king, Charles IX. The colony was strengthened by Jean Ribaut, who bore instructions to take up a position to the south whence he could pounce upon Spanish treasure ships from Mexico, heavy with bars of silver and gold. The route to Spain lay north of Cuba through what the Spaniards called, as on the old Spanish maps, Canal de

---

[1] For notes to chapter i see page 201.

COMING OF THE BLACK ROBE 3

Bahama. From Florida, then, the French could harass and possibly capture the coveted galleons of Spain, laden with the sinews of war for the European quarrels of Philip II. The French settlement must be destroyed. There was a man at hand who was among the strongest of his type. Don Pedro Menéndez de Avilés, Spain's first captain of the seas, was commissioned by King Philip to oust the enemy and was created *adelantado* or governor of Florida. He achieved his purpose completely and ruthlessly. The French were surprised and defeated in 1565 and St. Augustine was founded. In order to hold the coast it was necessary to establish settlements and the best way to secure settlements was through missions. Therefore it was that on May 3, 1566, Philip II wrote to Francis Borgia asking that twenty-four Jesuits be sent for the evangelization of his province of Florida.[3]

The failures and tragedies of the Jesuit Florida missions have of late years become more widely known.[4] It has recently been told how, of the first three Jesuits who came to the coast of Florida in December, 1566, Father Martínez was slain by savages even before the mission was begun; how others followed, headed by Father Segura, who with seven of his brethren founded the mission of Santa María in what the Spaniards called Axacán, on the shores of Chesapeake Bay, and how all these were slain early in 1571 by savages on the banks of the Rappahannock.[5]

The tragedy of the "martyrs of the Rappahannock" discouraged further Jesuit efforts on these inhospitable coasts. Two years later, Franciscan Fathers came to Florida. They founded missions which were to have a long and interesting history, leaving relics that still molder on the mainland and on the islands that fringe the shore. Other and more fertile fields were calling for the Jesuits.

Loyola, before he went to France to complete his studies at the University of Paris, had gathered around him, in Spain, men who were animated with a religious enthusiasm similar to his own. They fell away, however, when their leader went to Paris. Two of them found their way to America. One, Calixto Sá, became a merchant and sought gold by barter in the towns of Mexico and the Spanish Main. The other, Juan de Arteaga, became a churchman, and at the time of which we are speaking was about to take over the bishopric of Chiapa, south and east of Mexico. He was accidentally poisoned before he could reach his see, but during his residence in Mexico City he had spread abroad the fame of Loyola's men.[6] Other bishops came to desire the service of the Jesuits, among them the Augustinian Agustín de la Coruña, who held the see of Popayán, and Don Vasco de Quiroga, Bishop of Michoacán. The latter took definite steps toward bringing in the Jesuits. But his efforts came to naught. Loyola died in 1556, and when the Bishop went to Spain to negotiate with Loyola's successor, Lainez, the four Jesuits given him fell so ill at San Lúcar that he had to return without them. Soon he himself passed away.[7]

The following decade, things fell out with better fortune. In 1568 a wealthy cavalier, Don Alonso de Villaseca, put 2,000 ducats at the disposal of the Jesuit authorities in Spain to defray the expenses of sending some of the fathers to Mexico. Then the leading men of Mexico City, both in church and state, sent a petition to King Philip II asking that he take steps to expedite the sending of the Jesuits. The Viceroy, Martín Enríques de Almanza, wrote to the King; the Supreme Inquisitor, Don Pedro Moya de Contreras, wrote; so did the royal *audiencia* or supreme judges, the *alcalde* or local judge, and many other private persons, including Don Alonso de Villaseca. These letters reached Philip just after he had received communications from equally powerful persons in Lima expressing their appreciation for the arrival there of the Jesuit Fathers.

On March 1, 1571, the King wrote to Father Manuel López, Provincial of Castile, asking for twelve of his men for New Spain. They must be men of letters and of solid parts, said the King. Father López replied that this request could only be granted by the Jesuit General. The King therefore wrote forthwith to Francis Borgia, successor to Lainez. The request was granted since the men were available. They were to be taken, directed Borgia, from the three different provinces of Spain and to have Father Pedro Sánchez, a doctor of the University of Alcalá, at their head as Provincial. The group was to sail with the flotilla leaving Spain in the summer of 1571.[8]

But there were often difficulties and delays to retard venturers about to sail the seas. A century later, in the summer of 1678, a ship carrying a group of Jesuits from Genoa to Cádiz was beaten back three times from before the Strait of Gibraltar, so that they missed by two days the flotilla on which they were supposed to have taken passage. They had to wait in Spain for *two years* before another fleet should sail direct to the Indies. But, alas, in making its way out of the harbor the ship which carried the padres grounded on a rock. The captains of other ships in the *flota* consented to take some members of the group, but others were left behind for still another year. Father Kino was one of those disappointed; Father Joseph Neumann, famous in the Tarahumar mission, was one of those taken on.[9]

So, in 1571, Father Pedro Sánchez and his band were long delayed. Sánchez had gone to the court to pay his respects to the King before embarking with his group. These were to await him in Seville. He got in too late. The very day he arrived in Seville the fleet on which he and his missionaries were to have sailed slid out from San Lúcar without them. It meant a year's delay. But this proved a blessing, for the fleet of 1571 was wrecked by a storm off the coast of Mexico and all on board perished.[10]

Changes were made in the meantime. Some missionaries were withdrawn; but more were added, so that, when the year of waiting had passed, Pedro Sánchez found himself at the head of a group of fifteen instead of twelve. The day for embarkation finally arrived. It was the Feast of St. Anthony, the 13th of June, 1572. Persons of moment accompanied the fathers to the shore, among them being the Dukes of Medina and Sidonia. Two ships received the Jesuits.

In five days they were at the Canaries. A rest here of three days, and they put out across the broad Atlantic. The journey required close to three months, for it was September 9 when the fleet nosed into the harbor of Vera Cruz, the only port of Mexico on the east.

The Jesuits were expected and were recived with a warm and honorable welcome. Father Antonio Sedeño, one of the Florida group who had escaped martyrdom and had been working in Havana, had been ordered to Mexico to prepare for their arrival. At Vera Cruz the governor with his staff, the clergy, and the elite of the town came out to receive the fathers and accompany them to their lodgings. The commissary of the Inquisition wanted to provide the travelers with every comfort for their journey to the capital. They refused, however, wishing to travel, according to their rule, as poor men. They hired mules, and traveled in religious simplicity.

On September 18 the Jesuits set out along the historic route of Cortés for Mexico City, mounting up to the heights of the great central plateau and passing through the beautiful city of Puebla which rests in a valley two miles above the sea. This gem of a city is guarded on the west by its giant peaks, Iztaccihuatl and Popocatepetl, which are draped in everlasting snow. Far to the east Orizaba's lavender cone points to heaven. Passing to the north of the volcanoes over a divide, the fathers descended into the broad plain of Mexico City, which was to be the heart of their operations for two centuries of labor for the good of men.

The following years saw a marvelous development of Jesuit activity and a rapid spread of residences and colleges. The very year of arrival, the Indians of Tacuba—which is now a suburb of the city—were busy building a church for the fathers, and the following year saw the foundation of San Pedro y San Pablo, the first Jesuit college in North America, which was destined to have a long and honorable career. This same year, 1573, Father Juan Curiel was sent to Pátzcuaro to found a residence, which later developed into a college. Juan Sánchez and Hernando Suárez de la Concha were sent to Guadalajara; then north to Zacatecas and south to Oaxaca. Colleges were founded at Guadalajara, Valladolid (now Morelia), and Puebla; a residence was established at Vera Cruz and a foundation at Tepotzotlán, near Mexico City, which later developed into the novitiate for the spiritual formation of the young Jesuits.[11] All this expansion took place before the Jesuits were a decade in the land. It became evident to all in the capital that these men were going to have a large and fertile field for their activities. History has confirmed the prophetic thoughts of those who witnessed the initial success.

Chapter II

THE PERMANENT MISSIONS

THE DECADES which followed the coming of the Jesuits to Mexico were the most glorious of the Society of Jesus. The sway of Claudius Aquaviva, fifth General of the Order, who held the reins of government from 1581 to 1615, has often been called the golden age of the Society. Mutius Vitelleschi, another great Italian, took up the charge of government following upon Aquaviva and ruled efficaciously until 1645. Indeed, the whole century from 1545 to 1645 may well be called for the Society of Jesus a golden age.

Before Aquaviva's time, in July, 1570, a group of seventy Portuguese Jesuit missionaries sailed for Brazil in several ships, part of a flotilla, since safety was found in numbers against the prowling sea dogs of the English and the French. A galleon that carried five hundred colonists was overtaken on July 14 by the fiercest of French sea dogs, Jacques de Soria, a militant Calvinist,[1] who for fifteen years had been the terror of the Spanish seas. Forty Jesuits were among those on board. Not one escaped. With their leader, Ignatius Azevedo, they were slashed with the pirate's broadsword and pierced with his dagger, and their bodies were flung overboard to redden the sea. Another group of Jesuits escaped, only to be tossed by a storm upon the islands of Santo Domingo and Cuba. On their way from Havana to Brazil fourteen of these were on board a ship which was captured by a fleet of English and French corsairs. Three were shot, the rest thrown into the sea. Two swam to another boat, but then were taken by the enemy.[2]

This was the very year, 1571, of the martyrdoms of Florida. Japan in 1573 had eight missionaries; six years later it had twenty-nine.[3] In 1581 the Jesuits entered the Philippines from Mexico, and reports of 1595 show that already thirteen residences or missions were in operation there, including two colleges.[4] In 1583 Rudolph Aquaviva, nephew of the ruling General, was killed for the Faith with four companions on the island of Salsette just off the west coast of India.[5] But the

---
[1] For notes to chapter ii see page 201.

blood of these martyrs was not spilled in vain, for within the five succeeding years, 3,800 natives were baptized on the island.[6] In 1588 the first Jesuits entered Paraguay, the field destined to produce the most successful missions in all history.[7] In Japan, by 1589, baptisms numbered 11,500. This same year the Society established two residences in China.[8] Golden years, then, may well be spoken of by the historian, for not only were there brilliant successes at home, but the work went on also in the mission field in countries far from the European homeland and on the islands that sprinkled all the seas. Mexico, or New Spain, was a field of struggle and achievement in this world-wide campaign.

When the fathers left for Mexico in 1572, they were probably looked upon as missionaries. Historians of today speak of them certainly as such. Yet it seems hardly correct to give all of them in Mexico, or even in Peru, this unqualified appellation. Mexico City, when the Jesuits arrived, was already a wealthy and well-organized town, having known the rule of a viceroy since 1535 and having enjoyed the prestige of a university since 1551. It had its elite, its governing class, its wealthy miners and merchants. The year after their arrival the Jesuits would inaugurate their college. Its rector, Diego López, had been named by Francis Borgia even before the departure from Spain. They would not all be missionaries, then; many of these men were destined for the lecture hall and the pulpit.

As a matter of fact, the real missions, missions among the savage Indians—*entre infieles,* as the Spaniards called them,—were not to be begun until 1591. Missions, to be sure, were preached before that time in centers and among groups already civilized and within the fold of the Church. Thus in 1582 the traveling Jesuit missionary appeared in Guatemala, Zamora, and Guanajuato to preach the passing mission.

We begin to touch the permanent missions among the savages in a heroic figure, just recently become known to fame.[9] Gonzalo de Tapia, sprung from an old and noble line, was born in León, Spain, in 1561. At sixteen he entered the Jesuit novitiate at Medina del Campo, and in the progress of his spiritual and intellectual formation he developed a vocation for missionary life. He applied for the missions and was accepted. This fact was big with importance for the history of the West; from it sprang the development of the West Coast missions, the

PERMANENT MISSIONS

march of Spain's frontier northward into what is now the United States, and ultimately the development of the California coast to San Francisco with its missions and its Spanish background. Tapia was a forerunner of Kino and Salvatierra, of Serra and Lasuén.

Twelve years after the first band of Jesuits sailed for Mexico, a group of twenty-three arrived at the port of Vera Cruz. They sailed from Cádiz, June 25, 1584, and Gonzalo de Tapia was among them. Not yet ordained a priest, Gonzalo finished his spiritual formation in Mexico. His first work as a priest was at Pátzcuaro, where he labored among the Tarascan Indians. This was a sort of mild missionary activity, and did not satisfy the vaulting ambitions of the young apostle. The Tarascans were a docile race, and decades of Christianity had rendered them amenable to every Christian influence. Tapia wanted to work among the untamed savages, to risk his life in the wilderness amidst the warlike and naked Indians. His desires were soon to be satisfied. Just here we see the beginning of the permanent mission entre infieles.[10]

The United States of America had for many decades a frontier which marched westward over mountain and plain, and the fathers of that progress—men such as John Sevier and Daniel Boone, Meriwether Lewis and William Clark, Lieutenant Pike and Captain Frémont—will always be remembered in the annals of the Nation. New Spain long before this had an advancing frontier. And great names figure here, for the march of New Spain northward was rougher if slower than the march of America toward the west, and the names of her explorers and frontiersmen will never fade from her annals. Guzmán and Coronado and Oñate, Carbajal and Ibarra and Urdiñola—these were the men who helped to make the frontier history of New Spain. But that which gave permanence to the explorations and settlements was the mission among the savages, and of the missions of the West Coast Gonzalo de Tapia was the father. The Franciscans had long been in the field before the Jesuits came and had done noble work to the north and east, pushing on the frontier over mountain and plain. It was to fall out that the western coast with its rugged backbone of lofty sierra should be left to the Jesuits.

As with the far west of the United States, so with the north of Mexico, it was gold that speeded the onward march. By the time the Jesuits came, the frontier had taken great leaps ahead because of the northern mines, chiefly silver mines. San Luis Potosí, on a level with the present Tampico; Fresnillo, Sombrerete, Parras, Saltillo, and Santa Bárbara—these were the mining towns of the plains or on the fringe of the sierras; Guanaceví, Topia, San Andrés, and San Hipólito—these were the mines of the mountains.

The road which led from Mexico City through Querétaro to the northern towns was fraught with danger from wild tribes of Indians generically called by the Spaniards of that day Chichimecos.[11] The tribes could not be subdued by arms because of the roughness of the country and the roving habits of the Indians. The viceregal government at the capital devised what means it could for the protection of travelers. Military posts were established at intervals; soldiers accompanied the larger mine shipments; parties were grouped for protection, as in the caravans of the ancient desert; even armored wagons with towers on them were used—in vain. The "great north road" was still unsafe and the losses of every year discouraged the miners and the government.

The authorities—the viceroy, the audiencia, the governor of Guanajuato—came to see that the only way to subdue these tribes was to send missionaries to attempt with the cross what the sword was unable to accomplish. Franciscans had done some work with the Chichimecos and had met with some success; a Jesuit, Father Juan Ferro, had paid them a passing visit. But the time was now come to found some permanent missions among them. Gonzalo de Tapia was at hand. At two different periods, in 1585 and 1587, both before and after his tertianship,[12] he had labored, as we have seen, among the Tarascan Indians. He had made a name in and about Pátzcuaro for skill and success in dealing with the Indians. Now that an attempt was to be made toward taming the savages through the gospel, the governor of Guanajuato asked superiors for the services of Tapia, for it was along the northern border of this province that most of the trouble was occurring. The rector of the college at Pátzcuaro was willing, and the provincial approved. Tapia was to begin his missionary career among the savages.[13]

Father Tapia then went north from Pátzcuaro among the Chichimecos. He labored in the pueblos of Purbandiro, Yerepuato, Numanán, San Felipe, and others. He achieved complete success. From now on, if the wild tribes were tamed, if Spaniards could travel the "great north road" in security, if convoys and presidios of soldiers could be done away with, the success was in goodly measure due to Gonzalo de Tapia. He left upon the geography of the country and upon the history of the nation a permanent mark of his success in the settlement which he founded, become since a thriving town, San Luis de la Paz, its name a fit memorial to the taming of the Chichimecos.[14]

These first successes were enjoyed during the years 1588 and 1589. Meanwhile a companion had been given Tapia. This was Father Nicolás de Arnaya, destined to have a long and fruitful career among the Jesuits of New Spain. Together these two men rode farther north in 1589, this time to carry spiritual help and consolation to the Spaniards and Christian Indians of the mines of Zacatecas and Durango. At the latter place, then called usually Guadiana, a fine friendship was formed between the young apostle Tapia and the grizzled soldier, frontiersman, landowner, and cattleman, who now was governor of the province of Nueva Vizcaya. His name was Rodrigo del Río y Losa. The friendship was to have important results a year later. Tapia spoke to Río y Losa of his apostolic ambitions; the Governor encouraged him and indicated a virgin field for his endeavors, the province of Sinaloa on the western coast.

The following year, 1590, Tapia was ordered definitely to Zacatecas, and the early part of 1591 found him teaching an Indian school there. In the meantime the young priest had written to the General of the Order, Claudius Aquaviva, and had asked for a permanent mission career. There was as Jesuit Visitor in Mexico that year a superior of courage and vision, Diego de Avellaneda. The General in Rome wrote an encouraging reply to Tapia and wrote likewise to Avellaneda in Mexico City in favor of Tapia's request. Finally a definite and most important move was made, the mainspring of which was the Visitor: Tapia was ordered to put himself at the disposal of Río y Losa and with a companion to go to the district which the Governor should indicate for the founding of a permanent mission. Río y Losa, wishing to advance the frontier on the coast, indicated Sinaloa. Tapia, with his companion, Father Martín Pérez, set out accordingly for the west.[15]

On July 6 they arrived at the Río Sinaloa, and the great mission system of the western coast of North America had begun.[16] These foundations were slight at the start: two padres, a handful of neophytes. But

12   PIONEER JESUITS IN NORTHERN MEXICO

they advanced, they became great. Like the mustard seed, the mission system sprouted and spread beneficent branches afar. This organization made it possible for the frontier of Spain to push farther and farther north until it reached the very gates of Alta California. The missions advanced apace, spanning the rivers that fall from the Sierra Madre and crossing the valleys that lie between the hills. They passed west across the Gulf of California and began to ascend the coasts of the peninsula; they climbed farther north and pierced into the deserts of Arizona. Other missionaries followed Tapia and Pérez. When the Indians on the banks of the Sinaloa were Christianized, the fathers went to the banks of the Fuerte; and when this country was conquered for the Faith, they passed on to the Mayo and then to the Yaqui. The latter they reached in 1617 and followed up its stream to the Ópata and Pima Indians. They then passed on to the Río Sonora.

After a few decades the number of missionaries had increased to twenty-seven fathers and several brothers.[17] By 1631, just forty years after their first arrival in Sinaloa, the missionaries had baptized 151,240 Indians.[18] By 1654 the number of registered baptisms for the whole mission system amounted to 400,000.[19]

The missions of the coast were not the only establishments of the kind begun and carried on by the Spanish Jesuits of the sixteenth and seventeenth centuries. It is true that their finest successes were perhaps on the coast among its numerous and loyal nations from the Cáhitas at the south to the Pimas at the north. But in the Sierra Madre itself, which runs like a great backbone through Nueva Vizcaya, and on its eastern slopes, the Jesuits founded other and flourishing missions. The numbers baptized and civilized here help to make up the totals that we have just quoted. The missionaries went into the mountains of the Acaxée, Xixime, and Tepehuán nations; they went east into the plains and the tribes of the lagoon country; then finally they traveled north and west into the mountains of the Tarahumar nation, whence near the borders of Arizona they joined with the missions of the West Coast. It is a thrilling story. There was the great Tepehuán revolt that dyed red the soil of the eastern Sierra Madre and added eight Jesuit martyrs to the list of those who died that others might live. There were many smaller rebellions, marches and countermarches, plagues and floods, pueblos founded and Indians brought into the fold.

The story of the beginnings of the Mexican west coast missions has been told,[20] and the historian of the Franciscans of the west, Father Zephyrin Engelhardt, has given us the mission story of Lower California.[21] One of the fathers of Western history, Herbert E. Bolton, has described the marvelous work of Francisco Eusebio Kino.[22] The historian of the missions east of the Sierra Madre has a virgin field to cover and a tale of stirring adventure to tell from the first opening of the missions at Durango to the winning of the Hinas and Humis to the south and the opening of the Tarahumar country to the north.

Chapter III

EAST OF THE MOUNTAINS

IT WAS MINES, then, east of the mountains, that chiefly led the frontier north from Guadalajara and Guanajuato. And it was a toilsome advance. The great cordillera that reaches from the tip of Alaska to the tip of Chile elevates Mexico, not only into rugged mountain ranges and lofty peaks, but also into a great central plateau, cut here by ravines and blocked there by ranges which make the country rough when they do not make it savage. This plateau rises gradually from Chihuahua southward to Zacatecas, the latter being one of Mexico's loftiest cities, 8,010 feet above the level of the sea. From Zacatecas south, all the cities—Aguascalientes, Querétaro, Cuernavaca, Morelia—are lifted more than a mile above the ocean. Mexico City itself, surrounded by tall ranges and towering peaks, is 7,349 feet above sea level, and Toluca, a few miles to the west, is 488 feet higher than Zacatecas. The snow-draped peaks that guard the capital rise to almost 18,000 feet. When the frontier, therefore, began to travel north, it spread over high elevations until it reached Zacatecas, and then began gradually to descend.

Zacatecas sprang into being in 1548 when the near-by mines of San Bernabé, Pánuco, and San Benito were founded. Out of the soil, wealth was created overnight, and the pioneers Cristóbal de Oñate, Baltásar Temiño de Bañuelos, and Diego de Ibarra became the first millionaires of Mexico. With the miners seeking gold went the Franciscan friars seeking souls. Both miners and friars kept pressing north. In a series of explorations and prospecting ventures carried on from 1554 to 1562, Francisco de Ibarra, nephew of the millionaire, discovered the ore deposits of Fresnillo, San Martín, Sombrerete, and Nieves.

These were the days of a rush for gold and silver, and the roads were worn by fortune seekers. Reports of an iron mountain got abroad and the fever for gain carried men yet farther north.[1] Franciscans were still in the van, seeking out the Indians. Fray Gerónimo de Mendoza, reaching out into unexplored country from the mining camp of San

---

[1] For notes to chapter iii see pages 201–202.

Martín, had such success with the natives that in 1556 three of his confreres were sent to help with the work.

In 1563 Durango was founded and a new province, Nueva Vizcaya, was created to bound on the north that of Nueva Galicia. The prestige of Don Diego de Ibarra of Zacatecas was great, for with wealth he enjoyed high connections, his wife being the daughter of the Viceroy. Using his influence in favor of his nephew Francisco, he had him appointed governor of the new province, to which he himself gave a name, and at the end of 1563 Francisco founded Durango in the Valley of Guadiana, to be its capital.[2]

Francisco de Ibarra became one of the great explorers of the Mexican Northwest. In 1564 he marched, with one hundred and seventy picked men, from Zacatecas 250 miles north and west along the fringe of the Sierra Madre and then 50 miles west through the mountains, where the way led him along deep ravines and over savage ridges to the summits that girdle the vale of Topia. He descried from these heights a populous Indian village with fine houses; he hoped to find here another Mexico.[3] Obregón, the sixteenth-century chronicler, describes vividly the hardships of the mountain perils and the storming and taking of the Indian pueblo deep-set like a nugget in its frame of rugged mountains. "They passed over ranges of great altitude," he writes, "over numerous large mountains, cliffs, deep ravines, and ridges, unloading and reloading the cargoes of the packhorses. The latter very frequently fell because of the great roughness of the mountains." The Sierras de las Cruces was a region "surrounded and hemmed in by frightful cliffs, rocks, and terrible ravines." On this crossing of the sierra to Topia the expedition, according to Obregón, lost thirty-eight horses which froze to death. The *maestre de campo*'s mount was discovered one morning frozen stiff standing against a tree.[4] Today as one gazes from Tepehuanes into the blue sierra one can see the deep and narrow pass which leads into the mountains of Topia.

The village was stormed and conquered and the foundations of a rich mining town were laid. Into these fastnesses the Franciscan missionary had preceded the explorer by nine years, and a few decades later would visit this mountain spot again to console the Spaniards of the mines and begin the general evangelization of the Indians.

Father Santarén, of whom we shall read, would come here to found a permanent mission for the mountain savages.

Once Topia was subdued, the march was continued westward over the mountains and on to the coast. Ibarra advanced to the Fuerte River and, by founding on its banks the town of San Juan Bautista de Carapoa, took the first steps in the colonization of that western corridor near the sea along which Tapia and Pérez would trudge a quarter of a century later and through which up to its northern limits the missions of Sinaloa and Sonora would extend. Accompanying Governor Ibarra in all these perils, the bravest of his officers and the finest shot with the arquebus, was Don Rodrigo del Río y Losa, destined later to be governor. By that time San Juan de Carapoa on the Fuerte would have been destroyed and its inhabitants killed, including two Franciscan friars.

In these earlier days before the Jesuits came, it was most always the son of St. Francis who could be seen on or beyond the frontier. Franciscan Fathers were eyewitnesses of the creation of the province of Nueva Vizcaya and of the founding of its capital, Durango, for they accompanied when they did not precede every advance of exploration or conquest of Francisco de Ibarra. Father Gerónimo de Mendoza was with Ibarra on his earliest tours in the 'fifties. The three friars who later joined him in a mission into unexplored country were to be founders of Nombre de Dios. Fray Diego de Cadeña and Brother Lucas were the first white men to venture into the region of Durango. So beautiful did they consider the valley and so fine its river that they called it the Valle de Guadiana, and for a long time Durango knew no other name.[5] The two friars had labored in the vicinity before the founding of the town. Four others, headed by Pablo Azevedo, stood at the beginnings of San Juan del Río fifty miles north of Durango. Azevedo, with other friars, accompanied Ibarra across the mountains of Topia and was with him in his expedition farthest north to Paquimé, or Casas Grandes. He remained behind with a companion, Father Herrera, with the settlers of San Juan de Carapoa and with them was massacred in the Indian uprising of 1569.[6] When in 1567 Santa Bárbara was founded, some two hundred miles north of Durango, the friars were there. It was from Santa Bárbara in 1580 that Fathers Agustín Rodríguez, Francisco López, and Juan de Santa María fared forth into the deserts of New Mexico, accompanied by Captain Chamuscado and nine soldiers, to win new provinces for Spain and for the Church. Rodríguez and López did not return with the Captain and his men. They desired to remain behind to convert the Indians—and were killed.

Thus the first advance of the frontier east of the mountains is intimately associated with the missionary activity of the Franciscans, just as to south and west of the mountains in the period that followed the settlement of Culiacán by Nuño de Guzmán. The creation of Nueva Vizcaya and the founding of its capital, Durango, was aided by the presence of these missionaries. "To the Franciscan friars all credit is due for the spiritual conquest of Nueva Viscaya," says J. Lloyd Mecham, Ibarra's most recent biographer,[7] and Hubert Howe Bancroft celebrates the memory of Bernardo de Cossin, first martyr of the new province, who was slain late in the 'fifties; of Jacinto de San Francisco, familiarly known as Padre Cintos, who had been a soldier with Cortés but who later doffed the coat of mail for the gown and cowl; and of Pedro de Espinareda, one of the pioneers of Nombre de Dios.[8]

How is it, then, that since the Franciscans were in Nueva Vizcaya from the beginning and had an establishment in Durango from its earliest days, the Jesuits came likewise to share the work and to build up a mission system in these same regions? The answer is that the field was large enough to absorb the energies of more than one missionary society and to allow Jesuit and Franciscan to carry on their work side by side.

The Society of Jesus was in the full vigor of its youth, and the decades that followed the founding of Durango were indeed the golden age of its history. The Jesuits had come to New Spain with an immense reputation. The founder of the Society, Ignatius Loyola, had been a Spaniard. The third General, Francis Borgia, had been a grandee of Spain and an intimate friend of the Emperor Charles V. Even before his death he was looked upon as a saint. The fame of Francis Xavier, apostle of the Indies of the East, had rung over many seas and reached the far coasts of the Americas. The martyrs of the Rappahannock, closer home, had enhanced the Jesuit name, and the good repute the Jesuits were winning in Mexico City itself through their colleges and ministry was growing apace. Vocations became numerous; the Society was in a condition to expand. The far-flung fields of the north were begging for spiritual workers, and a constant complaint of the Franciscans was that they lacked numbers to satisfy the demands.

The friars had long wished to convert the tribes of the lagoon country, but for lack of men they had to forego their desire.[9] Though the district around Culiacán on the coast had been settled by colonizers and Christianized by the work of the Franciscan Fathers since 1531, at the end of the century there were no laborers to send into this field, so that the Jesuits had to come south from their own missions periodically to attend to the spiritual wants of the Tahue Indians.[10] Topia had been begun, destroyed, begun again; Cuencamé had been begun and abandoned.[11] When the Bishop of Guadalajara, Alonzo de la Mota y Escobar, desired to send men of God to the San Andrés mines, he looked for secular priests to fill this need. They could not be found, so finally he asked the Jesuits to take over the district.[12] Then death by martyrdom took its toll. At least five Franciscans were murdered in the midst of their missionary labors, in the early pioneer years of Nueva Vizcaya.[13] Two Franciscans were killed in Topia as early as 1562.[14]

Jesuits were therefore called upon also for the missions east of the mountains. Tapia was the pioneer there before going to the western coast. He visited Zacatecas and Durango in 1589 with Father Nicolás de Arnaya, and the following year was situated definitely at Durango. Then it was that he received orders to place himself at the disposal of Governor Río y Losa and was sent with Martín Pérez to Sinaloa. This was in 1591. Durango had still no resident Jesuits. Within three years, however, the fathers were to establish themselves in the capital of Nueva Vizcaya.

Neither the Governor nor the citizens of Durango had forgotten the religious zeal and the fruitful ministrations of Gonzalo de Tapia and of Nicolás de Arnaya during their stay among them. It was a broad-minded gesture on the part of the Governor to send Tapia and Pérez far from his capital city to the district which in his opinion most needed these apostles. It so happened, however, that in 1593, for reasons not known to us, Father Martín Peláez with a companion visited Durango.[15]

The success of the Jesuits' work here was phenomenal. By means of an interpreter they composed a catechism of the Christian doctrine in the Tepehuán language spoken by most of the Indians of the vicinity. Each day they gave instructions to both the Indian and the Spanish population and were assiduous in the hearing of confessions and other spiritual ministrations. Besides this they rendered a great social service to the town. For eight years a feud between two wealthy Spaniards had scattered smoke and fire over the settlement. The populace took sides and the whole community was torn by dissension. Peláez had repeated talks with each of the leaders privately and through his quiet reasoning was able to calm their quarrel. They consented to a compromise and were willing to forget their alleged grievances. They embraced publicly, after the Latin fashion, and sat down to dine at the same table. Peláez had mended a social schism and his prestige mounted apace.[16]

When the time came for the departure of the two fathers, they were pressed to see to it that superiors replace them by spiritual workers who should come to stay. These people of Durango were very much in earnest, especially the Governor, Río y Losa. Under his leadership the wealthy citizens of the town pledged a sum of 22,000 pesos for the foundation of a Jesuit house and college and promised also to put at the disposal of the fathers certain buildings to serve as a residence. Peláez responded to the earnestness of the capital and under date of March 31, 1594, sent a letter both to the General of the Society in Rome and to the Provincial of New Spain in Mexico City, Father Pedro Díaz. Peláez urged strongly the reasons for a permanent foundation in Durango, seeing that it was to become the center of all the mining, farming, and missionary activity east of the mountains.[17]

Matters, however, did not await a formal response to these documents. Before the end of the year 1593, an unidentified Jesuit was sent up to make his permanent residence in Durango, who should begin the work of education by teaching grammar to the youth of the town. He was soon followed by a confrere. In 1595 there were four fathers and two brothers in residence in a commodious dwelling and the work of the Jesuits east of the mountains can be said to have fully begun.[18]

Chapter IV
THE MISSIONS OF THE LAGOON

DURANGO WAS well chosen for the capital of the new province. Its elevation is 6,850 feet, so that its climate is relatively cool and salubrious. It lies in an immense valley with wide savannahs which, stretching in unbroken line to far-off hills, impress the traveler with the gigantic length and breadth of Mexico. Two cordilleras of the Sierra Madre enclose the capital in a distant frame and far to the southeast they may be seen rising clean and blue. This is the Valley of Guadiana, along which runs the San Pedro River making its way south and west to drop into the sea near Tepic on the western coast. The surroundings were fertile in the time of the missions; its lands are fertile today. Governor Río y Losa became a wealthy man and lived like a patriarch on his estates from the produce of these hills and valleys. His great flocks and herds, his shares in rich mines of the vicinity, helped to make of Río y Losa another of the millionaires of the north. In 1621 the city became the seat of a new bishopric which was made out of large portions of the diocese of Guadalajara to the south and of unlimited extensions of territory to the north. The Augustinian Fray Gonzalo de Hermosillo headed the long list of the bishops of Durango, whose portraits hang today on the walls of the chapter room of the magnificient cathedral. In June, 1891, the see became that of an archbishop.[1]

Although up to 1600 Durango did not have a population exceeding five hundred inhabitants, the surrounding country, because of the mines and farms, was, for northern Mexico, fairly well populated.[2] There were some thirty farms in its immediate vicinity, which produced close to fifty thousand fanegas of wheat and maize annually. This meant, besides the Spaniards, a far greater number of Indian laborers. Permission was asked and granted to import into the province for labor in the mines of Indé, Topia, Guanaceví, and the rest, a thousand Tlaxcaltec and Tarascan Christian Indians from the south, that these, added to native labor, might not only increase the output of the

---
[1] For notes to chapter iv see pages 202–203.

mines, but also act as a steadying influence upon the local tribes.³ Naturally enough, then, Durango became the mission center whence spread a radiation, in all directions, of evangelical laborers.

Yet the first beginnings of the missions east of the Sierra Madre were made not from Durango, but from Zacatecas. The Jesuits had come to the latter town two years before their permanent establishment in Durango. The energetic Visitor, Diego de Avellaneda, the same who sent Tapia on his career in 1591, provided for a permanent residence of the fathers in Zacatecas probably late in 1590. Two fathers, Agustín Cano and Juan de la Cagina, were sent to start this house of the Jesuits.⁴ Their first concern was for the spiritual care of the Spaniards of the town, but as laborers increased they began to think of missions among the Indians.

Now, Zacatecas takes its name from the Zacateco Indians, who inhabited a broad belt of country north and south of Durango and to the east. They were "a tall, well-proportioned, muscular people, their strength being evidenced by the great burdens they carried for the Spaniards." They were repulsive in appearance, having in an oval face, "long black eyes wide apart, large mouth, thick lips and a small flat nose." The men wore a breechcloth and the women a short petticoat of skins or woven maguey. They often smeared their bodies with clay of various colors and painted them with the forms of reptiles or other unseemly objects. This latter practice bore a triple effect: it beautified them in their own eyes, it kept vermin off their skin, and it shielded them against the sun's rays.⁵

Many of these Zacatecos had been accustomed to contact with the Spaniards, by whom they were employed in the mines and for various other forms of labor. Many of them had likewise been converted to Christianity by the early Franciscans of whom we have spoken. But to the north and east of Zacatecas, north even of Durango and east of the mining town of San Juan del Río, there was a virgin field for the missionary, for in the early 'nineties this district was beyond the frontier. The Franciscans were here in 1598, but everything indicates that this mission had not been permanent.⁶ The Jesuits in their thrust north and east from Zacatecas aimed at beginning here.

The first Jesuit penetration beyond the frontier to the northeast was made from Zacatecas by Father Gerónimo Ramírez and Juan Agustín de Espinosa in the summer of 1594, the year after the beginning at Durango.[7] Father Ramírez went north to the pueblo of Cuencamé, former mission of the Franciscans. The route to this district is easier from Zacatecas down the Río de las Nieves than from Durango, though the distance from the latter is far shorter, for from the capital the stretch is exceedingly dry, sometimes dangerously so, and a barrier of mountains is flung across the direct route.[8] Cuencamé is about sixty miles south of the modern Torreón, and from the environs of this city one can see today the parched and rugged dryness of those hills. Father Ramírez, like his fellows, was a dutiful son of his Society. He therefore kept in continuous touch with his superiors by letter. It is fortunate for the history of the missions, and indeed for the history of the development of all Mexico, that these missionaries wrote. We have such instructive details of the beginning of this mission in eastern Nueva Viscaya because the padre penned a long letter of his activities to his provincial in Mexico City from Cuencamé, August 31, 1594.[9]

Cuencamé was on the northern boundary line of the land of the Zacateco Indians. As the fathers approached their village the natives came out on horseback to meet them. The women too came out on foot. After a few days, caciques from the Río de las Nieves, hearing of the fathers' presence, came up with gifts of fruit and seeds. They were probably Indians of the laguna country, for Ramírez says he greeted them with no more than the four words of their language which he had learned on the way. Here at Cuencamé the finest house in the pueblo was given the padres for their use—indeed the only adobe structure in the whole district, which belonged to a Tarascan Indian of Michoacán, "an old Christian whom God drew here in order to help us." This was used for a chapel, while with fine good will the Indians built a porch and two rooms for their guests. They brought up presents of squash, watermelons, and fish, and an old Christian from Culiacán used to bring from time to time meat and milk.

Here, as generally, the first task for the missionaries was to perfect themselves in the language and to translate for the use of the prospective neophytes the catechism of the Christian doctrine. The missionaries did not begin baptisms immediately, for instruction must first be given, but they did baptize an old man and an old woman who were on the point of death. Ramírez closes his letter in a most sanguine mood. The Indians are delighted to be with him; they follow him with joy wherever he goes; if the Viceroy will see fit to send more workmen, a large harvest will certainly be taken in.

Father Juan Agustín de Espinosa's labors carried him not far from his native place, for he was born and bred in Zacatecas. I shall speak of him simply as Juan Agustín, for thus he signs himself in his letters and thus he is spoken of in the *anuas*. Starting out with Ramírez, Juan Agustín soon branched off for himself. He tells us that the pueblo he reached stood at the foot of the Cerro Gordo, a bold and rough range of hills, north of Cuencamé, at the foot of which reclined the town that bore the name of the sierra.[10] The cacique came out six or eight leagues on horseback to meet the padre and to beg his blessing. This was a consoling introduction, a result of the long contact these Zacatecos had enjoyed with those of their race who for a long time had been Christians. A site for an altar was selected and a first mass was said with the greatest possible solemnity to impress the pagans.[11] Then there began regular lessons in the Christian doctrine which the father went through with the Indians morning and evening. There were many old Christians in this district, though some were Christians only in name, having forgotten all that had been taught them.

Some of the Indians more than eighty years of age Juan Agustín thought it best to baptize, and a few of the children. He was greatly encouraged. He wrote: "God has put into the hearts of these people a great appreciation of the good that the coming of the fathers means to them and of what they hope from it." One of the old men came to the missionary and confessed that before the latter's arrival he used to drink each day to intoxication, but when he heard that the padre was planning a visit he said to himself: "I ought not to continue thus getting drunk, for there is coming a father through whose means I shall save myself. And though I had great difficulty I was so determined to reform my vices and sins that it is now four months since I have touched liquor or committed any other sins."[12] This and many other consoling things happened to Juan Agustín.

As the report spread that the missionary was in the country many other caciques came to see him. Three especially from the Río de las Nazas pressed him to come over to their rancherias, for the plague was there and many infants were dying. "We well know that you have not come to seek gold or silver, but only the salvation of our souls and to take us to Heaven. And since this is your desire you do not mind our poverty and our lack of clothes, for our souls are worth more than this." The Jesuit went from place to place and everywhere was warmly greeted. He baptized in one village seventeen or eighteen children sick of the plague. When he spoke of a permanent residence among them they were delighted and said they would gather about him, for salvation was worth all. Many who spoke thus were old Christians,[13] who had been converted by the Franciscans.

Here then we have a picture of the beginnings of the Jesuit missions entre infieles, east of the Sierra Madre. Fathers Ramírez and Espinosa had passed beyond the frontier; they had confronted the heathen with the gospel. And the general lines of the story run true to form: the Indian is mild, he takes readily to the gospel, his attitude is one rather of welcome than of hostility. This was often repeated on the western coast. As was the Zacateco with Ramírez and Espinosa, so was the Cáhita of the west with Tapia and Pérez. "They are a very docile race," writes Father Martín Pérez from Sinaloa in 1593, "and of good natural disposition, receptive of whatever may be taught them, especially the younger people of twenty-five years and less."[14] An anonymous account speaks of the "gentleness and affability" of the Indians.[15] All this often held true, but by no means always, as the narrative will abundantly show. Cabeza de Vaca at the end of his long tramp through Texas and northern Mexico made mention of the mildness and docility of the Mexican Indian, qualities which had touched his heart.[16]

In this part of the country, however, the chief work of the permanent Jesuit missions was not to be with the Zacateco Indians, but with the tribes that lay to the north and east. Orozco y Berra[17] gives the name of Irritila to the Indians living here, but they are called by the early padres De la Laguna, or simply the Laguneros, from the circumstance that they lived about a great lagoon that spread over the plain. Upon these Indians the fathers of Durango had early fixed their eye.[18]

From Durango east, after the divide is passed, the elevation drops to five thousand feet above sea level. The drainage of the eastern slope of the Sierra Madre in the latitude of Durango is gathered up mainly by two streams, the Río de las Nazas and the Río de las Nieves. It was down the valley of the latter going north that Ramírez and

MISSIONS OF THE LAGOON   25

Agustín went to the farthest Zacatecos and close to the Laguneros. Modern maps indicate two large lagoons, Laguna de Mayrán and Laguna Viesca, as formed by the rivers just mentioned, which drop their waters here and leave them. But, as a matter of fact, large modern irrigation ditches take this water as it flows in the rainy season down the river beds which at other times are dry and distribute it far and wide over the level land. This distribution helps to create the present fertility of the Laguna Country.

In the days of the missionaries it was otherwise. There was no system of irrigation to guide and distribute the water as it flowed down the Río de las Nazas, and a lagoon sprawled over this level land like a giant pool. It was called by the fathers the Laguna Grande de San Pedro. If there was, some miles to the south and over a ridge of hills, another lagoon, formed by the Río de las Nieves, it is never mentioned in the reports and letters.

The lands lying close to the lagoon were fertile; a few miles away, especially among the hills, the soil was rock-ridden and parched, fit mother of the thorny cactus and the dry sage. The Laguna de San Pedro rose and fell as the river flooded and dried up. It measured in the days of the missions 120 miles in circumference when it was low; when high, as much as 200 miles. In this country more than twelve thousand Indians lived.[19]

The first mission to be founded in this district, however, was many miles removed from the verge of the muddy lake, and separated from it by a fertile pass running between hills and watered by a stream with high and irregular banks which winds an uncertain way to flow into the lagoon. Twenty years before, the Franciscans had a settlement here which they called Valle de Parras. This first Jesuit mission was called Santa María de las Parras (St. Mary of the Grapevines) because wild grapes, as Ribas tells us, grew abundantly in the area.[20] Parras still exists, reposing on sloping ground and set like a gem on the skirts of a vast mountainous country which today, as one looks to the west and south, can be seen from the town stretching away in blue ridge or pointed peak. A full stream from these mountains rustles through a lane fringed with willow and the housewives bend over its brink to wash their linen. The grapevines too are still here, but cultivated now so that their juice, cured in local vats, centuries old, is made into a delicious wine for which the place is famous. And this old, quaint town is still redolent of its mission days. The ancient church, though restored, is still here, with old-time relics, altars, retables, and paintings, and the entrance through old wooden doors testifies to its antiquity. Later a fine college building was put up and another church built by the Jesuits. These too stand hard by the ancient fane.

Santa María de las Parras lies northeast from Durango almost two hundred miles, and over a country so difficult and so dry that for those who would make their way there at certain times of the year "it was necessary to carry water in casks."[21] In spite of these distances the capital of Nueva Vizcaya became the base whence the padres approached the whole district of the lagoons. The approach from Zacatecas, though easier, down the valley of the Río de las Nieves, was a little longer, nor did the Jesuits maintain a base in that town. But when Father Arista first entered the country from Durango, he went south to Zacatecas and then north down the river, traveling about four hundred miles.

The fathers had no high idea of the lagoon Indians. Half men, half beasts, says the writer of the anua of 1596.[22] They lived partly on the water and partly on land, but nowhere did they hold to a definite location. They neither sowed nor reaped, and they went practically naked. They lived chiefly on fish. After the flood season, when the waters would slowly recede, fish—especially the *matalotes,* which made fine eating—would become imprisoned in pools or easily caught in shallow estuaries. The Lagunero had a novel way of catching duck. He would cover his head with the dry shell of a gourd, with two holes in it to see through. Then he would submerge himself in shallow water with only his head above its surface, appearing to the unsuspecting fowl as a floating shell. As the duck paddled by, the Indian would reach up from below and clutch it by the legs or the feathers of the breast. It later became hard to persuade the Indians these were not fish and might not be enjoyed on Fridays. The natives lived likewise on the flour they made from a species of reed mace, and the fathers praised its quality. They danced rhythmically around bonfires all night long and became intoxicated from the juice of an herb called *peyote,* which, says the missionary, robbed them of their meager intelligence.[23]

MISSIONS OF THE LAGOON

Superstitions, of course, abounded among these Laguneros. They harbored great fear of the whirlwind. When it appeared, they fell to the ground and shouted "Cachinapa," their devil's name. The women, after childbirth, abstained for six or seven days from fish and game. Their belief was that should these things be eaten by the mother after the birth of a child the living animals would feel injured and flee the vicinity. As did all these primitive tribes, they had traffic with troublesome spirits and wicked spirits. With horrible visage and haughty mien, wrote Ribas—probably exaggerating,—with fire flowing from their eyes and blood from both eyes and ears, the spirits would appear, urging the savages to evil. The Indians murdered with facility; they slew their own sons, especially the first-born; they did away with their sick and aged. It was the convinced judgment of the Jesuits that evil spirits led these children of the hot lowlands to many an evil practice.[24]

Yet these children of the plains were not ferocious; they were only wild and as yet untamed. We can understand the fears of the fathers of Durango in 1595. Gonzalo de Tapia had been murdered in Sinaloa in August, 1594, and for a while it looked as if this western venture might have to be abandoned. After the increase of numbers in Durango, and because there were now four fathers resident in the capital, the missionaries turned their eyes to the Laguneros. It was thought advisable not to organize, so soon, a permanent mission among them, but to send fathers from time to time in order that gradually these savages might become accustomed to the padres' presence.[25] The years 1595 and 1596, therefore, saw temporary visits. Results were encouraging. The Indians listened to the explanations of the missionary and sometimes asked questions which were more intelligent than some that are asked now. In 1596 one asked the classical question: "Why was it that if God created all things He created poisonous snakes which did no good?"[26]

It was Father Juan Agustín de Espinosa, now evidently belonging to the group at Durango, who achieved through the mildness of his manner the chief success with the Laguneros. By the beginning of 1598 it was decided that a permanent mission and pueblo should be organized among these Indians, and there existed at the end of the eighteenth century an ancient report of these beginnings made by order of Captain Diego de Robles, from which we learn of the details.

Juan Agustín left Cuencamé for the Laguna country to start a permanent mission on January 23, 1598, accompanied by Captain Antón Martín Zapata, who had persuaded some Tlaxcaltec Indians from a colony at Saltillo to accompany him and aid in the foundations.[27] At the same time fifteen caciques of those who had been baptized by the missionary consented with all their people to gather themselves together into a "reduction," a pueblo, there to live with their padre and enjoy a constant contact with him, they and their children. This infant village of Christian Indians was given a name, above alluded to, which has perpetuated itself upon the land. It was called Santa María de las Parras, and its birthday was February 18, 1598.[28]

Thus began a mission started by the tiny nucleus of Santa María. It was destined to grow and to spread its beneficent influence throughout all the lagoons, to the solid advantage of the province of Nueva Vizcaya. Father Juan Agustín de Espinosa seems to have been a particularly successful missionary, like Gonzalo de Tapia and Cristóbal de Villalta on the coast; like Salvatierra in Baja California and Junípero Serra in Alta California. His success at Santa María de las Parras was swift and widespread. Hundreds were gathering into the new pueblo, and he had baptized most of the children and was preparing the adults. Soon in the vicinity some five thousand Christian Indians would be settled.[29]

The details of the padre's own letter give us a fine insight into his successes at Santa María. The devotion of the children; the assiduity of the adults; the conscientiousness of the father's adult helpers, namely, *fiscales* and catechists, were all a source of consolation to him. For the Christmas of 1598 he prepared a joyous celebration. Spaniards from near-by *encomiendas* or ranches were invited to participate. Christmas morning, the three Masses which the padre was able to say were attended with reverence and devotion. That night the neophytes were given permission to dance a *mitote* which was joined by pagans as well as by Christians. "For not only ten or twelve enter," explains Ribas, "as in Europe, but one hundred, two hundred, or more. At the celebrations in Mexico City for the beatification of Ignatius de Loyola, the Mexican Indians came out of their plaza for this dance . . . in numbers of two or three thousand adorned with their plumes and feathers."[30]

So here at Santa María on Christmas night the mitote was danced, but after the Christian fashion. Bonfires were lighted in the plaza and near the door of the chapel. Then a cacique of the Irritila nation led the merriment. First, in the church, there was the adoration of the child Jesus and His mother; then the Indians poured out into the plaza for the dance, the Spaniards looking on with interest, the padre with love and pride. Joining in the festivities with the Irritilas were Miopacoas, Neviras, Hoeras, and Maiconeras who belong to the valley in which Santa María lay. And added to these were others from closer to the lagoon: Poagas, Caviseras, Vasapayes, Ahomames, Inavopos, and Daparavopos.[31] "These nations I have wished to mention," writes Juan Agustín to his superiors, "because the adoration which they made that night seems the fulfillment of the universal prophecy: All nations will come and adore before the Lord."

They danced adorned after their own fashion with plumes and feathers and all Indian finery, holding arrows in their hands. The young made up the greater numbers; of the aged, who were stubborn about joining themselves to anything the padre organized, only one old man called Maigosa entered the melee. They called out in the midst of the dance the divine praises in their own language and after their own fashion. Literally translated, some were: "Let us adore the place where stands our most holy Mother." "Worthy to be praised is God our Lord." "The feast of Our Lady makes us very joyful." "Fragrant is the hat of the Lord."

All this delighted Juan Agustín's heart, "for now they did to honor God what before they performed to honor Satan," he writes, alluding to the mitote, which was formerly a pagan dance. When morning broke, they feasted from heifers which had been roasting all night long. Dishes of maize were likewise served. It happened to be Friday, but the abstinence was not observed owing to the solemnity of the feast. The padre, by this liberal humaneness, so won their hearts that the Indians averred that even should he wish to leave them they would hold him by force. This the Black Robe considered the finest compliment the Indians could give, proof of their loyalty and devotion.[32]

On New Year's Day Father Juan Agustín organized the pueblo politically, as was always the custom with the Jesuit missionaries. Indeed, such organization was the desire of the Spanish government, evidenced by the express command of the kings from the days of Charles V.[33] This meant that under the supervision of the padre, or, if there was a military post, of the captain, Indian officials were elected from among their own number to attend to the proper governing and ordering of the pueblo. Sometimes these officials were simply appointed by the Spanish authority. First there was often a governor of the pueblo, a *gobernador,* appointed or elected; then alcaldes or *regidores,* who were officers of justice and order; *fiscales,* to look after all things belonging to the ordering of the church, and spiritual things, such as the instruction of those who needed it and information to the missionary concerning those who were dying that he might come to them; and, last but not least, the *temastián,* or catechist, who was, however, always appointed by the padre himself. His duty was to aid the father in the instruction of the children and catechumens. The fiscal, besides his other duties, sometimes turned catechist.

Therefore, on New Year's Day, 1599, these elections were carried through and the pueblo received its political organization. Here, as elsewhere, the chief Indian officials were allowed to dress in the Spanish fashion and were given swords, that they might carry greater authority.[34]

On the Feast of the Epiphany, January 6, those Indians who were considered by Juan Agustín to be properly instructed were baptized, and many were married after the Christian fashion. And the father adds in his letter: "Outside of the constant exercise of the catechism and instruction, I have to baptize, confess, marry and pacify not only the savages, but also strangers and Spaniards."[35] He overthrew a notorious idol on the Feast of St. Lawrence the Martyr, and was consoled by the heroism of one of his young neophytes who preferred death to the destruction of her chastity.

Thus did Father Juan Agustín de Espinosa make a splendid beginning, laying strong and deep the foundations for a fine group of missions among the Laguneros. However, if the work was going to spread he must have helpers. He had need of a companion, too, for the consolation of his spirit, which at times was subject to harsh fits of desolation. He utters a cry of agony in a letter written to one of his confreres: "A few days ago I was so filled with tedium, sadness, and aridity that it repented me of my very life. Oh! how much patience and confidence in God is necessary for this kind of ministry! How many occasions of sin there are! What loneliness, what journeys, what waste solitudes, what hunger, what bitter waters and vile odors! What nights spent in the open, what heats of the sun, what pests of mosquitoes, what thorns! What childishness of the people, what deceits (*tlatotles*) and contradictions from *hechiceros* [medicine men]!" In spite of all this, however, he closes his letter giving evidence of his desire always to do the will of God.[36]

A companion was soon to be sent him, and then still others would come, and his generous work would be carried on until the whole eastern part of Nueva Vizcaya could be claimed for Spain and rendered safe for the mines and the ranches of the Spaniards.

Chapter V

THE TEPEHUANES

THE COUNTRY of the Tepehuán Indians lay west of that of the Zacatecos and of the Irritilas or Laguneros. Of all the tribes verging toward the northwest of Mexico, the Tepehuanes, though less numerous than some, occupied more territory than any other either east or west of the Sierra Madre except possibly the Pima Alto far to the northwest, whose area of activity extended into present Arizona. The Tepehuán nation spread over territory that runs south almost as far as Zacatecas and north to Parral and Santa Bárbara. On the east they dropped down into the wide levels of the plain of Durango. On the west, both south and north, they mounted into the ruggedness and coolness of the mountains. Many of the mining towns already familiar to these pages were set in Tepehuán country, so that when Francisco de Ibarra fared forth to his explorations and conquests north from Zacatecas the greater part of his marches east of the Sierra Madre threaded along territory occupied by this nation.

Sombrerete, Durango, Nombre de Dios, Indé, Parral, and Santa Bárbara were all in the land of the Tepehuanes. San Juan del Río lay just outside its borders. These savages occupied all the banks and tributaries of the Río de las Nazas north and west of San Juan del Río until the river dropped into Zacateco and Lagunero country. It was only in the middle district, in country east and south of Culiacán, that they did not run deep into the mountains, for this part of the high sierra including Topia and San Andrés was occupied by the Acaxée Indians, while south of them was the Xixime nation. The western Tepehuán border formed a semicircle, the hollow of the crescent being occupied by the Acaxées and Xiximes. North lay the great Tarahumar family.[1]

The Tepehuanes were a noisy, unruly, and warlike race—though at first the missionaries did not recognize this. They were accustomed to bully their neighbors, especially the Acaxées and the Tarahumares. They were the ancient kidnapers and gangsters of northwest Mexico. They would make raids into neighboring territory and carry off

---

[1] For notes to chapter v see pages 203–205.

women and girls. These they would either keep as wives or hold for ransom. Their weapons were like those of the other tribes: the bow and arrow, the knife, and the pike or club of brazilwood. They made wine from mescal, and, as usual with barbarians, they had frequent carousals. Their homes were made of the branches of trees or of stone and mud. Superior to many other nations in dress, the women clothed themselves in wool or cotton, though the men went almost naked.[2]

This was the nation among whom the most disastrous revolt of all Mexican mission history broke out. Yet at the beginning this people gave good promise of civilization and Christian conduct. The Spaniards entered their territory with little difficulty. Though there were some affrays and skirmishes, no war of conquest was necessary. Because of the rich mines which dotted their plains and mountains, crowds of Spaniards came into their country. The Tepehuanes profited by this contact, becoming expert in some of the Spanish frontier usages. They were employed not only for mine labor by the Spaniards, but likewise as *vaqueros,* and thus learned to be skillful cowboys and horsemen. They could hurl a spear from horseback with the dexterity of a European cavalryman and became adept in the use of such firearms as they were able to loot from the Spaniards. This was never a serious danger to their conquerors, however, for they knew not the art of making powder.[3]

The fathers of Durango showed from the start a distinct favoritism for the Tepehuanes. The reports about them from the superior at the capital appear in all the more favorable light when compared with what the same padre wrote concerning the Laguneros: "It is sufficient to say that the Tepehuanes have great advantages over the Laguneros for receiving the faith, because they are naturally more mild and more given to reason. They even enjoy a bit of political organization, which those of the lagoons entirely lack.... They educate their children with love and care and it looks as if God were inviting them into the Faith."[4] Such optimism in a missionary fresh to the field is understandable and pardonable. But disillusionment would follow fast.

The first Jesuit to go temporarily among the Tepehuanes was Father Gerónimo Ramírez, the same who had been with Espinosa among the Laguneros.[5] He brought back distinctly favorable reports. He esteemed their language above all the others and counted this the most successful and pleasurable of all his travels and missions. "They receive baptism with joy, they gain a good concept of the sacrament of penance and they ask for it with real sincerity." Ramírez met one with so fine a memory that, hearing an instruction on the catechism one day, he could repeat it word for word the next. This man he made his catechist, to help him instruct the others.[6] True, they feared the Spaniards and harbored some suspicion because of past encounters, but they impressed the first Jesuits who went among them as being appreciative of the peace and security which Christianity brought them, and the coming of the Black Robes tended to allay their suspicions of the Spaniards in general. Even before Ramírez went to live permanently among the Tepehuanes, they gathered themselves together to the number of two hundred in several rancherias, thus to be better able to foster the Faith.[7]

It was in the Lent of 1596 that Gerónimo Ramírez took the first steps to carry the gospel to the Tepehuanes.[8] All the sources agree that the success of his activity was encouraging from the start. Ramírez began his labors at Sauceda, a mining center almost forty miles north of Durango and the closest to the capital of the more populous districts. The modern railroad north from Durango passes through Sauceda, which is known today by the name of the larger town, Canatlán. The missionary's introduction to the Tepehuanes was indirect, for at Sauceda his first sermons and instructions were to the numerous Tarascan and Mexican Indians brought up from the south by the Spaniards to work in the mines.[9] These southern Indians had long ago been Christianized, but, on their moving north, much of their religion, for lack of ministers, had shriveled in their minds and hearts. While Father Ramírez, then, would be trying to revive the feeble Catholicism of the old Christians, the Tepehuanes, led by a "laudable curiosity," says Alegre naïvely, used to gather round to hear what the padre had to say. Their first understanding of Ramírez' instructions was of the vaguest kind, for they scarcely understood either Mexican or Tarascan. Yet this piqued curiosity and this dim understanding were something; it was the first slipping in of a thin wedge which opened for the padre a little crack through which he could gain that direct contact which he desired.[10]

Gerónimo Ramírez began gradually, with that skill which so many of these missionaries possessed, to win over the barbarous Tepehuanes through kindness, through little gifts of beads and of glass, and through the ease and charm of his manner. He knew, besides, a bit of their own language, which delighted them. To offices of religion he attracted them by that color and pomp of ritual which is one of the richnesses of the Catholic Church. In such ceremony the Spanish temperament led the colonists of the New World generously to indulge; in this same splendor the native Indian with childish instincts took delight. The Mass, the adornment of the altar, the penitential processions of Lent, all attracted the savage Tepehuán. The ceremonies of Easter deepened the impression and added to his delight. On this feast in 1596 the Spaniards and Christian Indians marched in procession clad in white, the women and children adorned with beads of glass, shell, coral, and snail, while they heard the sound of trumpet, oboe, and flute.[11] The Feast of Pentecost this same year was celebrated at Sauceda with a religious procession in which both Spaniards and Christian Indians joined with the singing of hymns, the display of banners, and the sound of the horn and the flageolet. The Tepehuanes looked on as children, their curiosity high but satisfied, their delight keen at the novelty of color and sound and form.[12]

Already at Low Sunday a Tepehuán cacique expressed a desire for baptism and was willing to be instructed; there followed him a number of his people. Pentecost was the day assigned for the solemn event. The neophytes made part of this solemn pentecostal procession with hair flowing loose and head garlanded with flowers. Colored feathers completed their personal adornment. Preceded by a cross and a line of Christians carrying lighted candles, these catechumens were led to the baptismal font by their godparents in orderly ranks. The font itself had been decorated with foliage and fragrant herbs. A large crowd of pagan Indians stood about, looking on idly and curiously, as the Mexican Indian still does today. Some, however, who desired to be baptized but were not yet sufficiently instructed, had to be put off. These showed by tears their sorrowful disappointment.[13] Ramírez was pressed by these savage children to remain at Sauceda till the Feast of Corpus Christi, which he did. On this day the Tarascan and Mexican Indians executed a dance while the pagan Tepehuanes emulated them in their own fashion.[14]

Thus had Gerónimo Ramírez within a few weeks become among the barbarians a focal point of religion, of culture, and of friendly intercourse. He had achieved a great success this Lent and Eastertide of 1596 among the Tepehuanes, and he left Sauceda to return to Durango with the satisfaction of having been invited to revisit the district and of leaving some catechumens there to be baptized at a later date.[15]

Among the first group baptized at Sauceda was an old man whose conversion can be called a notable one. It was so typical of the missionary's experience and so illustrative of a certain phase of Indian religious psychology that it is worth recounting in full. This man belonged to the class always troublesome to the missionaries, the class which can be said to have stirred up practically all the troubles and rebellions that the padres had to contend with through the centuries. The Spaniards called these men *hechiceros* or wizards. They were in fact the native priests whom the English-speaking explorer and settler called medicine men. The Spanish name is well chosen, for wizards or sorcerers these personages certainly were, pretending to cure sickness and to avert evil through practices of black magic. By such means they sometimes seemed able to have traffic with spirits of the other world, provoking phenomena which surpassed the powers of natural causes and which filled the superstitious savages with awe and dread, elevating high among them the prestige of the hechicero. The padres called the spirits thus evoked by the wizard evil spirits or devils, and certainly the effect of contact with them was consistently evil and destructive: it invariably induced pride and an obstinate rejection of Christianity, when it did not lead to ridiculous superstition or revolting cruelty.

A belief that communication may be had with disembodied spirits has been entertained by many a Christian theologian and philosopher, and instances have been recorded throughout the centuries from the Biblical account of Saul and the witch of Endor to the writings of certain moderns who have claimed a like experience.[16] The Gospels tell of demons speaking through the mouths of persons possessed. The Church has long had prayers for the driving forth of demons.[17] The barbarous blacks of Africa who were transported to America as slaves brought with them their practice of intercourse with evil spirits, as the Jesuit scholar Joseph J. Williams shows with respect to the black inhabitants of Jamaica.[18] And even as recently as the year 1935 there was published, as of a current happening in the United States, an account of a diabolical possession and the remedy of exorcism invoked by the Church.[19]

Just so did these poor children of the northern Mexican wilds have unhappy traffic with evil spirits, who made sport of them and often tormented them. Taxicora, a cacique and hechicero on the Fuerte River, west of the mountains, was said, while mounted on a horse, to have raised himself and the beast from the ground in order to defy and confound the missionaries.[20] On the upper Fuerte a spirit tortured a converted hechicero, appearing to him in monstrous shapes and bellowing like a bull.[21] On the Yaqui, Ribas reports that shortly after the coming of the missionaries an evil spirit appeared to many, speaking in a loud and terrifying voice and threatening dire punishment should the Yaquis not forsake the padres and Christianity. This all but stirred up a rebellion.[22]

Pérez de Ribas made a study of such phenomena out of a book written on this subject by the Jesuit scholar Martín Antonio Delrío[23] and thought he discovered that all the European scholar brought forth concurred with what he himself had witnessed among these Indians of the northern Mexican coast.

Ribas, together with most of the other missionaries, accepted too uncritically the word of the Indian in these matters. Delrío himself, to whom Ribas gave his confidence, was a victim of the witch superstition of his age, and undoubtedly gave aid to the cruel practices of the witch persecution of the times.[24] But it is not too strange that phenomena such as those related by the missionaries should appear among rude or barbarous peoples. Their ignorance, their credulous stupidity, their closeness to earth, the weakness of their wills—all this makes of such peoples a fertile field for the deceits of the hechicero and his controlling spirit.

Thus, Gerónimo Ramírez, in writing to his superiors about this his first entry among the Tepehuanes, described his spiritual conquest of an old and hardened hechicero of seventy years. For forty of these seventy the old man had been in contact with an evil spirit. He used to carry about with him a small stone idol, shaped like a human skull, which, he averred, spoke to him. He kept the idol hidden and filled the people with awe, for, said he, if they should once look upon it they would die. These speaking stones seem to have been more often in evidence among the Tepehuanes than among the other nations.

The father expended upon this old fellow all his tact and kindness, for it was always a special victory to win an hechicero to Christianity, and old people carried great authority with the tribe. Ramírez spoke to him of death, but he said he was immortal, for this was promised by his spirit; the padre threatened the vengeance of God, but this the old man laughed to scorn before a public group. One night, however, he was attacked, as some thought by a wild animal, and appeared the next morning ready to submit, his confidence in his spirit completely broken. The father was right, he said; the devil had fooled him with an immortality he had no power to give. The wizard renounced his idol, asked for baptism, and was willing to appear forthwith at the religious exercises. Baptized soon afterward, he was honored with the father's own name.

What was the beginning of this savage's contact with an evil spirit? He told Ramírez his story: One day as he was sitting with others a stone rolled toward him and when he took it up a voice came from it saying that should he keep it and respect it he would have all good fortune—victory in war, health and strength for the chase. Gradually the voice became more familiar and began to prognosticate the future. When it prophesied war the stone would be covered with blood. Sometimes the idol would disappear and then come back to view, giving him to understand that more honor should be shown it. Later the hechicero began to feel the evil effects of his sorcery—great debility of body, for instance, and fears of different kinds. But, declared the convert, now that he had been baptized he experienced great relief of spirit and his fears were replaced by happiness and joy.[25]

The idol became an object of fearsome curiosity, for the evil spirit had spoken through it. Should anybody look upon it he would die. Ramírez acted here as so many of the other missionaries acted in similar circumstances and usually—though not always—with good effect. He walked up to the idol and dared not only to touch it, but to fling it contemptuously to the ground. He did this publicly, of course, that the devil might be publicly confounded. When nothing happened—

THE TEPEHUANES 39

when the padre was not struck dead, the earth shook not, nor did a great wind blow, nor the sky collapse—the Indians saw that their fear of the idol had been unfounded. The idol was a small stone about the size of a large apple, wrapped about three or four times in very subtle veils or membranes which Ramírez and some other Spaniards thought might be that which covers the cerebellum of the human brain.[26]

After this his first *entrada* among the Tepehuanes, Father Ramírez returned to the Jesuit house in Durango, where this year, 1596, there were four fathers and two brothers.[27] The Superior was so pleased with the success of Ramírez during the Lent and Easter season of this year that later on, possibly in the fall, he sent the missionary a second time among the Tepehuanes. The anua tells us that this second mission lasted three months, that to the high delight of the Tepehuanes Ramírez penetrated forty leagues from Durango into their territory, and that he obtained a great deal of valuable information concerning the habits and customs of the nation.[28]

In Lent of the following year Ramírez revisited the districts of his former missionary activity. He first went to Sauceda, where he made contact again with its near-by rancherias. Then he journeyed north, turned west over the hills, and dropped into the valley of Atotonilco down which flow to meet each other the Río de Santiago and Río Tepehuanes to form the Río de Ramos. There were five pueblos of natives in the valley and they received the padre with manifestations of pleasure. He was welcomed likewise by the Spaniards, some of whom had farms upon which they employed old Christians from the south. Holy Week was at hand; Ramírez was petitioned to prolong his stay until Easter. He did so, glad of the opportunity of going through all the offices of Holy Week with the Spaniards and Christian Indians, that the pagans might be impressed. There was a public procession, a scourging, a carrying of the cross, and then a glorious Easter celebrated by Mass, music, and a solemn baptism of the children, whom Ramírez had instructed in repeated lessons during each day of his sojourn.[29]

After Easter the missionary returned to Sauceda. Here he found an increased number of the Tepehuanes who had been driven down from their mountains by hunger. To these for the first time he preached Christianity. He heard there was a pagan settlement not far distant in the hills. To this he went, disabused the Indians of strange ideas they had concerning baptism and the Church, and before departing promised to send them a cross and a catechist, that they might be ready for baptism the next time the father should come. Ramírez pierced deeper into the hills and for eight days threaded arroyos and clambered over ridges seeking for wandering sheep. His efforts were rewarded finally, though at first the savages fled from before him like frightened deer. Upon his return to tamer country, numbers of these mountain families followed and settled into a pueblo on lower ground where they could be reached later for instruction and baptism.[30]

One morning in a pueblo, six miles distant from Sauceda, while the padre was getting ready for Mass and a group of Spaniards were standing about waiting for the Holy Sacrifice to begin, a pagan girl finely dressed in the Mexican fashion came up, accompanied by her parents and family. She asked Ramírez if she might be baptized. Considering this merely a piece of curiosity and love of novelty, he replied that he would gladly baptize the girl provided she should be willing to go through the usual course of instruction. Both she and her parents affirmed that she had already done so; the padre might quiz her if he would. He put question after question to her and on no single point did she give an erroneous reply. Ramírez was thunderstruck. He baptized her that evening, together with several others. The girl, a stranger to this particular rancheria, had been instructed by that Indian catechist of long memory whom Ramírez had left behind him the preceding year.[31]

Encouraged by the phenomenon of this well-instructed Indian maiden upon whom he had never before set eyes, and more and more fully persuaded of the good work his catechists could do, Ramírez decided to visit himself the pueblo from which the girl had come. He found that his catechist had done his task well: the Tepehuanes of this village in which he had never before set foot came out, all together, to meet him. Not only the young and middle aged thus received him, but also the old—an encouraging sign, for these were more set and stubborn in their paganism.[32]

The missionary then returned, aglow with the fine feeling which spiritual success brings, to the environs of Sauceda, and now he met again the old hechicero whose conversion the preceding year had been so dramatic. The latter's greeting was enthusiastic and affectionate.

THE TEPEHUANES   41

"It is some years now," he said, "since I have been in contact with the Spaniards, but none took any notice of me. You alone respected me and helped me with the waters of baptism, and named me with your own name, which is Gerónimo Ramírez. I have fulfilled all that was commanded of me. I pray to God and when I am alone in the fields I cry out to Him, asking with all my spirit that He pardon my sins."[83] The kindliness and strength of Ramírez had here accomplished much.

The padre could not leave Sauceda until after Pentecost, so pressingly did both Spaniard and Indian urge him to remain. On this feast was another celebration participated in by pagan savages of various tribes of the Tepehuanes. They smeared themselves all over with a hairy herb resembling wool. Some covered their faces with masks and danced their wild dance, holding staffs in their hands. Others, dressed like demons, beat rough drums in the dance and brandished horns of the stag, in mysterious fashion feigning to write in books, using horns for pens, that which pertained to the Faith.[84]

After all these good results in the vicinity of Sauceda, Ramírez made his way north and west, back toward the valley of Atotonilco. Here he revisited his neophytes of the early part of the year and then turned south again to follow up the Río de Santiago, which flows north behind a mountain barrier that blocks off the country from the broad valley of Durango in which Sauceda is situated. Up this stream was Papasquiaro, a mining settlement, and he had heard that in this district, too, hunger had driven many of the Tepehuanes down from their mountains. Word of his approach got about the country and before he could reach Papasquiaro bands of Indians came down one or two days' journey to meet him, from the mountains and from the mining town itself. They came carrying crosses instead of arms, "with every sign of benevolence, as a people courteous and friendly." They listened with docility to the sermons of their missionary, and as the group enlarged the father thought this a splendid opportunity for the formation of a Christian pueblo. On this point too the savages listened to his suggestions; they were willing to remain here under the protection of the Church and the King of Spain, assured by Ramírez that they would be unmolested by the Spaniards of the mines twenty miles up the river. The padre himself would instruct the Spaniards of the vicinity to leave this pueblo in peace.[85]

So it was done. An Indian pueblo was founded here on this fresh spot, a delightful place on the banks of the Río de Santiago.[36] The settlement consisted entirely of Christians or prospective Christians, and it was given a political organization. Besides the Indian governor, other officers, alcaldes or *alguaciles,* were elected under the supervision of the padre, and an Indian fiscal was appointed. Ramírez wrote that in all this district there was hardly anyone who refused the Faith. "In this," writes the author of the previous anua, "we can see the strength of the truth that is preached and the infallibility of divine predestination which in its own good time out of wolves has made lambs that they may enter into the fold of Christ."[37]

Thus was founded in 1597 the important pueblo of Santiago Papasquiaro, which has enjoyed so long a career in the mission annals of northern Mexico and which sits today serenely on the banks of its ever-flowing river a few miles south of the junction with the Río Tepehuanes, in a valley, then called Atotonilco. The beauty of that valley's narrow vales even today strikes the traveler with joy. The fathers early knew the importance of this new pueblo, for Ribas assures us that it became a place of note since it was situated at the pass and gateway to all the mines of the sierra and to all the commerce of the mountains.[38] And so it is today, while the railroad follows close to the ancient route of the miner and the padre.

From this newly formed pueblo Ramírez went down the river and, reaching its junction, threaded up the Río Tepehuanes, which flows down the valley southeast. Having traveled some thirty miles, he reached a district where the Tepehuanes were known to be less friendly, indeed particularly surly, hostile, and barbarous. The padre was protected by friendly Indians, probably from his newly formed village, who accompanied him on horseback and armed with bow and arrow.[39] Ramírez preached, but these savages were cool and rebellious. Finally, after repeated efforts on the father's part, an old woman broke in upon one of his sermons and raised her voice in a vehement harangue. She rebuked the tepidity of these her tribesmen; the good father had come a long distance to visit them for their better interests, and she at least would harken to his word, act upon all he exhorted, and petition the waters of baptism. The speech had a fine effect. The savages, influenced always by the old, became more friendly and soon

THE TEPEHUANES 43

assented not only to future baptism, but even to the formation of a pueblo upon a site indicated to them.

The new pueblo was organized on July 16 by the gathering together of those who had formerly lived scattered in the vicinity and by the building of huts in a group clustered about a plaza. They named it Santa Catalina. It was situated "at a distance of one league from the Sierra Madre where the road from Topia to the Tierra Caliente emerges." It was formed on a hill that commands "a fine view of the river which they call Los Ahoreados. The stream runs swift and full in the rainy season and is shaded by many beautiful groves."[40] The mission remained and slowly grew into a town, the present Tepehuanes, whose ancient church of Santa Catalina attests the glory of its mission days. The visitor knows that the description of the site given in the sources is exact, and it fits today in every detail the beauty of this lovely spot.

The seal was set upon this new Christian center by the public celebration of the baptism of the children. This took place with the usual colorful display, to the delight of the childish-minded savage. All the infants and children of the settlement and a few of the more advanced adults were made Christians. A celebration had been planned for a general baptism of adults, which was fixed for the Feast of St. James, July 25. But some trouble occurred and a number of the Indians pulled up stakes and went back to their old haunts in the mountains. Ramírez then left this district and went north to Guanaceví.[41]

In spite of the setback at Santa Catalina, the Black Robe was so encouraged by his new and unlooked-for success that he wrote to his superiors he could make this whole section Christian in two years' time. But this was not to be without trial and sorrow, even after it was first accomplished; for at this second organized pueblo of St. Catherine twenty years later the first flames of the murderous Tepehuán revolt broke forth and spread over the country.

From Santa Catalina north and a little west sixty-five miles over hill and dale, over high mountain summit and along sinuous gulch and canyon, lay the mining center of Guanaceví. Thither from the south Ramírez now made his way. The Indians here were cast in milder mold than those of Santa Catalina, and after a brief lapse of time Ramírez was able to enjoy the third of his great triumphs of the year's work. The celebration of the public baptism, because of the help he had from the Spaniards and the old Christians of the mines, was particularly brilliant. A theater was thrown up in front of the church used by the Spaniards and in this they raised an altar in honor of Santiago, adorned with many spears. In front was the baptismal font, curiously decorated. In the morning there was a Solemn Mass, and singing and instrumental music; in the evening, around the church a procession of the catechumens, dressed all in white, the children holding candles as they marched toward the font. After the rite of baptism, some of the young men and women just made Christians through one sacrament were united in the bonds of wedlock by another. The Tepehuán pagans looked on in mild-eyed amazement.[42]

Among those baptized at Guanaceví was a youthful cacique who had become attracted to the father while the latter worked at Santa Catalina. He was of fine appearance—had a well-knit body and a handsome face. His manners were courteous and gentle; and his talents were as great as his other gifts. He was conspicuous among those baptized, robed in white silk and with a silken cape thrown over his shoulders. He took the name Gerónimo in honor of his padre, to whom he professed eternal devotion. In the evening, he was married to a noble maiden of his own race. Gerónimo the Tepehuán proved a golden treasure to Gerónimo the Jesuit. The latter formed his neophyte into a brilliant catechist and he became the Black Robe's most faithful assistant. He was a born teacher. The clarity of his exposition of the Christian doctrine and the force of his exhortations to his brother Tepehuanes excited the admiration of padre and layman alike. These various gifts, added to the nobility of his birth, made of him a nucleus of attraction for all the parts contiguous to Guanaceví. Many, including his formerly pagan family, came to settle in the town, so that this mining settlement became a third Christian Indian pueblo of newly converted Tepehuanes.[43]

Thus did Father Gerónimo Ramírez conclude the successes of this year, 1597: three pueblos of Christian Indians formed, with two of the three enjoying that political organization which further confirmed their permanence. Hundreds had been baptized, children and adults. At this time, certainly, the Tepehuán mission promised to become the most flourishing of all that lay east of the main Sierra Madre range.

Chapter VI

THE HEART OF THE SIERRA

As WE HAVE watched the Jesuit missionaries going up the western coast in 1591 and starting missions on the Sinaloa River, the very rim of civilization, and then making a permanent residence east of the mountains in Durango late in 1593, we shall not be surprised to learn that soon they penetrated the mountain barrier itself and set missions in the very heart of the sierra.

Shortly after the discovery and conquest of Topia by Francisco de Ibarra in 1563 and 1564, silver mines were opened up in this wild country "surrounded and hemmed in by frightful cliffs, rocks and terrible ravines,"[1] as the ancient chronicler Obregón describes it. There was a rush for the mountains, and soon there lived here an isolated colony of Spaniards seeking wealth from the bowels of the earth. Neither they nor the Indians, however, were spiritually neglected. The Franciscans, just as they had accompanied Ibarra in his explorations and conquests, just as they had founded convents and missions in Nombre de Dios and Durango, founded also a house in Topia even before Ibarra's time. They called the mission San Pedro y San Pablo del Valle de Topia. Little is known of this foundation. It was begun in 1555 in the Valley of Topia barely twelve miles as the crow flies northeast of what became the mining town. In 1559 it received the official status of a convent, with two resident Franciscans. Three years later the convent was destroyed by the savages and the fathers killed. In two years the foundation was restored, and it may have been still existing at the time the Jesuits first came to Mexico.[2]

It seems certain, however, that when the Jesuits started up the west coast in 1591 there were no Franciscans in the mines of Topia, just as it seems certain there were none in Culiacán during the following years, and none in Cuencamé when Ramírez and Agustín de Espinosa founded their mission in 1594.

The first Jesuit to enter Topia was Gonzalo de Tapia. The Spaniards there had heard of the successes achieved by Father Tapia on

[1] For notes to chapter vi see pages 205–206.

the banks of the Sinaloa and they desired that such an element of stabilization as this energetic personality should come into the mountains to quiet the Indians and give spiritual comfort to the Spaniards.[3] Besides, he had been suffering from ill health and it was thought that the more salubrious air of the mountain mining town would improve his condition.

Tapia arrived in Holy Week, 1592. He preached to the Europeans in Spanish; he heard their confessions, offered Mass for the satisfaction of their devotion, and gave wise counsel for the proper management of their affairs. A number of Tarascan Indians were there, working in the mines for their Spanish employers. The Tarascans were old spiritual children of Tapia, among whom he had exercised far in the southland his maiden priestly functions. To these Christians too he was as much a consolation as to the Spaniards. Before returning to the banks of the Sinaloa late that same year, he went among the as yet untamed and unchristianized Acaxée Indians who inhabited all that district of the mountains. He learned their language and went in among them to their deep vales and rugged mountainsides and carried to them the gospel of Christ. Shattering superstition, he had an idol overthrown, and on the point of departure he promised the savages a permanent padre as soon as this could be arranged.[4] In the Valle de Topia, highly walled about by the sierra, Father Tapia organized a pueblo of these Acaxée Indians and called it Santa Cruz del Valle. This means, as we have noted earlier, that he appointed an Indian governor for the village, a *corregidor,* to see to the good behavior of the inhabitants, and a fiscal to look after the spiritual well-being of the community. As Tapia's stay could not be permanent, Franciscan fathers moved into the pueblo and saw to the permanence of his organization.[5]

By Christmas Tapia was back in Sinaloa. A year and a half later he was a martyr for the Faith, slain by one Nacabeba, a rebellious cacique of Tovoropa off the fringe of Sinaloa town.

The thin edge of the wedge had therefore been inserted by Gonzalo de Tapia among these mountain tribes of the Acaxée Indians and further effort would result in what should become known as the missions of Topia and of San Andrés, which would include an Indian nation living farther south, the Xiximes. Hernando de Santarén would be the first Jesuit to found a permanent mission among these mountain tribesmen. He entered the country to stay, in 1598.

Who were these Acaxées? Andrés Pérez de Ribas, historian of these missions, who himself labored sixteen years among different tribes of the west, describes their habits and character at first hand: They had their dwellings not on the summits of the mountains, because of the cold, but lower down among the deep folds of the hills, difficult of access. Their houses, for all their mountain wildness, were better built than those of the Indians of the plains, and from all descriptions of those who dwelt among them at this time the Acaxées were generally more advanced in culture than their cousins of the lowlands to both east and west. For whereas in the lagoon region the missionary upon entering a village could find but one house built of adobe, some of these mountain dwellings were made of stone and mud, some of poles and straw. In Topia there was a sort of fort, with embrasures for defense against an enemy. Thus it was that when the Spaniards first looked down from the tops of the mountains upon the Valle de Topia they thought they saw another Mexico, and they had to storm the fort before they could command the district.

At the end of the 1500's the Acaxées numbered from twelve thousand to sixteen thousand souls. Corn and beans made up their principal diet, with smaller legumes or seeds as delicacies. Honey was not unknown to them and "it was as white as the snow on the peaks of their mountains." Their clothing was scant, woven from the fibers of the agave. Contact with the Spaniards led to improvement of their dress. Not only the women, but the men also took particular care to arrange and decorate their hair, binding it with fillets to different shapes. They adorned themselves with strings of white pearls which they got by barter from those who lived near the sea. Thus ears and nose, bored through from childhood, and arms, too, carried the white ornament of the pearl.

Their medical skill was dull and blundering, by the low standards even of that age. When fatigued they would bleed their legs with a sharp-pointed stone or shell, and when suffering from headache they would bleed their temples. In time of war they selected a maiden to perform a vicarious penance for the tribe through rigid fasting. The girl was allowed but a bit of toasted corn each day. Absolute silence, too, helped the victim to placate the god of war. Excited by combat, these savages descended to cannibalism, and when Santarén first entered among them he was shocked at beholding a mound of close to two thousand skulls—of their enemies, whose flesh they had fed upon.[6] "[They] practice cannibalism," says Obregón. "Countless bones and skulls of those whom they had killed and eaten were found."[7]

They indulged in human flesh chiefly after a victory. First they propitiated the god of war by leaving for him as they went to battle an offering of an arrow or a bone of a former member of the tribe. This was deposited at the foot of a *sapota* tree which they had planted near their huts. After a victory, they acknowledged the favor of the god with feasting. We do not read that like the Guaranís of the South American Chaco, for the more exquisite indulgence of their appetites, they fattened their prisoners through idleness and pleasure and then cut them to pieces that the old wives might throw the parts of their victims into earthen caldrons to cook.[8]

These Acaxées of Topia dragged their victims dead from the fray, and placed their limbs, not broken but severed at the joints, on flat stones near the entrance to their huts until it came time for feasting. The parts of a single human corpse were thrown into two large urns to be cooked all night by a slow fire watched over by two old men of the tribe, while the others danced and shouted the song of victory, holding the head of the victim. In the morning they removed the bones from the cooked flesh and kept them in their strong houses or forts, or collected them gradually in piles near the entrance to the forts. The flesh they mixed into a kind of stew and feasted on it, seasoning the portion with beans and corn. Each one who danced all night received a share of the repast, but not until a sufficient offering had been made to the gods and to the slayer of the unfortunate victim.[9] Their cannibalism was not entirely limited to their enemies. The Acaxées themselves were divided into multitudinous factions and intertribal strife was frequent, often terminating in the devouring of human flesh.[10]

These Indians were relatively chaste; and they did not steal or lie, considering such practices the vices of children. They were nevertheless much addicted to the worship of evil spirits. Indeed, their superstitions were as stupid as their habits were brutish. They worshiped idols, usually of stone, through which an evil spirit spoke. When Tapia had the idol overthrown in Santa Cruz del Valle, and the earth did not quake nor the heavens fall, these people began to realize the crass stupidity of their former beliefs. In various spots of their mountains they had built shrines made of nothing more than piles of stones. Their hechiceros could summon forth a spirit by going into a dark hut at night, shaking timbrels and calling aloud for the spirit to appear. The spirit harkened to these petitions, appearing in the form of a dog or stag or mountain lion. The Acaxées adored, besides, eagles, fish, and stones shaped like human skulls. Five hundred such idols were destroyed upon their embracing the Faith. In time of drought these stones were flung into the streams. If rain fell not, they were replaced by others.[11]

After Gonzalo de Tapia left the mines of Topia there appears to have been no resident priest in the mines themselves to attend to the spiritual desires and needs of Spaniards and of the Indians, both Tarascans and the few Acaxées newly converted. Tapia had left a great reputation behind him, enhanced after August, 1594, by his honorable death, for he was considered another martyr of Holy Church. Another fine character and another martyr, killed later in the Tepehuán revolt, was destined to be the founder of the permanent Jesuit missions in the mountains and in the mountain mines of Topia, San Andrés, San Bartolomé, San Hipólito, and Las Vírgines.

Hernando de Santarén had already had a brief missionary career before he inaugurated permanently the mission of Topia. Born in Cuenca in Spain, his father was *corregidor perpetuo* of the city of León. A maternal uncle had been founder of the Jesuit college in Huete. Here the boy spent his years of schooling before entrance into the Jesuit Order at fifteen years of age. He early evinced a desire for the Indies and was finally sent over in 1588 in company of the Jesuit Dr. Pedro de Ortigosa, who in Mexico became his professor of theology. After tertianship, Santarén was made minister of the college at Puebla, and then, together with Pedro Méndez, was sent on the mission to Sinaloa. This was the result of a trip Tapia made to the capital to ask for additional men.[12]

The usual route to Sinaloa was north from Mexico City to Durango, and then across the mountains through Topia to Culiacán and up the coastal corridor to the missions. On his way through the mountains with Méndez, Father Santarén had experience of the Indians he was later to evangelize. At San Andrés those working in the mines, which had been established subsequent to those of Topia, begged him to tarry. Here he exercised a passing ministry, and later with his companion arrived at Culiacán, June 29, 1594, just eleven days before Tapia's murder.[13]

When things quieted on the Sinaloa, Santarén was given his first missionary work. He was sent to the lower river to evangelize the mild Guasave Indians. Here in the pueblos of Guasave and Ure he labored for two years with full success. On one occasion at Guasave he threw down a stone idol worshiped by those pagans, and with the help of Spaniards had it brought to Sinaloa, where it was profaned and held up to public ridicule by the Christians. It is said that a great wind blew, that night, and the Guasaves, frightened and horrified, fled to the mountains, whence to coax them back cost Santarén weeks of patient labor.[14] After four years on the Sinaloa he was called away to Topia and was succeeded on the lower Sinaloa by his old traveling companion, Pedro Méndez.[15]

What was it that caused Hernando de Santarén to be sent permanently from the lowlands of the western rivers to the bleak and savage mountain country of Topia and San Andrés? It was the need there existing. He had preached a passing mission in the mountains in 1597, after closing a mission at Culiacán. He and his companion enjoyed a resounding success. They visited thirty pueblos and saw the Indians coming out to meet them with raised crosses, chanting the Apostles' Creed. The missionaries soon had them coming to the sacraments and reciting the rosary and doing penance.[16] These were evidently old Christians, whom the Franciscans had already converted.

Watered though it was by its rapid mountain streams which freshened the physical beauty of these wilds, spiritually a large part of the district was dry and parched. The Franciscan foundation ministered only to the Valle de Topia; the mines and the mountain country in general called for a missionary of venturesome spirit. As new recruits were being sent to Sinaloa, superiors were able to release a man for the mountains. They decided upon Hernando de Santarén and in 1598 he arrived at his new field of labor.[17] His central mission house would be no longer Sinaloa, for these more southern mountains were placed under the jurisdiction of Durango, the general superior being resident there.

On his way to Topia, Santarén passed through San Andrés, where the Indians of the mines begged him to remain. Two hundred savages knelt before him and in tears implored a longer visit. He was forced to accede to this legitimate request. Then he went on to Topia. Much work awaited him there. Drunkenness was a vice with the laboring Indians of the mines. During his first days he beheld four or five intoxicated. He rebuked them and led them to penance. They came to his hut, flogged themselves with whips as a sign of their contrition, and "took the pledge." His manner being such as gained him immediate good will, it soon happened that the Acaxée Indians from round about came to Topia to visit him.[18] This was the beginning of the conversion of that whole numerous nation of mountain savages.

The Spaniards helped the padre in the beginning of his mission. The first thing necessary was a translation of the catechism into the Acaxée language. This accomplished, the missionary was able to begin instruction. The usual method of the fathers was followed here. Some of the brighter young men who had well assimilated the doctrine were made into catechists, who, baptized before the others, went about instructing their tribesmen in the truths of Christianity. These young men exercised their office, we are informed, with the greatest diligence, begrudging the time that was needed for other duties.[19] They had a novel way of memorizing the prayers and the answers to the questions of the catechism. It must have been Santarén's idea, for it was intelligently practical, making up the deficiency of books, and it is comparable to modern standards of realism in education. Set off in groups, the Indians made a circle of small stones and on each stone they wrote a word. Thus all were aided in the work of memory, and knowledge kept spreading fast. These word-bearing stones were placed in front of their dwellings, especially if they harbored sick, in order that those within might profit.[20]

Early in 1600 the work of Santarén was facilitated by the arrival of Father Guillermo Ramírez and by the substantial coöperation of the secular arm. Captain Diego de Ávila was one of the large landowners of the district, a wealthy *encomendero* of broad and scattered acres. This gentleman, fine Christian and good Spaniard as he proved to be, received an official commission from the Viceroy to aid the fathers in the labor of reducing the Indians to pueblos, where, gathered in from far-off wilds as into a school, the savages might be instructed with ease and frequency. Orders to this effect came to the Captain on February 27, 1600. It is a compliment either to the thoroughness of the Viceroy's supervision or to the Captain's eager desire to prove his obedience to his higher superior that the details of this his spiritual activity during that year were attested by the notary Martín Duárez and several other witnesses.[21]

Captain Diego de Ávila lost no time, beginning work it would seem that very day. With Santarén and some other Spaniards he succeeded in persuading the Indians of Ocotitlán and Ayepa, Indian villages not far from San Andrés, to migrate to a more fertile and accessible place. A new pueblo, which they called Santa Ana, was formed with some ceremony. Before a raised cross the padre and then the Captain prostrated themselves in veneration and the other Spaniards present followed suit. Then the savages, exhorted thereunto in the Acaxée tongue by Santarén, imitated these pious demonstrations. The site for a church was selected at once and the missionary that very day began his series of instructions. A catechist, Juan Tomás, was appointed to help the padre and to the joy of the Indians Captain de Ávila promised bells for the church and a picture. The catechist was to solicit wax for the candles. Fifty-seven persons had come together to make this beginning of the new mission of Santa Ana.[22]

The following day a greater success was achieved. The Captain and some other Spaniards were accompanied this time by three priests, the two Jesuits and the curate of the mines of San Andrés, Luis de Cuevas. They came to a little pueblo of only three or four houses in the encomienda of Alonso de Ávila, six miles from the mines and on the banks of the Río de los Remedios. The Indians from the surrounding rancherias were called together here that the Captain might give them the message of the King: they were to become Christians and thus earn the protection of His Majesty, and no Spaniard was to use them for labor without pay. As a mark of respect for the Church the Captain taught them how to kiss the hand of the fathers, himself setting the good example. By next morning one hundred and thirty persons, young and old, had gathered here, and here they were persuaded to remain. It was a new pueblo, a new mission. San Martín they called it. When the Indians asked for hatchets to build their new homes, the Captain gave them notes to present in the mines of San Andrés and to their delight they were given what they desired. The men were persuaded to cut their long hair that they might appear more in the Spanish fashion. Farther up the river and about fifteen miles from San Andrés, another such mission was begun with an initial number of 170 persons. Then the pueblo of San Pedro was formed, twenty-four miles from San Martín, the people coming down from their former settlements of Coapa, Saicos, and Macos and gathering here. Some of these groups asked for a full political organization, but only fiscals and catechists were conceded to them. All the rest of that year, new Christian pueblos were being formed. Idols were smashed or broken, individually and often in whole heaps and collections.[23] Father Alonzo Ruiz now comes to the help of Santarén.

Thus the work of Santarén met with phenomenal success. He continued going from pueblo to pueblo, baptizing thousands of children and preparing the adults through instruction. Neighboring tribes became interested and invited the padre to visit them. To attract him and give earnest of their good will they raised crosses in their vales and on their mountainsides. Once, a group came to demand baptism on the spot. They had of course to be put off for instruction while their attitude towards Christian marriage had to be determined. One, however, who was sick, received the saving waters. When Santarén visited the pueblo of San Bartolomé he found that the cacique had held his people in such excellent disposition and had so exerted himself for their instruction that in a very short time he was able to baptize fifty adults and marry them in the church. Idols throughout the whole pueblo were knocked down and burned or otherwise destroyed, and for baptism the Indians submitted to the cropping of their long hair, of which they were habitually proud. Some pueblos opened hazardous paths for Santarén over rocks and beetling cliffs; to some others he was not able to go until helpers should be sent him.[24] He was invited to come south to a place called San Miguel in a country just opened up. This he had to refuse. He was able, however, to make contact with the Naperes to the south, where they built two chapels for him.[25]

Santarén's hardest work was during Lent. Ribas estimates that each year at this season he traveled fifteen hundred miles. On each Sunday in Lent Santarén delivered three sermons. Two were at San Andrés, one for the Spaniards, the other to old Christian Indians of the Mexican language, imported from the south for labor in the mines. The third was delivered to the laborers of the Acaxée tongue. That same day he would leave San Andrés for Culiacán, traveling a distance of seventy miles to preach there on Wednesdays. From here he would journey back into the mountains, traveling almost another seventy miles to Topia, passing the three hundred fords up the canyon before reaching the settlement. Here on Fridays he preached another three sermons, as at San Andrés, to accommodate the babel of tongues. Thus for every week during Lent he completed this large and fatiguing circle.[26] These labors produced their fruit. The year 1601, for example, recorded four hundred baptisms of children.[27]

It was evident that Father Santarén needed help. Not physically robust, such a round of labors and exertions would wear him out. Besides, the safety of the Spaniards in these mountains demanded that all the Acaxées be converted. This appealed to the Viceroy, who wrote to the Jesuit Provincial asking for men. Finally the Provincial of New Spain, Father Francisco Váez, influenced by an account of the work of the missions by Father Francisco Gutiérrez and by a long letter of Santarén, sent two additional priests to the mission of Topia. They were Fathers Alonzo Ruiz, who came in 1600 or before, and Andrés Tutino, who seems to have come later,[28] replacing Father Ramírez, who left.

Santarén could now expand his work. He had already five thousand persons under his charge in four missions. But he speaks of the ranges north and west of Topia, called Baimoa, where three thousand more natives dwelt. These, witnessing the peace and tranquil life of those who had become Christians, had asked that padres be sent to them. This could now be done. Likewise there could now be permanently reached a district near Baimoa on the fringes of the Tepehuán country in the vicinity of the Sierra de Carantapa. Here on a journey which Santarén made alone in 1601 he visited four hundred people. In the south the pagans waged perpetual war with the newly made Christians, in the districts of Guapexuxe, Xoxotilma, and Campaña Grande.[29] It is quite evident that Ruiz and Tutino would have plenty to do.

But the vicissitudes of the missions were many and life among the savages, especially in the beginning, was a hazardous existence. Here among the Acaxées, just when things gave such promise of advance, trial and danger came upon the padres as well as upon the settlers and Christian Indians. Revolt flared up in a flame among Santarén's new charges. Spaniards including the fathers were marked for death, and the mines—San Andrés, Topia, San Hipólito, San Gregorio, and Las Vírgines—were threatened with destruction. Let us tell the story.

Chapter VII

A MOUNTAIN REVOLT

THE REVOLT began among the Acaxées for reasons that were common in the history of early Spanish America; it was continued among a cognate group, the Sobaibos, in circumstances as amusing as extraordinary. The ordinary cause was the same as that which stirred up the Mixton War sixty years before when the nations south of Culiacán rose against the oppression practiced in Nueva Galicia by Nuño de Guzmán and his followers; it was the same as that which, in the following century, led the Inca chief, Tupac Amarú, to a general uprising against Spanish rule in the viceroyalty of Peru. The Acaxée country, as we have seen, was rich in silver mines. Topia was first developed; then mines were opened up at San Andrés, San Gregorio, and San Hipólito; most recently, the mines of Las Vírgines, thirty miles southwest of San Andrés. In connection with the working of these rich veins of silver the Spaniards, as so often before, exploited the Indians. The mine owners assumed a haughty and domineering attitude, worked the Indians without consideration or mercy, and sometimes even enslaved their women and children. This was against the law of Spain which prescribed that the Indian be not subjected to enforced labor, and that he be paid reasonably for his service.[1]

Impatience under the discipline of the newly founded pueblos was a contributing factor. But against repeated warnings from the missionaries the mine owners defied the laws, which were of Spain, as of Christianity. It was the old story of greed, the lust for gold.[2]

Disaffection was noticed both by the missionaries and by the other Spaniards. The Indians ceased coming to church or to listen docilely to the instruction; the growing sullenness of their manner was a cause of uneasiness and anxiety. The fact is that after a short while some five thousand were thus evilly affected and joined the party of revolt.

The chiefs took counsel together, to decide what best to do. They would destroy mines and kill the Spaniards. But what of the fathers? Should they slay them too? Here the leaders were divided, but the

---

[1] For notes to chapter vii see pages 206–207.

A MOUNTAIN REVOLT 57

majority were at first for sparing the lives of the missionaries. These men were not like the other Spaniards, they said, and had done them no wrong. Indeed, they added, the padres by their kindnesses and services of various kinds had obligated strongly all their nation. The other leaders recognized the obligation, but advanced a seemingly strong if specious argument for the slaughter of their benefactors also. How could they, said the opposition, resolve to put to death all the Spaniards and then spare the very individuals who by their authority and influence over the people and themselves held the greatest power for the suppression of their revolt? The argument seemed to be that if they were to revolt at all they might as well go through with it. This opinion finally prevailed and the lives of the fathers were forthwith designated for sacrifice. September 8, 1601, the rebels rose.[3]

The first to perish were five Spaniards of a prospecting party, led by Captain Juan Ruiz, who were going deeper into the sierra, lured by the age-old rumor that there was gold farther on, that richer veins of silver lay within those deeper folds of the mountains. The party stopped one night at a small pueblo, and the Indians, covering over their real feelings, pretended to receive them with sincere and even joyous hospitality. The party lodged in a rude chapel built of poles and straw. In the middle of the night the savages surrounded the hut, set fire to it, and prevented the escape of the prisoners. Every man of them, the five prospectors and their servants, perished in the flames, and upon their burnt flesh the rebels swore to exterminate their enemy the Spaniard. Quickly through all the country the news was spread and in the twinkling of an eye throughout the land the Indians were up.[4]

"Marauding bands seized the roads and fell upon Spaniards, mulattoes, Negroes. No life was safe; robberies, burnings, murders threw the whole district into terror. What pueblos and churches could be reached were soon reduced to charred ruins. The maddened natives carried the dead bodies away for old-time feasts and dances. More than a thousand bowmen, joining together, bore down on the mining camps."[5] At San Hipólito the rebels killed thirty persons; four of them were Spaniards, the rest Negro slaves. This havoc was wrought September 26.[6] The rebels thus harrying the country destroyed forty rude chapels, coming now for murder to the hallowed spots to which they had formerly gone in piety and devotion. Then they made for the mines of Topia, of San Andrés and Las Vírgines. At all three places they worked havoc, falling suddenly upon the districts and forcing both workers and owners to flee. They burned the wooden machinery, they destroyed the workshops, and they vowed to put to death every Spaniard and Christian Indian in all three places. The mines at Las Vírgines were utterly destroyed, and many Christian Indians and Spaniards slain. At San Andrés the revolt flared up at its worst. Here were the firm Sobaibos of the south. They had determined to kill Father Alonzo Ruiz; but the padre was saved by a combination of circumstances. One of the neophytes warned the missionary by a message sent through his son. Ruiz rushed by night to San Andrés to warn the Spaniards and Indians there. Though the rebels attacked San Miguel where Ruiz had been staying and though they had the roads to San Andrés guarded, the padre escaped both the one and the other group and got to the mines before the attack. But his house and church at San Miguel were destroyed.[7]

Nevertheless, the attack at San Andrés came swiftly enough to work destruction. A rebel band of more than a thousand fell upon the mines. This was the vigil of the Feast of St. Michael, and would be, therefore, September 28. The Spaniards warned had fled to the church. Here the rebels besieged about forty of them, including Father Alonzo Ruiz. This was at seven in the morning. Fortunately the Spaniards had guns, though mostly unfit, and some powder. They could thus hold off the savages, and at three in the afternoon they made a sortie, which relieved the close pressure about the church, driving the rebels farther off. But the besieged lacked provisions, and hunger soon declared its presence. Besides, the powder would be giving out.

Another sortie was decided on. By the advice of some Christian Indians the time was fixed for very early the following morning when it was hoped they should catch the enemy asleep. The ruse was so far successful that some of the rebels were slain and all were driven back, giving opportunity to gather in supplies from fields of corn that lay hard by the church. Father Ruiz came out with the rest all unprotected, holding high a crucifix and showing himself boldly to the enemy. He was hit by no arrow, for it appears that his former spiritual children did not even try to slay him in spite of plan and resolution. They still held for their padre a reverence and affection that stayed their murderous intent. But some of the Christian Indians were slain in the act of getting in supplies, and as the surrounding rebels could not be put to flight, there was nothing for it but to return into the church. It was still early morning, so that the padre said his Mass, gave Holy Communion to the beleaguered, and exhorted them to Christian fortitude and readiness for death in the Christian cause. So the time passed and the fifteenth day of the siege came and went—then relief and the raising of the siege.[8]

At the first flare of trouble swift messages had been sent to the nearest of the towns, to Culiacán, fifty miles out of the mountains to the west, and to Durango, one hundred and fifty miles south and east. But especially to Mexico City was word sent to the Viceroy and to the Governor of Nueva Vizcaya, Rodrigo de Rivera, then in the capital of the kingdom. The latter was dispatched immediately north with orders to draw upon the royal treasury at Zacatecas and Durango and muster a force sufficient to repress the revolt. But the lieutenant of the Governor was sent ahead, probably from Durango, to raise the siege of San Andrés. His force was not large, but he was aided by several hundred Indian allies, fine bowmen from the Lagunero country. At their approach the hostiles fled and those beleaguered in the church at San Andrés were delivered from their peril.[9]

The Governor finally arrived in person with his forces. Things progressed slowly, however, and great difficulties beset his path. The ruggedness of the country and the wide dispersal of the rebels throughout the rocky summits or into deep folds and barrancas made it impossible to suppress the rebellion at a single stroke. Pursuit would have to be slow, and reconquest accomplished piecemeal. In the meantime, traveling was dangerous and commerce between Culiacán and points east had all but ceased. Once, when a mule train did attempt a journey, there was murder and pillage. The Governor seems to have suffered from discouragement, for in a letter of January 28, 1602, he writes from San Andrés complainingly to the Viceroy, petitioning for further supplies of munitions and men. But in the spring of that year there was success. He drove almost three hundred rebels to a *peñol* or craggy peak, and on March 23 attacked them there with sixty soldiers. From early morning until late afternoon the attack was pressed until the remnant surrendered after one hundred and thirty were killed.[10]

But this single success was far from ending the rebellion. There were many other rocky summits thus to be taken, many ravines and gorges cleared. But it was thought well, after the success of the Peñol de Pospa, to try conciliation and diplomacy and Hernando de Santarén was chosen for this dangerous work.

Santarén was the best-beloved man of all these mountains. He was the Indians' first father and through the waters of baptism he had brought a large number of them into the fold of the Church. The Governor considered that if peace were possible at all Santarén could effect it. He was sent therefore with a handful of soldiers to try to bring the Indians to proper mind. He met with no success. He pleaded that he was their father and that he would answer for the conciliatory intentions of the Governor and his soldiers. They replied that he was not their father and they were not his sons. With that they took leave of him. He made several other efforts. On one of these occasions they consented to meet him provided the soldiers should be left behind and he, the padre, should come alone into one of their deep ravines. It looked like a design upon his life. Nevertheless he consented. They did not kill him; but he had no positive success. "Disowned by his spiritual children," he withdrew to Culiacán.

In the meantime Don Alonso de la Mota y Escobar, Bishop of Guadalajara, enters the story. His Excellency came into this ragged country in 1601 to encourage the neophytes and console the Spaniards and old Christian laborers of the mines. When the revolt broke out he did not leave, and he was far from inactive. He went about the country doing what good he could. He even made the dangerous journey to Topia, accompanied by a guard of forty soldiers. He traveled from mine to mine, from pueblo to pueblo. Once, his soldiers met the rebels, and in a skirmish some of the latter were killed. The Bishop now made an attempt at conciliation, for which reason he summoned Santarén, "the great conciliator," from Culiacán. The missionary made another effort in the direction of peace. He sent a faithful and trusted Indian to one of the chief retreats of the rebels, a deep *quebrada* most difficult of access. He sent this messenger with a white banner and a cross, emblem of peace. The result was encouraging: the hostiles indicated their willingness to confer with the Black Robe, provided he would come to them. The padre accepted, and he wanted to penetrate alone into the savage fastness, but the Spaniards would not allow it. They sent to accompany him an escort of ten soldiers. This time Santarén enjoyed better success: the rebels were willing to negotiate if he, Santarén, would guarantee the terms of peace.[11]

Bishop Mota y Escobar seconded the efforts of Santarén. He too sent them emblems of peace, namely, his miter and pastoral ring. These tokens were sent by the kindly offices of friendly Indians. When the latter did not return, the Spaniards lost hope, thinking they had been killed. Not so the Bishop. As a matter of fact, his benign gesture added its influence to the efforts of Santarén and effected the submission of a large part of the rebels in the quebrada of Topia and over the more eastern section of the country.

According to a letter of Juan Fonte, Captain Mateo Canelas, the Bishop accompanying him, pursued a group of five hundred Acaxée rebels to the foot of a peñol upon the rocky summit of which the hostiles stood at bay. The Captain wanted to give battle and storm the height. He was making preparations to do so when a most extraordinary thing happened. The rebels flung a wooden pole down the precipitous flanks of the peñol, and as it came tumbling and sliding down, the Spaniards at the base noticed that objects were tied to it. A closer view revealed the curious gesture of the Indians and their wholly original manner of signifying peace: tied to the pole were the miter and ring of Bishop Mota! The soldiers revered and kissed the miter to impress the Indians with the importance of the episcopal office, while both Bishop and Captain made signs of accepting the seemingly proffered peace. With that, the rebels from the rocky top of their peñol signified surrender by running and tumbling down its sides, shouting in their own language the word "peace" and other terms of amity and friendship. They too now revered and kissed the Bishop's miter while their leaders were embraced by both the civil and ecclesiastical leaders of Spain.

After this, Bishop Mota y Escobar on his way back to Topia went over to San Andrés to aid in the conciliation there, and soon afterward the Spaniards at Topia saw a thrilling sight. Santarén had been in the wilds with other submissive rebels for several days. It was agreed that he should lead them into Topia so as to make the reconciliation visible to the eye. Santarén marched down the winding path into the pueblo at the head of the caciques of eleven pueblos. These chiefs came with their people, three thousand of them, displaying the white flag of peace. Streaming down the mountain trail they came, carrying the white banner and the cross which Santarén had sent them. Gathered into the town, they promised before Governor Rivera, Bishop Mota y Escobar, and Santarén, submission to the King of Spain and good conduct for the future. All the mountain country rejoiced; the backbone of the revolt was broken. These various events took place probably in the early part of 1603.[12]

The details of the submission were consoling. Governor and Bishop embraced each pacified rebel in turn. Governor Rivera then harangued the crowd, defining the conditions of peace. Bishop Mota y Escobar offered a Mass of thanksgiving and preached sentiments of gentleness and brotherly love; presents of cloth were given to the reconciled; Santarén stood by to see that all should be steady and well confirmed. It was his influence that gave assurance of permanence to this peace. Rivera returned to Mexico, thinking that his work was over.[13]

Unfortunately, the work was not yet over. To the south and west large numbers of rebels still held out. These it seems were the Sobaibos, and they were being kept in disorder by a strange, if amusing, development. A cacique by the name of Perico, native of Chacala in the west, gave himself out as bishop; nay, he went further still, he proclaimed himself as God the Holy Ghost: the prestige enjoyed by Bishop Mota y Escobar was perhaps too much for his jealous nature. The tribesmen should follow him, he said, for he enjoyed all the powers of the Bishop and more. He met with a degree of success that bloated him into a real and dangerous rebel, for these simple and stupid children believed him and called him "Bishop" if they did not call him God. He pretended to rebaptize those to whom the Jesuits had administered the sacrament; he divorced couples married by the fathers and remarried them to others. In short, he pretended to take upon himself all the powers of the priesthood and the episcopacy. This leader and this section of the rebels now had to be dealt with.[14]

Father Santarén went into their country and enjoyed a partial success, six pueblos submitting to his persuasions of peace. Others, however, held out and railed at those who submitted. The padre sent word to Mexico of the continued trouble and went to Durango to seek help.

A MOUNTAIN REVOLT 63

Here he secured the services of Captain Juan de Castañeda, who came west from Durango over the mountains and arrived in the rebels' country just in time to be close by when they waylaid a mule train coming with merchandise from Culiacán. The rebels killed the two Spaniards in charge and made off with what goods they could carry.[15]

In the meantime, the messages of Santarén were being acted upon at the capital. Governor Rodrigo de Rivera resigned his office and the Viceroy appointed a man who was to figure largely in the early history of the northern frontier, Francisco de Urdiñola. Appointed on May 23, 1603, he took possession of his office before the *ayuntamiento* of Durango on June 23 following. Well aware of the smoking and sputtering embers of the rebellion, he took the field immediately, though in the midst of the rainy season, and sped west in pursuit of the leaders. Santarén was with him. Urdiñola enjoyed swift success. The two ringleaders, the would-be bishop and his chief aid, were captured and executed in punishment of their crimes and murders, the gentle padre assisting at their death and reconciling them to their lot.[16]

The leaders gone, the rest, in the hands of an able man like Urdiñola, was only a matter of time. The new governor rode all over the disaffected country, extinguishing the still smoking faggots of the revolt, not by harshness, but by an understanding diplomacy. Having shown his strength, he could now afford to be kind. Besides, the law allowed force only after all efforts of benignity and diplomacy had been exhausted.[17] Once, he came upon a band of women and girls separated from their husbands and fathers. They were taken and held for a while, the Governor issuing strict orders that not one of them be molested by cruel or dishonorable treatment. When he felt that the right effect had been produced, Urdiñola sent them back under escort to their men. Savages though they were, they appreciated this magnanimous action. They admired a man who, though possessing power, yet employed the means of tempered diplomacy and kindness.[18]

It was now time to send Santarén on his last mission of conciliation. He went, and succeeded. The rebels said that although they had vowed eternal enmity, their hardness was melted by the generosity of the new governor. As earlier in this revolt Santarén had gathered and led into Topia the chiefs and people of eleven pueblos, so now he had a similar success with nine pueblos of the south and west. As happened so often on this frontier, these savages, reduced to a conciliatory spirit, seemed as anxious now to conform to authority's desire as formerly they had been determined to run counter to it. As on other fronts, they were willing to hand over for special punishment the leaders of the trouble. The number executed this time was large, forty-eight in all; which reminds us of the forty-three captured by ruse just three years before this on the Fuerte through the energy of Captain Hurdaide and executed where they were caught, with the exception of one who escaped and another who was pardoned. But the hanging corpses of thirty-six of these Acaxées were strung at intervals along the road leading to San Andrés that all who passed might know the ultimate price of murderous rebellion.[19]

Soon every sign of hostility was gone from these mountains and the work of recuperation was begun. The miter of Bishop Mota y Escobar, which had figured so prominently in the earlier stages of the revolt, was hung up in the church at Culiacán, a lasting memorial of the peace. Governor Urdiñola, so successfully terminating the first activities of his new office, did not return immediately to his capital, Durango, but traveled directly north to visit the flourishing missions of Sinaloa. It was now early December, 1603.[20]

Chapter VIII

SUCCESS AMID HARDSHIPS

THE REBELLION over, the work of the missionaries immediately picked up and advanced apace. The year 1604 was encouragingly progressive for the mountain missions of Topia and San Andrés. This year twenty-five hundred persons were baptized, of whom only four hundred were children, which brought the total number since the uprising to thirty-seven hundred. More than seven hundred couples were married in the Christian manner, and during Lent three hundred went to confession. The devotions of Holy Week were gone through with all the exterior fervor of the Latin Christianity of the Counter-reformation. During Lent, on Mondays, Tuesdays, and Wednesdays many scourged themselves privately in the church; on Thursdays and Fridays penitents marched around the church in public procession during which the participants scourged themselves to the flowing of blood. *Disciplinas de sangre* is the term used throughout all these missionary annals for this kind of public demonstration. "Those who the year before," wrote Santarén to his provincial in Mexico City, "did not hesitate to shed the blood of Spaniards now made their own blood to flow with great sorrow for their evil deeds and in repentance for their sin of rebellion." The Governor had impressed upon the Indians the respect they must have for the fathers. Therefore, whenever a padre entered a pueblo they came out, carrying small crosses, to greet him.

Because these mountain missions of the south progressed so well, Santarén asked for more fathers. The work was becoming too widespread for himself, together with Ruiz and Tutino, to handle it. Besides, Santarén had great visions of expansion, which were encouraged by the fact that a new mine in the Sierra de Carantapa northwest of Topia had been discovered in 1604. There was another gold rush north from Culiacán. The Real de Carantapa was founded; machinery was hauled over the rough trails; a new though brief period of local prosperity had begun. This meant greater facility and safety for the expansion of the missions.[2]

---

[1] For notes to chapter viii see pages 207–208.

Governor Urdiñola seconded the padre's request with a letter to the Viceroy. The latter, inclining a favorable ear, wrote to the Provincial for men. The Governor requested bells and ornaments for the churches damaged during the uprising, and royal alms for the establishment of a school for the sons of caciques, that they might serve in the Church and later be able to govern the Christian pueblos with loyalty and justice. To these requests, except perhaps for funds for the Indian school, the Viceroy acceded. He asked for four fathers and the Provincial dispatched them. With them came bells, ornaments, paintings, and musical instruments: flutes, flageolets, trumpets, and bassoons.[3]

The necessary divisions of work were now made, the district being divided off into *partidos,* and a change in administration was made, Alonzo Ruiz becoming local superior of the Jesuit group.

At least four missionaries arrived in 1606 and 1607 and by the fall of the latter year were well at work. The charges were redistributed: Alonzo Ruiz, the superior, took the country around San Gregorio, at which place he resided with two or three assistants. San Gregorio is some miles south of San Andrés and was, at the time of our story, on the borders of the Acaxée nation at the fringes of the Xiximes. This is far up the quebrada of that name, down which canyon in the rainy season tumbles a stream called the Río de los Remedios, which drops into the sea under the name of San Lorenzo. Lower down from San Gregorio, where various forks meet to form the Río de los Remedios, is Otatitlán. This was the residence of Father Diego Gonzales Cueto, to whose charge were given the restless Sobaibos. The central mountain district with Topia and San Andrés fell to the lot of Father Gerónimo de San Clemente, who resided usually at Tamazula, midway between Topia and Culiacán. The more northern districts of Baimoa were taken by Santarén, who was given charge of the Sierra de Carantapa, and by Floriano Ayerve, who lived at Atotonilco, northeast of Culiacán and far distant from the other Atotonilco which is east of the mountains. Santarén and Ayerve organized a new mission unit in the district of the new mines, at Partido de Carantapa, which included the three Indian villages of Tabanetu, Tecuciapa, and Baimoa. Finally, Fathers José de Lomas, Andrés Tutino, and Alonso Gómez worked with Alonzo Ruiz near San Gregorio and took charge of other Acaxée pueblos.[4]

SUCCESS AMID HARDSHIPS

The greater part of this country was wild and savage in the extreme. We have already seen the mountains about Topia; the rest of the districts were similar. On the way from Culiacán to Topia the Quebrada de Topia with its stream had to be crossed two hundred and seventy times, and south of Culiacán looking east one can see today in the blue distance the sharp serrated outlines of these gruff sierras. From the plains to the mountains the fathers went from heat to cold, and when the waters of the rainy season swelled the rivers the labor of travel was as hazardous as it was fatiguing.

Father Alonzo Ruiz writes of the dangers two of his subjects had to undergo in traveling down to Otatitlán after a meeting of the local missionaries at San Gregorio. They had waited in San Gregorio six days for the floods to abate. Then they departed. Arrived at the stream which they had to ford, they first tried sending a mule across with a pack of the sacred vestments and articles and of books. But the animal was swept off his feet by the force of the current and everything was thoroughly drenched. The mule and pack were salvaged only with the greatest difficulty. The next mule sent across was ridden by one of the padres. This almost led to disaster. The animal was carried away and the padre leaped into the stream. An Indian saved him at the risk of his own life, but his books and manuscripts were lost. It was only after a delay of fifteen days, with the discomfort first of wet clothes and then of scanty food brought by the Indians, that the two missionaries were able to cross in safety.[5]

In 1607 there was a grand celebration at San Gregorio over the dedication of a new church the Indians had built. The fiesta lasted eight days, on the first three of which a Solemn High Mass was celebrated. A procession each day was enlivened by an orchestra and singers, and two barrels of powder were consumed in salvos and fireworks. The church itself was decorated for the occasion with silken hangings and tapestry of gilt and tinsel. Visitors from thirty miles around came in to see the celebration and for all the eight days were housed and fed. All were entertained with mock combats of horsemen and foot soldiers, the gaping Indians looking on in astonishment.

During Holy Week of that year four hundred Indian men took part in a penitential and flagellant procession, and communions amounted to two thousand. If it happened that on a Sunday Ruiz would be absent from the pueblo his neophytes would assemble at the church, led by their Indian fiscal, to pray and to rehearse the catechism. Indians, coming into the pueblo to barter for salt or for knives, saws, and other tools, were edified to see their fellow tribesmen gathered in church and listening to an instruction by the padre.[6]

The adventures of Floriano de Ayerve were thrilling and his missionary experiences consoling. He came to Baimoa, as we have seen, with Santarén in September, 1606. A large group of savages had waited for three years for the padres to come to them and had remained within reach of an accessible spot near the Sierra de Carantapa. Recently, their patience worn out, they had dispersed to their three original districts, one of which was almost absolutely inaccessible. The other two places could be reached by the fathers. While Santarén took the districts farther north about the country of Tecuciapa, Ayerve was to visit the pueblos near Atotonilco, which was his residence.[7] To reach them, he wrote, he had to follow through the rough country a forky mule path which crossed the stream, a branch of the Río Culiacán, two hundred times. But his people were happy to see him, and within a month he had baptized two hundred children and one hundred and ninety adults, and had joined in legitimate wedlock twenty-nine couples, having persuaded that many braves to dismiss their other wives.[8] "Ayerve describes the eagerness of the people in learning the *doctrina,* counting out their little stones with admirable perseverance, and the recitation of the prayers aloud as the *temastián* drilled his groups." The new converts were zealous to bring others down from the mountains; they were willing and ready to surrender their idols.[9]

In December Ayerve had gone off many leagues into the mountains to visit a section of the country allotted to him. But he was caught by continuous rains and found it impossible to traverse the pass leading back to Atotonilco. A few beans and tortillas of maize were a day's food, and so short was he of wine and hosts that on Christmas Day he had to forego two of his three Masses. Later he had to cross swollen streams, and more than once he was in danger of drowning as his mount was swept off its feet in midstream and carried down by the flood. In one of these mishaps his books were soaked and his manuscripts lost. At last, worn out and shaking with the chills of fever, Ayerve got back to Atotonilco.[10]

Consolations of the spirit balanced hardships of the body. Twelve savages once came to the padre, naked and carrying bow and arrow. They had traveled far to invite Ayerve to their pueblo that he might baptize them. He dared not go because of the season. Should he arrive in their country and the rains begin, he would be there for months. The place was accessible only in February, March, April, and May. The Indians would not be put off, so after eight days of preparation the padre administered the baptismal sacrament.

When the rains were over, Ayerve went to their pueblo. They carried him across the swollen river on a raft which four of them propelled with their heads as they swam. Fifty came out to meet him and conduct him to their settlement, which nestled in a delightful glen. Here awaiting his approach were seven hundred boys and girls, men and women, crowned with garlands of cattail and carrying branches of palm in their hands. When Ayerve beaming with delight came up to them, they dropped to their knees and together intoned the Credo: *Oneya quevava ni Dios Tacaca nevincame* (I believe in God the Father Almighty). The padre was struck dumb with joyful amazement. He came as to ignorant and pagan savages of the wild, and discovered that the whole tribe of them knew the Apostles' Creed and could sing it in their own language! How did they learn it, he inquired. Why, they replied, the twelve whom a few months ago he had instructed in eight days and baptized had returned bringing with them their new-found knowledge. They had been good teachers, they had taught the Creed to all the tribe. No need to delay long with instruction here; the padre's work had been prepared before him. Father Ayerve baptized four hundred and eighty-two at this visit, which, added to the rest to whom he had administered the sacrament in the pueblos of his district, swelled the total to fourteen hundred. At his return he visited the pueblos of Chanmayo, Batocomito, Atotonilco, and San José. As in all these missions, the padre destroyed hundreds of idols. When later his superior ordered him to Culiacán for some passing work Ayerve brought with him a few of his neophytes.[11]

Prospects were not at first so encouraging in another district, where the savages refused to descend from their mountains and derided the missionary from afar. The Church is like a woman, they said, which possesses neither bow nor arrow; it can neither hurt us nor defend itself, and so is not to be feared. They had no dread of Spanish arms, for they considered their fastnesses sufficient protection. Some of the former rebels and false Christians joined this group and grew more stubborn in their hostile attitude. Yet even here perseverance led to a measure of success. First, two hundred and fifty were willing to group themselves into a pueblo. Soon, five hundred others were added to the number. They set themselves to building a church and when Holy Week came they underwent the flogging to blood as if they were old Christians. Soon they were baptized.[12]

Some of the soldiers who were staying with Santarén wanted to accompany Ayerve into his new mission, but he would not have it. "If the Indians had attacked me," he writes, "only I and the two boys would have been the victims. Moreover, there were not so many soldiers that they could have saved me from the hands of these barbarians, and the bad example of the soldiers probably would have been an impediment to the teaching of the gospel."[13] The savages expressed wonder that the missionary dared come into a strange and unknown country alone. They asked what would happen should they kill him and devour his flesh. He gave appropriate answers. Some of those still pagan, seeing on one occasion the respect shown by some Spaniards at Mass, thought this honor and adoration were given to the padre himself, and they began to be extravagant in their manifestations. He restrained their zeal and proffered the correcting explanations. After having been for many months greatly consoled by the devotional reaction of his neophytes to the Faith, Ayerve, now worn out with hardship and illness, was ordered at the end of 1607 to Topia and was succeeded at Atotonilco by Father José de Lomas.

Father Santarén had good success with his Sierra de Carantapa during the three or four years following the revolt. The center of Santarén's labor was Tecuciapa on a branch of the upper reaches of the Sinaloa River, almost as many miles north from Atotonilco as the latter was from Culiacán. This padre had a consoling experience similar to that of Ayerve, and, strange to say, with some of the latter's people. "These Indians," writes Santarén, "came from thirty leagues away to beg me to go to them. The better to clinch the matter, they went to gain over to their cause the captain of the mines of Carantapa, presenting to him some metal from their land." The padre put them off; they were too far away for instruction and he could not spare the time to go to them. Their disappointment was keen, but their resolution great. They took matters into their own hands, left their rancherias, and came all the way, one hundred and thirty of them, to Tecuciapa to seek baptism. Not one of them returned to their old haunts; they preferred to remain with the padre. They became homesick, however, for their families and companions and clamored for them. Santarén found himself obliged finally to make the journey with the captain of the mines over country so rough that five leagues a day was good traveling. He met a hundred and fifty persons. Of these, thirty came to Tecuciapa with him; the rest promised to follow. The padre was waiting for them when he wrote his letter.[14]

Others also, who called themselves Sicurabas, gathered about Santarén for baptism, to the number of ninety. In 1607 he baptized twelve hundred and married four hundred couples. He destroyed his two hundred idols, and Ayerve his three hundred. At Tecuciapa, called Santa María, the padre had a pueblo of five hundred Christians; at Yamorinoa, called San Simón, he had a pueblo of the same number. Four hundred were at San Pedro y San Pablo de Bacapa, and three hundred were at San Ildefonso de Tocorito.[15]

Santarén had his adventures, too. Once his mule slipped on the edge of a declivity. The box containing his effects was shaken loose and rolled down the steep slope. It landed at the bottom broken to pieces, and books, pictures, and altar furnishings were scattered over the rocks. This mishap lost him a day.[16]

Father Diego Gonzales Cueto this same year wrote a glowing account of the devotion of his neophytes, manifested in the recitation of the rosary, in confession, and in religious processions. The Lenten devotions among Cueto's children were most encouraging. A thousand neophytes would go out at night for a "procession of blood," that is, to scourge themselves publicly, the darkness partly dispersed by the dim light of torches made of fagots or dry grass. A Spaniard who witnessed one of the processions of the Blessed Sacrament in which the Sacred Host was carried in a rude wooden box covered over with coarse cloth averred that he was more moved by this sight than by the rich and splendid processions of Mexico City. The pueblos of Otatitlán and Las Vegas were witnesses to such beginnings in Christianity.

Stories of edification abounded. One Indian swam across the river swollen with the rains in order to come to confession. Another, one of the most promising of Cueto's flock, fell ill. With all his promise and his fine piety, there was a great flaw in the practice of his Christianity; he had not been able to keep the law of Christian chastity, living as he did with his two sisters. He fell ill—so ill as to lose consciousness. Father Cueto came, the neophyte revived sufficiently to make his confession; then, upon the reception of the sacrament of extreme unction, he entered upon a state of absolute recovery. During his period of unconsciousness, he averred to the father, he had had a glimpse of the other world. As for this world, his appreciation of the value of it underwent a radical change. He left his two sisters and subsequently shone, writes Cueto, in the splendor of his chastity. If ever trouble came to him thereafter he would call to mind the glimpse he had caught of the future life and his soul would thereby be made strong to resist.[17]

A great deal of Cueto's work was at Las Vegas, not more than twelve miles from the mines called Las Vírgines and not far distant from Culiacán. In the mountains east of this town three Christian pueblos were formed, Vadiravato, Conimeto, and Alicamac, and a school was organized. At Carantapa good progress was made for a while, but the mines petered out, the Indians dispersed, and no lasting mark was put upon the land.[18]

The old pest of the fathers, the hechicero, was present among these Acaxée Indians with somewhat greater frequency than elsewhere. Ribas wrote, "It is certain that you always find among them certain ones, sorcerers or others, who are possessed by the evil spirits, which fact as during the life Christ is discovered by the light of the gospel." These wizards threatened evil or promised reward, "health or sickness, ease or labor, plenty or famine, life or death." Indeed, asserts the padre here quoted, some of these *hechiceros diabolicos* succeeded in procuring the deaths of certain Indians.[19] Here, it appears, was black magic indeed, and, on the part of the padre, of seventeenth-century superstition.

The wife of a wizard died. The hechicero and his friends spread it about that through the power of their incantations she would rise from the grave and slay those who were near by, especially the chil-

SUCCESS AMID HARDSHIPS

dren. This created a scare. Then one night the three or four who were performing the incantations suddenly fell to the ground speechless, which caused a whole pueblo to flee. The padre was summoned. He came and at his presence those lying as if dead revived, but they looked as if they had suffered a serious illness. The dead woman at this same time appeared to an old man of seventy, who likewise became forthwith speechless and so stiff of body that his arm could not be doubled. The missionary gathered all the pueblo before him, thundered against the vile superstition, and ordered the guilty to be immediately punished—flogged by their own Indian alcaldes. He strengthened the weak and the fearful by telling them of the force of prayer, and he said a Mass and prayed that God disperse the powers of evil. The pueblo remained thereafter quiet and such disturbances were not heard of at this place again.[20]

During a visitation among the Baimoas of the dreaded *viruelas* or smallpox, so fatal to the Indian, an hechicero, it was said, gathered the men, women, and children of a pueblo into and about his hut and summoned up not only one, but five or six demons. One of the Christians hidden under a blanket conceived so great a fright that he called out the name of Jesus, at which a clap of thunder rent the air, the demons scampered, the hechicero was howled over, and the roof of his hut shaken and undone, while those within stood aghast with fear.[21] But, in spite of all, such abundance of food was raised in and about Otatitlán under Cueto's supervision in 1607 that this district was able to send supplies to droughty and hard-pressed Culiacán.[22]

Thus were the fathers tried; thus did they succeed. Sometimes as a last resort they would have to call in the military to quell a disturbance and to punish an hechicero. But, in spite of all superstition and demon worship, Christianity spread apace and letters coming in to headquarters from other missionaries tell the same story of success for the years that followed the Acaxée uprising. If in the year after the revolt thirty-seven hundred persons were baptized, and if within two years Santarén alone could organize four new pueblos containing in all seventeen hundred new Christians, one will not consider that Pérez de Ribas exaggerated when, writing in 1643, he recorded that in these parts of the mountains among the Acaxée Indians and the Xiximes south of them fifty thousand had been received into the Church.[23]

Chapter IX

THE LAGUNEROS WON OVER

THE INDIANS of the lagoon country were, as we have seen, the first with whom the Jesuits made contact east of the Sierra Madre. We have seen how in 1594 Gerónimo Ramírez and Juan Agustín de Espinosa from Zacatecas went up among the Zacateco Indians who lived near the lagoon. These missions were only temporary, and we soon read of the two fathers as resident in Durango. Although the records of 1595 are silent, we know that both missionaries were on the road in 1596. Juan Agustín went back to the lagoon country and among the lagoon Indians, but this time alone, for that spring Ramírez, with the success we have seen, made the first Jesuit entrada among the Tepehuanes to the northwest. Juan Agustín was still alone in 1598[1] and it was, one may suppose, loneliness joined with other suffering that wrung from him the letter quoted above.[2] This year seems to have been the first of his permanent residence among the Laguneros and it was the year of his success, the founding of the first Christian pueblo of the region, Santa María de las Parras.

The field was large and it was evident that with the expanding efforts Juan Agustín would need assistance, for living in and about the lagoon of San Pedro were twelve thousand Indians. Besides, the Spaniards to the west wanted these Indians Christianized for the greater safety of their farms and mines. The Viceroy, therefore, communicated with the Jesuit Provincial in Mexico City and with the royal officials. The Provincial was asked to send men; the officials were ordered to give out of the King's treasury what was needed for the expansion of the new mission: bells, sacred vestments, ornaments for the proposed chapels, and musical instruments.[3]

The Provincial, Francisco Váez, was able to satisfy the demands of the Viceroy. He had a man at hand whom he would send, Father Francisco de Arista, and, with fine circumspection, he sent up with him, as it were to start him off well and to look into the condition of the new field and it's possible demands for the future, Nicolás de Ar-

[1] For notes to chapter ix see pages 208–209.

THE LAGUNEROS WON OVER 75

naya. This was the same Arnaya who had accompanied Tapia north in 1589. He was therefore familiar with this part of the frontier. Arnaya was to visit the mission at Parras and then to go to Durango to be Superior. In 1601 from Durango he sent the reports of the anua down to Váez, and in 1613 he was Provincial of the province of New Spain.[4] In 1599 then, the three fathers, Juan Agustín de Espinosa, Francisco de Arista, and Nicolás de Arnaya, having met either at Zacatecas or Durango, went together into the Laguna country by way of the cordillera of Zacatecas, or down the valley of the Río de las Nieves.[5]

Arnaya looked well over the field and when he had satisfied himself as to its details of the present and possibilities for the future he departed for Durango by way of Río de las Nazas and from the capital sent his report to the Provincial. He had remained twelve days in Santa María de las Parras and was enthusiastic about all that he had seen. There were sixteen hundred neophytes about the pueblo, he said, and there would be need of two more missionaries, because ascending the banks of the Río de las Nazas on his way to Durango he passed through a populous country where the fathers hoped to organize four or five settlements. While Arnaya was at Parras a cacique arrived with some of his followers asking that all his people might settle there. Nine other chiefs coming in made similar overtures, so that soon, thought the Black Robe, Parras would be a center for some five thousand Indians. Therefore he considered that in no place could workmen be employed to better advantage than here.[6] One chief gave Arnaya his idol, a small hard rock with the shape of a human head. "I shall send it to Your Reverence," writes Arnaya to the Provincial, "that you may see what sort of thing these people adore."[7]

When Father Arnaya departed for Durango he left Francisco de Arista behind to be companion and helper to Juan Agustín. Arista was soon ardently engaged in the work which was to hold him for sixteen years, and after three months he sent in to headquarters a good report. He visited surrounding rancherias, accompanied by the caciques who acted as messengers to gather in the scattered people that the padre might speak with them. Word of the good treatment the Indians might expect at the hands of the Black Robe had gone abroad, so that larger and larger numbers gathered to the mission of Santa María de las Parras. "They have come up to this new pueblo by the hundreds and hundreds with their families... seeking information and making trial of this new mode of life that they might return to report back to their respective settlements and discuss the advantages of joining perpetually the pueblo. Some have already departed and others are preparing to leave, for the rainy season is at hand.... It looks as if Divine Providence were about to accomplish the salvation of this people."[8]

One has to admire the tolerance and the liberal spirit of these two missionaries, Espinosa and Arista. Well did they understand how through kindness to gain the good will of their neophytes. From time to time they invited the chiefs to dinner and on certain feast days they supplied a repast for all the people. After the meal there would be a general dance according to the Indian custom, "but spiritually and with Christian hymns," writes Arista, "which we have translated into their language from the Mexican." The place of merriment was the plaza in front of the church. Arista says that the Indians were pleased to have the fathers at these dances and adds that the fathers were as pleased as the Indians to be there. The boys and girls had their own fun when they gathered each evening for instruction.[9]

Juan Agustín de Espinosa built well from the beginning. To each Indian family newly arrived from outlying rancherias to make their permanent dwelling at Santa María was given a plot of ground on which to erect their hut and to use as a kitchen garden. Adjoining was a small field for sowing. The dwellings and gardens were laid out in orderly fashion between straight streets as in the Mexican pueblos, and the padres visited the Indian homes from time to time to see that order and cleanliness were kept, so far as these wild children of the plains and lagoons were able to keep them. Though the Indian was lazy by nature, this distribution of lands and gardens aroused his interest in cultivation, and he never before worked with such diligence. The neophytes were aided in their household problems by supplies furnished from the treasury of the King. Corn, salt, chilli, and garments were doled out to the Christians. At times some interested Spaniards would give the fathers a supply of beef and they in turn would dispense it to their charges. Of meat these savages were most greedy and they would fall like famished things upon a quarter of beef till nothing was left but the bone.[10]

A small chapel had been built for Mass, with a house near by for Juan Agustín when he was alone. When Arista came, the neophytes made him as comfortable as they could. Already, before the latter's arrival, five caciques with their people had gathered into Santa María, which brought the number to a thousand souls. Some had already been baptized, like Don Juan Maiconera, Martín Pacho, and Antón Martín Irritila. But others were pagan like Don Francisco Dui, Calaraque Lacateco, and Mainara. Some of the Christian caciques desired to go to Mexico City to offer obedience in person to the Viceroy, to thank the Jesuit Father Provincial for the light of Christianity now shed upon them, and to see the greatness and the splendor of the city of the Spaniards. The pagan adults were being prepared for baptism when Arista arrived on the scene. Juan Agustín had given them instructions from the catechism, which was translated for them into two languages, the Irritila, the idiom proper to the valley, and the Mexican, which most of them could understand but could speak only poorly. The children gathered every evening for instruction and the speed with which they learned was remarkable to the padres. On feast days a sermon to all the pueblo was given.[11]

Every day the children came for Mass. They understood they had three duties for each day: to hear Mass in the morning, to come to instruction in the evening, and to keep the church in orderly condition and clean with sweeping. They would be up before the sun and would gather in front of the church, and would keep up a chatter and laughter until the coming of the padre. Sometimes they would awaken those who were still asleep that they be on time for Mass. The older boys were less eager, however, for these things, and some of the old men were so indifferent that they often put off baptism, even, until they were in danger of death.[12] "On some of the principal feast days," reported Arista, "we organize processions during which all the new Christians carry crosses of flowers in their hands. At the Mass which follows they assist with such reverence and attention that they demonstrate more and more each day their good will and their intelligent conception of the divine offices of Holy Mother Church."[13]

Thus after three months could Father Arista describe to his provincial the activities of the mission of Santa María de las Parras, which Juan Agustín had begun the year before and to which Arista was sent to help carry on and expand. One is not surprised at the enthusiasm of the Jesuit's letter and, reflecting on these facts, one comes to the conclusion that these poor children of the wilds on the rim of the Spanish frontier were especially attuned to the Faith, so ready and even eager were they to receive it. From such events of history the modern reader comes to a knowledge of how the people of Mexico became Catholics and realizes the truth of a statement made by a great scholar that "it was thought worth while to improve the natives for this life as well as for the next."[14]

In a subsequent letter to his provincial, Francisco de Arista speaks of the possible organization of those pueblos which Nicolás de Arnaya had mentioned. The Jesuit describes them as a fine field for the exercise of his apostolic zeal. "Besides the pueblo of Parras," he writes, "which at present Father Juan Agustín and I administer, there are in this district five others which the Society might take under its charge to the great glory of the Master." His letter presents a good example of the exact information concerning the Indian settlements which the writings of the missionaries afford. One district was Santa Ana, forty-five miles to the west, where lived a group partly Christian and easily handled.[15] The fathers had already visited this pueblo from time to time. If only eight or nine caciques of the district could be got together, a settlement of five hundred families could be formed. This land, with mountain, valley, and stream, was fertile in the production of fruit and grain and in the chase. The second place was at the mouth of the Río de las Nazas where its waters were spread into the lagoon of San Pedro. It was more than fifty miles from Parras. Thirty caciques lived in the vicinity, ruling over a numerous population, gentle, docile, and desirous of baptism. The land was exceedingly fertile. Any kind of fruit or grain could be grown here and there was excellent fishing and hunting. Hills were near by, with wood and rock for building.[16]

A third good place was one, some distance up the river, over which the cacique named Aztla held authority; it became known as San Ignacio. It was rich in wood for building, especially ash, and had this advantage over the other two places, that the water from the river could be easily drawn off for irrigation. There would be five hundred families here, Father Arista calculated, were the Indians reduced to a pueblo. The fourth district comprised the rancherias which went

THE LAGUNEROS WON OVER

by the name of San Francisco, farther up the Río de las Nazas. The people here were already Christian and enjoyed some organization. There were only three hundred and fifty families in this group, but they could not be moved to another place because of the advantages of soil and climate where they were and because of their attachment to their own group. Then there was a fifth settlement, the most populous of all. It was ninety miles to the north on the other side of the lagoon. It was called Quatro Ciénegas. Into this valley at certain seasons of the year came Indians from other districts, from the valley of Herradura and from a region called Tlaxcala, and from the banks of three other streams. Could this place be properly organized, thought Arista, two thousand families could be got together into a Christian pueblo, for the people were well disposed and of fine quality."[17]

Such was the large area for the exercise of apostolic fervor over which the newly arrived missionary cast a wistful glance in 1599. It was impossible, however, for two men to administer spiritually to a district in which the outlying pueblos were distant fifty and ninety miles from the center. More men were needed if this ready fruit was to be gathered in. So Arista argues. And he speaks of the multitudinous details of his activity which pressed with absorbing demands upon all his time. "The missionary has to go with these children to sow and to gather in the crops, he has to teach them how to build their houses and their churches, and he has to instruct them in Christianity and in the organization of their pueblos; above all, he must give them their rations and support them until they harvest their corn and have the wherewithal to live. With all this," concludes the Black Robe, "what time is there remaining in which to visit other settlements, to teach the Christian doctrine, and to learn different Indian languages, since there is hardly time enough left over to recite the breviary and to recommend ourselves to God?"[18]

It was evident that more fathers were badly needed. However, the energetic Espinosa and Arista, though carrying the full burden of Santa María de las Parras, still found time not only to visit the far distant groups of which Arista wrote, but even to organize some of them into pueblos as he had before suggested to the Provincial.

A beginning of organization was made in 1601 with the groups that lived at the mouth of the river. The padres named this pueblo San

Pedro, and its numbers were augmented by four hundred Zacateco Indians who made their home here and by some Indians who came in from the islands of the lagoon. Santa Ana was likewise started, and its numbers also augmented by three hundred Zacatecos.[19] The lands of the cacique Aztla farther up the river were organized by 1603 and the principal pueblo here founded was called San Ignacio. By this time two smaller settlements were organized not far from San Pedro, which were called *de visita,* which is to say, Christian settlements without a resident priest. These two were San Gerónimo and San Tomás. Names were given likewise to two smaller places near San Pedro, and they have come down to us as Santiago and San Nicolás. By reason of this progress we are assured that, by 1604, fifty-five hundred Indians had been baptized.[20]

When we consider that Santa Ana was forty-five miles west of Parras and that San Pedro was fifty-four miles northwest, we may appreciate the burden put upon the fathers and the hindrances to a rapid advance in districts so far removed from the central pueblo where the missionaries resided. Four more workers were sent, however; and it was all the more necessary now because the founder of the mission, Juan Agustín, died on April 27, 1602. Juan Agustín de Espinosa had entered the Society of Jesus in his youth, and, if the record be correct—if he had been a Jesuit only seven and one-half years,—he was ordained priest just after his novitiate and sent immediately to the missions. A native of Zacatecas, Juan Agustín lived, labored, and died in his native valleys.[21]

The coming of the new padres was facilitated by the desire of the Viceroy and the frontier Spaniards to have this country well Christianized, for mines were being discovered to the east where Governor Urdiñola was soon to found the important city of Saltillo, up to this time but a settlement.[22] It was very important for the safety and expansion of the province of Nueva Vizcaya, therefore, that these Indians of the lagoons be Christianized and the tribes safely reduced.[23]

Four Black Robes arrived in 1603 or 1604.[24] Among the number were Fathers Diego Díaz de Pangua and Diego Larios.[25] The chief pueblos other than Santa María de las Parras—namely, Santa Ana, San Pedro, and San Ignacio—now had their resident missionaries, and the work advanced apace. This year, 1604, the number of baptized was augmented by various caciques who came in from the hills. The young Chief Llepo came with fifty of his people. What helped greatly was the introduction into these missions of old Christian Indians from the south. We learn of Tlaxcaltecos coming into the mission together with the Mexicanos. These Indians were accustomed to a political organization of the pueblos, and, because they loved the fathers, they were a wholesome leaven among the neophytes of the lagoon.[26]

It was not an easy enterprise, however, as a letter of Diego Díaz de Pangua indicates. Stupidity, disease, superstition, inconstancy, and sometimes even violence, the missionary had to work against. One of Pangua's confreres describes the difficult soil graphically enough: "Many are so barbaric, coarse, and unfit by nature, especially the older ones and those who come from the extreme wilderness into the pueblo, that they do not appear to be human at all. The natural light of reason is so darkened in them that they cannot grasp anything that is spiritual or anything that is reasonable. Their greatest happiness and all their worry is caused exclusively by eating and drinking. They always think of food, they always speak of it as if it were the highest and most important thing in this world.... Therefore they are neither frightened by hell nor moved by heavenly glory, unless heaven is presented to them as a place where there is abundance of all kinds of food and hell as a place in which there is nothing but extreme poverty, hunger and thirst.... They are so stupid that after many days or months of careful and diligent instruction they will hardly have learned an iota of the catechism. Only a few natives speak the same language; almost every village has its own dialect, which is entirely different from that of other pueblos. It is very difficult to make them live together and hence more difficult for us to instruct them in the Christian Faith. Often they rove in bands through the wilderness and we must go after them to return them to the pueblos. Those in the villages are restless and flee without our knowledge back into the wilds...."[27]

Thus is described the initial difficulty of that pueblo forming which the missionary considered necessary for the proper instruction and education of the savage. It may have been the only practical method of evangelizing large numbers of the savages, but it had the one great drawback that it facilitated the spread of disease, which in this very mission of Parras some years later decimated the tribes.

But in spite of all initial trials and drawbacks the four centers above mentioned progressed speedily and by the end of 1607 many new contacts had been made. In the final months of the year, two hundred and eighteen souls had received the holy waters; one hundred of these being adults, of whom seventy-eight were married in the Christian manner.[28] It simplified the work of the padres in this bedlam of languages that most of these tribes understood something of the Mexican idiom, for in this the missionaries were well versed.[29] The churches of the pueblos, which up to this time had been poor affairs of mud and straw, now gave place to durable and more substantial structures. A beginning was made at Parras with what the padres considered a beautiful building, with a painted façade, which they called the Sanctuary of Our Lady of Guadalupe. The ancient fabric still remains to sanctify modern Parras. Its walls have been renewed and freshened, but within hangs the odor of centuries, and old images and retables are redolent of long ago.

The manner in which the fathers finally succeeded in winning over and organizing the children of these missions is admirable, and the new missionaries fell in with the methods employed by Espinosa and Arista. The adult catechist, our now familiar temastián, was the fathers' aid in instructing those to be baptized. Here among the Laguneros as with the Tepehuanes the fiscal was appointed in each pueblo to look after the affairs of the church and sometimes to be catechist. There is an amusing bit of information concerning these missions of the lagoon country. The fathers appointed *fiscales chicitos,* or boy fiscals, who had a double duty: to see to it that the children of the pueblo should be faithful at Mass and that none played truant from the instructions which these young catechists were trained to give. A number of them were appointed in each pueblo. They were boys, however, and they too were sometimes missing from their post of duty. So seriously did the other children take it that they would go in a band to seek out the truant in field or thicket and bring him to his post. Next morning he would have his own fiscal upon him with a scolding and a punishment. "This procedure was as pleasing to the fathers of the flesh," says Ribas, "as it was to those of the spirit."[30]

On the Feast of the Holy Innocents, December 28, the padres kept a yearly custom of preparing a dinner for the youngsters. On this day they would invite the boys to a dinner in the patio of the church, where a sumptuous meal and delicacies were served *a los barbarillos*. At the beginning of each course a salvo of trumpets was given by those who had been taught to use the horn. Christmas was a time of prayer and devotion blended with joy and jollity for all. Spaniards who had ranches in the vicinity were from time to time invited to participate in both the one and the other. Christmas Night bonfires, lighted near the entrance to the church, in the plaza, and on near-by hills, spoke far and wide of happy festivity. This kind of Christmas happiness, introduced at Santa María by Espinosa, spread to the other missions as they developed. In like manner, recurrent feasts such as Easter and Pentecost were celebrated, thus diffusing happiness throughout the months of the year. The Spanish Black Robe understood well the workings of the Indian mind and knew well how to attach the neophyte to the Faith. Indeed, in the processions, the decorations, and other colorful externals of these religious fiestas, the way of worship of the Spaniard of Counterreformation days approached closer to the tastes of the simple neophyte than did the colder and more sedate devotions of the European nations of the north.[31]

Here indeed was a fine and fertile field for the six padres to work upon, a field to be plowed, sown, and harrowed. If the sowing became a success and produced a rich and abundant crop it was because the ground had been laboriously prepared; it was because the soil had been broken and the surface well harrowed through trial on the part of the missionaries and sacrifices on the part of the natives. Although these tribes were naturally of a docile temperament, and although there was comparatively little of idolatry and superstition among them,[32] nevertheless here too was the hechicero, whose influence had to be combated and killed. From moral death the wizard sometimes rose to life again to tear down the fabric the Black Robe was endeavoring to upbuild. Here too, though in a less degree than among the Acaxées and Tepehuanes, superstitions were to be overcome and idolatry to be thrown down.

When an Indian wife was delivered of a child, the husbands went to bed and fasted from meat and fish five or six days to prevent contamination. At the end of the fast an hechicero came over to the hut and lifted mother and babe by the hand from their pallet. With this the father became again a free man.[33] A woman dreamed that some relatives dear to her had died; upon awakening she killed her newborn babe.[34]

As the gateway to life was darkened by superstition, so was the departure. Should any man or woman of the Pachos witness the death of another, he or she too would die. It was death to gaze upon the dying. Accordingly, these poor savages either buried their sick and old alive or carried them out into the fields and thickets or into caves and there abandoned them to end their hours alone and unprotected. One old woman they carried out to bury for no other reason than that she was useless. Of the death of children they made no case at all. Indeed, some of the women were accustomed to kill their first-born. The corpses were buried under stones in caves. Then the dirge began. Friends and relatives gathered at the place of burial, mornings and evenings for days on end, and with begrimed faces set up a ghastly plaint in honor of the departed. Father Pérez de Ribas heard these same lugubrious howls and whines when he himself was missionary among the Ahomes of the west coast and he describes with sufficient realism this gruesome custom.[35] But here east of the mountains it was a little different. There were not only plaints of sorrow, but likewise songs of praise for the valorous deeds of the dead. They celebrated a man's valor in war; also his skill in the chase, and how thus he had been a good provider for his family.[36]

Strange superstitions were connected with the stag's head, especially those of stags that had been killed in the chase by the father of a family. These were preserved with fearsome reverence. A missionary was called to a dying man. He found the patient surrounded with the heads of stags with the antlers arranged well in order. Here were also Indians, and, of course, some hechiceros, striving, as the padre says, to win this soul for hell. The missionary ordered them to throw the heads into the fire. They replied that should the smoke touch them they would all die, and they proceeded to hide away the heads. "Numskulls, all of you!" shouted the priest, and with that he seized what heads he could still reach and flung them into the fire. The Indians ran out as if fleeing death. But when they saw that the padre, for all that he was in the smoke, did not die, they were greatly impressed; and the stupid rite was abolished, for news of the thing went abroad.[37]

We must not look for any kind of consistency in the superstitions of the savage. If he feared like death the smoke of a stag's head when a man was dying, so at other times and for other purposes he burned the head in a bonfire. If one had died in the course of the year, the relatives and immediate family at the turn of the new year left the house of the dead man at nightfall, sending lugubrious wails to heaven. An old woman carried the head of the biggest stag the person mourned had killed. They would make a fire, throw arrows into it, and over all place the antlers that they might burn. Around the fire, savages passed the night, the old woman wailing, the others singing and dancing till the dawn. Then they buried the ashes, with which was also buried the memory of the man who had killed the animal.[38]

Another kind of stag dance they had around a bonfire all night long. In this, an hechicero, instead of throwing into the fire the whole head of a stag which a certain dead man had killed, threw in only bits of the horn cut from the main branches of the antlers. The savages watched these pieces burn, persuaded that when all was consumed the skill and strength of the hunter who killed the beast would enter into them. Finally, they gathered the ashes, mixed them with water, and drank the potion, that they too might become strong and skillful hunters.[39] Once on the Feast of St. John the Baptist when the padre knew they were going to celebrate such a dance, he rebuked them for the ridiculous superstition. They took the scolding in such good part that after Mass the Indian governor of the pueblo and the fiscals went about to all the houses collecting heads of stags. These were burned in a heap and the practice was abolished forever. In place of stags' heads now they put crosses in the huts, an earnest that they had become better Christians.[40]

This last incident, narrated by Ribas, gives us an idea of the ease with which these savage children of the plains and the lagoons followed the lead of the Black Robe in what concerned most of the details of their life. Easily frightened by an hechicero, when his deceits were discovered the savage was ready to give a far deeper confidence to the Jesuit. The Spanish captain of arms could easily overawe these savages and press them to submission and often to servitude; the padre gained them chiefly by love and kindness. The miserable rites of the savage were replaced by the picturesque ceremonies of the divine office and instead of fearsome devils there were offered the sweet and consoling figures of Christ and His mother."¹ It is no wonder, then, that the Indian's loyalty to the missionary surpassed by far that which he formerly gave to his native priest and that the bonds that tied him to his gracious father were of more enduring form than those which bound him to his Spanish conqueror, become too often his exploiter.

These missions, then, advanced and multiplied under the kindly and skillful leadership of the Jesuit missionary. Although harrowing trials did befall here, as we shall see, they were visitations only, while the happiness and prosperity and peace of this region were of lasting quality. A vast section of Nueva Vizcaya was being added to the frontier of New Spain.

Chapter X

NORTH INTO THE MOUNTAINS

AT THE Tepehuán mission, Father Gerónimo Ramírez had evangelized the Tepehuanes who lived in rancherias about the Spanish settlement of Sauceda and he had gone from there north and founded on the banks of the Río de Santiago the flourishing pueblo of Santiago Papasquiaro, and, twenty-five miles distant from this, Santa Catalina, and then Guanaceví, much farther north. He worked alone for some years after 1595, the date of his first entrada, and certainly after this first year, at least, he returned to the central house at Durango. Whether after this period he remained in the mission permanently it is impossible to say. However, by 1601 he had a companion.

Nicolás de Arnaya, superior at Durango in that year, informs us that there were then eight fathers belonging to the house; that six of these labored in the three missions and that the other two with two brothers remained at home to administer spiritually to the capital of Nueva Vizcaya. The three missions Arnaya refers to were those of the Laguna, of Topia, and of the Tepehuanes. Espinosa and Arista were at Santa María de las Parras; Santarén and Ruiz were laboring in the mountains of Topia and San Andrés; this leaves Ramírez and a fellow laborer for the Tepehuán mission. The companion's name is Alonso Gómez, and he was with Ramírez as early as 1600.[1]

It was necessary soon to send more workers. Santiago Papasquiaro had grown appreciably. Besides its natural advantage of location on the riverbank close to the arteries of travel to and from the mines, and besides the attraction exerted by the affability of the padres, there was another reason why groups of Indians came to this Christian pueblo. The famine of 1597 in the mountains led the pagan Indians, as we have seen, down from their deep canyons and lofty summits to look for food. Ramírez preached to them, and they were willing to give ear to his message; he used upon them his accustomed tact, and they became willing to stay. Their greater security here against a return of the famine was a very strong motive for both the one and the other.

---
[1] For notes to chapter x see pages 209–210.

Thus were the members of Papasquiaro augmented.[2] Through various circumstances and through the help which Ramírez received in 1601, Santa Catalina likewise grew in population, and by 1600 most of the Indians here had been baptized.

To the north, at Indé, another beginning was made. At first ill success was Ramírez' lot, for Indians who had consented to gather there went back to their wilds. But in 1600 or 1601 the settlement was permanently established,[3] and Arnaya at Durango judged, therefore, that this mission needed more padres. The man who arrived in 1600 was Father Juan Fonte. By 1604 four fathers were in the mission. This increase would release Ramírez from his charges of the original pueblos and make it possible for him to stretch out his ambitions farther toward the north.[4] More work, the padre thought, could still be done here in the district south of Indé and Guanacevi.

Down the Río de Santiago northeast, up the winding vale of the Río Tepehuanes northwest, then over some rough ridges, and the traveler comes into the beginning of a beautiful and fertile valley watered and drained by a stream, called Río de Zape, which flows almost directly north into a branch of the Río de las Nazas. The rolling valley lies between Santa Catalina and Guanacevi, some thirty miles from the former. Here the padre began to make contact with the natives and to introduce Christianity among them.

Though Ramírez had formerly gone farther north than this, namely, to Guanacevi, he was still far from home. Santiago Papasquiaro was eighty-five miles as the crow flies northwest from Durango, and this new district he now entered lay more than sixty miles again north of Santiago. And it was virgin country. Many families here gathered about the kindly Black Robe to listen to his message. They became willing to remain with him and to receive from his hands the sacrament of baptism. It seemed good, then, to organize them into a pueblo, and they were willing. They let him choose the site. The foot of a towering rock which thrust out from a steep ridge like a powerful bastion was watered by the pleasant Río de Zape which flowed close to its base. Here in this picturesque spot the northern pueblo was founded. It was called Nuestra Señora del Zape, and the village still at the site bears today the name which it gave to the stream that waters it.

The towering rock which overshadows Zape is the first thing which strikes the eye of the traveler as he makes his way northward over that centuries-old highway and swings over the shoulder of a low-lying hill a mile from the town. The rock, in layers now tipped on end, runs north more than a mile, but with diminishing height, and for most of the way its base is washed by the stream. The rest of the country is open.

Many a tale of Indian lore these ancient stones could tell. Time has written beautifully upon their face, for ancient lichens have spread, with the passing of the years, in green and orange, and lavender and red. Upon this surface in prehistoric times the aborigines scrawled their hieroglyphics, and the perfect image of an antlered deer attests the art of long ago.

This rocky bastion has been cleft by the primeval workings of nature, and in its lower reaches it has been carved by the slow wearing of wind and water. Indians doubtless lived early in the shelters thus created, for here their markings are most abundant. In a narrow crevice near a spring Ramírez discovered many idols, which he destroyed, and round about, he said, he found the ruins of ancient dwellings. Thus with the founding of Zape and with the older Guanaceví and Indé the fathers were firmly established in the northern Tepehuán country and near the heart of their northern mountains.[5]

During the years that followed, owing to the arrival of new workers a steady progress was made and the conversion of all the Tepehuanes was envisaged.[6] It is true that progress was slower among these mountains and less spectacular than among the Indians of the west coast. There the conversion of whole nations was rapid and brilliant and thousands were baptized within the space of a few months.[7] But these Tepehuanes of the mountains were a colder and less generous race and it took the gospel a longer time to win over their hearts.

And they, too, had cruel customs which the missionaries had to combat. For instance, when illness visited them they would kill a child or children in order that the sickness of one or more of the living might consume itself in the dead. Idols and hechiceros, here as elsewhere, were obstacles to progress. Nevertheless, in other things the fathers had less to contend with, as in the introducing of Christian marriage. For these people were a chaste race, as savages went, and far less than most of the others were they given to polygamy. The unfaithful wife was abandoned by her husband and no one else would have her. So too, no one would marry a girl who had lost her virginity. Neither were they much given to theft. But their great weaknesses were superstition, sorcery, and idolatry, and the pest of petty war and raids upon their neighbors.[8]

In 1603, when Father José de Lomas was with Santarén at Tecuciapa in the west among the Acaxée Indians, the Tepehuanes, whose borders are close to the district, ran amuck. They murdered a Christian cacique and threatened Santarén with death. The padre was obliged to keep to this pueblo and to guard the church from attack with fifty armed neophytes whom he kept always near him.

At last he thought it safe to depart in order to visit other places, Father Lomas likewise leaving for other settlements. Hardly was Santarén gone when a cacique of Tecuciapa came running up in haste, begging him to return if he would save his people. The Tepehuanes had destroyed a whole pueblo, he said, farther up the river, and only one had escaped to tell the story. The trouble had started when, a short while before, the Tepehuanes kidnaped three daughters of a Christian chief of the Acaxées and threatened them with death if they refused their captors what they desired of them. Father Lomas, who knew the Tepehuán language, went into the Tepehuán country to endeavor to get the girls released, but he could not approach, since the troublemakers had persuaded an entire settlement formerly Christian to quit the fathers and the Church. Finally Santarén dispatched thirty of his finest bowmen, and they succeeded in rescuing the captives. Now the Tepehuanes had returned to burn a pueblo; such pests had they been constantly to their neighbors the Acaxées. But as their conversion to Christianity progressed, these hostile attacks diminished and finally ceased. Then there reigned a peace upon the border never known before.[9]

As for their sorcery and idol worship, the Tepehuanes were sometimes persuaded by the padres through their catechists to do away with the idols, and often before the Indians were baptized these objects of superstition were thrown into the river. There is one story of an hechicero and his idol which Ribas narrates with great prolixity. But there is instruction in the story because of its similarity to others. We have already seen (in chapter v) how these people had traffic with evil

NORTH INTO THE MOUNTAINS 91

spirits.[10] And here may be added another story of the same type: the stone was half buried in the ground when it spoke and demanded attention, offering favors of various kinds. It began to demand food, and the unhappy victim felt himself obliged to bring corn and frijoles for the supposed satisfaction of the spirit.

In spite of such drawbacks as this, progress continued, especially after the arrival of Father Fonte in 1600 and of others in 1604. Santiago Papasquiaro exhibited the finest example of a Christian community among the Tepehuanes, where matters were advanced by the presence of numbers of old Christian Indians—Mexicans and Tarascans—who worked in the mines. Here at Christmas time it was customary to hold a festive celebration; these old Christian Indians helped make it a success. They dressed as shepherds and at Mass came up to the crib to offer Christ some gift which they carried. One, having nothing else to offer, gave his soul, a pious gesture which impressed the newly converted Tepehuanes.[11]

After Father Fonte's arrival, hundreds of children in the rancherias near the pueblos were baptized into the Faith, and trusty fiscals and catechists were left in these more out-of-the-way places, that the seed sown be nurtured and the older people be gradually prepared for the sacrament. The political organization already described was extended to the new villages. The country was settling down to a civilized life.

By 1607 Father Juan Fonte had penetrated farther to the north and east, beyond Zape and Indé, to a district called Ocotlán. Fonte first entered this region in January, 1607, and on October 24 he returned to instruct and baptize the neophytes. He had most encouraging success with these Tepehuanes, who were of the northern borderline which separated them from the Tarahumares. Fonte's first contact with them had been in 1603, when he had been friendly with one Gigibodari, a leader in the north. Two years later, the chief came to see the padre and told him of a cross raised in his pueblo and a chapel finished.[12] Since in 1606 another encouraging contact was made, the field was ripe by 1607 for beginning permanent labors at Ocotlán.[13]

Fonte thought highly of these Tepehuanes of the extreme north. He praised their honesty, for they neither lied nor were given to theft, and the chastity of their women was remarkable. "If a girl loses her maidenhood it becomes difficult for her to procure a husband; if a woman is faithless to her husband she will be divorced." The caciques, however, and the hechiceros could have two wives. Even drunkenness was not so frequent as in other parts of the nation. And, as under Santarén in San Andrés, these northern Tepehuanes learned their prayers by placing stones upon the ground and making each stone correspond to a word of the prayer they were learning.[14]

There was a famous idol here. The natives called it Ubamari and gave its name to the pueblo which was situated near by. This place was fourteen leagues east-northeast of Zape.[15] The idol "was a stone," writes Fonte, "five palms in height, with the form of a human head at the top, the rest bearing the shape of a column." It stood at the summit of the hill at the foot of which the pueblo rested. The natives made offerings to the idol—old arrows, pots of clay, the bones of animals, and fruits and flowers. "But," continues Fonte sincerely, "so soon as they had acquired sufficient knowledge of the true God and of the way in which His Majesty ought to be honored," even without insinuation or command from the missionary, led by the cacique of the place, and on the very day of their baptism, they threw down the idol and flung it into the deepest part of the river which watered their valley. They then came and told the father what they had done.[16]

Fonte on his second visit, in October, baptized these Indians, at which they exhibited a spiritual joy that touched his heart. They made a great cross, covered it with flowers and fragrant herbs, and, forming a procession, carried it to the place where for so many years the idol had been honored. On the way, they chanted the Credo in their own language. Arrived at the spot, the neophytes planted the cross as a symbol of the grace of their rebirth in Christ. And this day the pueblo itself was baptized to a new name. Ubamari was dropped and forgotten; Santa Cruz became the designation of its new and happy life, and the town of Santa Cruz today is reminder of the change. Father Fonte could not remain here, however. He must return to his permanent pueblo, Zape, but he promised soon to be again among this newly won people of Santa Cruz.

Here on the border there had been almost continual war with the Tarahumares. The Tepehuanes of the Valle del Águila, particularly, had suffered. They decided to seek the advice of Father Fonte, who was many miles to the south in Ocotlán, persuaded that whatever their missionary said they would follow out, whether to continue the war or to come to an understanding. They felt that the Tarahumares would be willing to treat with them, once they were supported by the authority of the padre, for it was now a commonplace thing among those mountains to the north that whatever the Black Robe said must be done. Fonte listened to the delegation. His advice was, of course, to cease fighting and come to an agreement. The Tepehuanes of the district, who were not all as yet Christians, set themselves to carry out this counsel of peace. They found the Tarahumares amenable to reason and the result of the whole maneuver was that a harrowing hostility of many years was brought to a close.[17]

Fonte entered the country again in the spring of 1608; a long and enthusiastic letter, dated April 22, describes his activities. He had for interpreter and ambassador a friendly and capable Tepehuán cacique. Between them, they brought no less than eight hundred and forty-two Tarahumar warriors to the desire for baptism. Representatives of this group went to Durango to ask the Governor that missionaries be sent them. The Governor consented to ask the Viceroy of Mexico for three extra missionaries, two for the Valle de San Pablo, about forty miles west of Santa Bárbara, and one for Ocotlán. Fonte was delighted. He had come without Spaniard and soldier, and the Tarahumares were asking for the Faith. Fonte wrote that since he was young and vigorous he would spare no effort or labor in reaching even the most remote part of the nation, and that he would bring Juan del Valle with him into the new mission.[18]

But the padre's hopes were for the present doomed to disappointment; the necessary missionaries could not be spared, and he had to content himself with a continued friendly contact while he perfected his evangelization of the district of Ocotlán and the pueblo of Santa Cruz. Good work had been done, nevertheless, and the peace begun some time before continued to reign on the border, in and about the Valle de San Pablo. A test of its stability occurred in 1610. It was again a Tepehuán hechicero who almost succeeded in undoing the work of Fonte and precipitating another war. This wizard persuaded ten of his relatives to join with him in the murder of a Tepehuán catechumen, a cacique of the Valle de San Pablo, at the very time that two of the fathers were working there. The relatives of the murdered chief, infuriated, thought only of revenge. What gave them pause was the safety of the missionaries, whom they urged to flee from danger. The savages then prepared for war, sending at the same time a delegation of twelve Tepehuanes, headed by the dead chief's son, to Durango to ask Governor Urdiñola for help against the hechicero and his men. But the Governor was then engaged against the rebellious Xiximes and could do nothing for them.

It soon transpired, however, that the Governor's services were not needed. The troublemaker, either fearing punishment or touched with remorse, came to the missionaries, asking pardon for his misdemeanor and petitioning baptism. Peace was thus restored in the Valle de San Pablo, and the Black Robes, returning, were able to baptize a large number in the valley, winning it for Christianity and using it later as a gateway into Tarahumara.[19]

Father Rodrigo de Cabredo, Provincial and Visitor since March, 1609, visited Durango in December, 1610, and held a meeting of the fathers, who came in from all the missions. Cabredo witnessed here a ten days' celebration of the beatification of Ignatius de Loyola. There were lights and decorations and music, sermons and solemn Masses. This all seemed to Cabredo to show forth the love of the Durango townsfolk for the Jesuits.[20]

Nor did the Provincial forget the missions. He ordered the two missionaries now resident at Papasquiaro, Fathers Juan del Valle and Bernardo de Cisneros, to go south among the recently quieted Xiximes and evangelize the pueblos of Hucoritame, Orisame, and Humase. To Father Juan Fonte, resident at Zape, he gave orders to go a second time to the borders of the Tarahumar country and to begin the Christianization of that nation.[21]

In 1611, therefore, Father Fonte went a second time to the Valle de San Pablo, gateway to Tarahumara.[22] He was accompanied by a band of his faithful Tepehuanes, which included four caciques, only two of whom were Christians. When he remonstrated that a boy to accompany him as servant would suffice, they replied that they wished to demonstrate both to the Spaniards and to the Tarahumares how greatly they esteemed his person and how happy they were to be with him. The Jesuit visited many wild places in the vicinity of the valley and was able to persuade three thousand Tarahumares to leave their fastnesses and come and live in the valley, side by side with the Tepehuanes. Such development spelled success. Fonte revisited here many of his former children, the Tepehuanes who lived near the valley.[23]

The Black Robe then passed for the first time beyond the valley of San Pablo and penetrated fifty miles into Tarahumar territory. He found that many of these savages lived in large caves in which there was room for several houses. The women, he noted, were bashful and retiring, and were good weavers of the fiber of the agave. These Indians buried their dead in cemeteries, placing food near the grave for the journey to the other life. The house in which one had died they destroyed, and in grief they cut their hair. Fonte found these people more gentle and docile than the Tepehuanes.[24]

Word of Father Fonte's approach had preceded him and when he came within five or six miles of one of their larger pueblos some spied him from a hilltop and signaled to the others his proximity. They all came out, men, women and children, to meet him, the chief with his lance and his feathers, and everyone with hand on head in token of respect. Arrived at the pueblo, Fonte made them a speech. He was happy to be with them, he said; it was love for them that brought him to their country. The Tarahumares offered food, for himself and his Tepehuán escort. Parting for the night, the savages next morning gathered around the padre and spoke their happiness at seeing him in their country. Fonte's letter says that "the women at first shrank away in bashfulness, but later, seeing the men free and easy with me and myself speaking to them as sons, the women too came up to speak to me as to their father. They as well as the men petitioned that I return to see them in their country once again."[25]

Before departing from Tarahumara, the missionary was able to make a beginning by baptizing several children. He was told of a dying child. He went to it and found that it knew something of the Faith from proximity to the Christian Tepehuanes. This child he baptized, as also another sick of the smallpox, and four other children, to the delight of their fathers. He spoke to them of the necessity of baptism for all. They informed him that in the district he was now traversing there were thirty-one hundred and seventy Tarahumares not beyond reach who could be prepared for the sacrament. The missionary appointed four fiscals to instruct in the Faith this part of the nation. He divided the districts and instructed these catechists to come to visit him in the Christian pueblos from time to time that they might report on the progress made.[26]

As Fonte went from one pueblo to another, the Tarahumares followed; and when finally he left the Valle de San Pablo to get back into his Tepehuán country, they sent eight or ten Indians with one as captain to accompany him. Shortly afterward, Fonte journeyed to Santa Bárbara to beg the Spaniards of that mining center to show friendship and good treatment to the nation. For this journey the Tarahumar chiefs sent him thirty men as escort. The padre demurred at so large a bodyguard, but they insisted, saying they wanted the Spaniards to see how much they esteemed him. They provided food for the journey and attended to his wants.

What especially pleased Fonte in all this was his brilliant success at the Valle de San Pablo, where he had succeeded in getting the Tepehuanes and the Tarahumares to live in amity. This he would not have been able to achieve had it not been for the aid and influence of an old and authoritative hechicero, half Tepehuán and half Tarahumar, who took a great liking to the Jesuit. Through the devoted coöperation of this old but now repentant sinner, Father Fonte was able in the Valle de San Pablo to lead the Tepehuán lions to live with the lambs of the Tarahumar.[27]

His affairs thus prospering, Fonte went to Durango to treat with the Governor concerning plans for the conversion of the entire new nation. The time-honored arrangements were discussed. The Governor would write to the Viceroy that he in turn should get in touch with the Provincial, so that more fathers might be sent for this new mission and gifts of bells and ornaments for the churches be got from the royal treasury. Unfortunately, a black storm soon to burst upon the missions postponed for many years what promised to be an abundant harvest in so fruitful a field.

Chapter XI

URDIÑOLA SUBDUES THE XIXIMES

THE RÍO DE LOS REMEDIOS, on the west coast, which as it approaches the sea is called the San Lorenzo, is the dividing line between the Acaxée and Xixime nations. The linguistic affinities of the Xiximes, as of the Acaxées, are obscure, and, compared with our knowledge of other nations lying north, there is little information about them.[1] The Xiximes were the most warlike of all the tribes of the mountains, and the Spaniards remembered them chiefly for their cannibalism. Ribas averred that they were a people as strong, proud, and rebellious as any who lived in the sierras and that their warlike propensities were exercised upon their neighbors the Acaxées as on the Spaniards themselves. Many of them lived in the most inaccessible parts of the Sierra Madre, which made approach to them, for Christianization, almost impossible.[2]

They were more addicted to cannibalism than any of the other tribes, and issued from their fastnesses only to hunt and kill their enemies, the Acaxées, and return to make fat dishes out of their flesh. This horror became apparent to the eye, for in different parts of their country were mounds formed by the bones and skulls of those whom they had eaten. Likewise, they liked to adorn the doors and inner walls of their huts with the bones of their victims after they had dragged them in great pride to their dwellings.[3]

With their continual victories over the Acaxées their pride and insolence had swollen to most ugly proportions and they bade fair to exterminate their neighbors to the north, now on the way to complete Christianization. Even when the Spaniards aided the Christian Acaxées, no headway could be made, and the white man lost in these frays both life and reputation. The Xiximes enjoyed two advantages over the Spaniards: the wildness of their country, and their great dexterity in ambush. They struck quickly from thickets and from behind rocks, and were gone before they could be hit by musket ball or arrow. They were strong and well-built men, of great energy. They

---

[1] For notes to chapter xi see pages 210–211.

were well clothed; but they enjoyed no art or industry, and, unlike many of the savages, they were given to deceit.

The Jesuit annual letters give a description of some some of the customs of these Indians.' They lived in two kinds of houses, of stone and of straw. The former were painted in various colors. Their houses they built and grouped together four or five in number, so as to form a sort of stronghold with an open space in the middle, protected by the dwellings. At each corner of this plaza or courtyard were loopholes or embrasures through which to shoot arrows. The entrance into the courtyard from outside the houses was so small that it could be easily blocked by a shield or other covering and protected by one man against successful attack. Their spears and shields and quivers they decorated with the brilliant feathers of birds, especially of one which they called the *guacamaia*. The points of their spears, arrows, and knives were made of hard red wood like the brazilwood. From the fiber of the century plant they could weave rich and curious garments. For food they raised or used corn, beans, squash, potatoes, and various plants and herbs, including of course the fruit of the cactus. They even made a preserve out of the agave which they called *mexicale*.

To achieve success in war they had a curious custom similar to the practice of certain tribes farther north near the coast. They carefully reared a maiden to bring them luck in time of war. While the actual fighting was taking place, they kept the girl in a cave carefully guarded. So long as hostilities continued, this "Vestal Virgin" had to keep a rigorous fast, eating only once a day and at that only a bit of ground corn with water. If victory perched upon their arms, the Xixime warriors, together with the women and children of the near-by village, released the fasting virgin and brought to her the skull of one whom they had killed. This she fondled as if it were the object of her greatest affection, and then she was allowed to have her fill of food. A dance always followed upon victory. The fasting virgin was the honored one. She took as partners in the victory frolic the men and women of the group, and all the while she carried the skull of the fallen enemy. When tired from this exercise, the victorious Xiximes fell to eating the flesh of other victims who had been slain in the war.

URDIÑOLA SUBDUES THE XIXIMES

Should these same warriors lose in battle, then the fasting maiden was in disgrace. She was criticized and derided. Her fasting was not sufficiently austere; she was disloyal to the tribe. Henceforth she was in disfavor and must even quit the tribe. Such was the barbarity of these cannibalistic Xiximes, neighbors to the Acaxées and waging against them an almost perpetual war.

But the Acaxées, almost all of them being by 1607 Christians, were become part of the great Spanish colonial system and were consequently under the protection of the King of Spain. Security from habitual enemies was one prized advantage which the aborigines appreciated upon entering the fold of the Church. The famous captain in Sinaloa, Don Diego Martínez de Hurdaide, made good this protection to every tribe of the west coast desiring to embrace the Faith, beginning with the Ahomes in 1604 and extending the strength of his shielding arm north over the rivers to the Ópata and Pima nations in the upper Yaqui drainage. We have just seen how when the northern Tepehuanes became Christians they were able, through the prestige of their padre, Juan Fonte, to bring to an end hostilities of many years with their neighbors to the north, the Tarahumares. Therefore the Acaxées resolved to appeal for help to their highest immediate superior, the Governor of Nueva Vizcaya himself, Don Francisco de Urdiñola, who in 1603 at the time of their own rebellion showed himself possessed of qualities both strong and humane.

The Governor's reply and his method at this juncture support the assertion of his biographer, Vito Alessio Robles, that, though an able soldier, he endeavored always to exhaust the resources of diplomacy before taking up arms—though there were times when this policy carried him too far, as we shall see, on the road of costly delay and seeming weakness.[5] Urdiñola bade the Acaxées capture some Xiximes and bring them to him that he might inquire into their character and advise them. After a sharp skirmish, the Christian Acaxées captured two Xiximes. One died of his wounds, but the surviving captive they brought to the Governor.

Urdiñola treated the savage kindly and fed him well and after a few days let him go that he might carry back to his nation the story of this benevolence, which would dissipate misunderstanding. He charged the man, too, with a message. Let the Xixime tell his people that the Spaniards were willing to live in peace and harmony with them, but if they should not cease from their atrocities and depredations he would come with a powerful force into their country, however rough, and impose upon them a punishment to be remembered. He dismissed the Indian proud and happy because the Governor had honored him with the gift of a Spanish cloak, which he wore on his return, and had one of the fathers accompany the Xixime for his protection as far as the mines of San Hipólito, which were below the frontier of the Xixime country. Moreover, Urdiñola instructed Captain Bartolomé Suárez de Villalta, of the presidio at San Hipólito, that should any of the Xixime nation approach with the intention of offering peace, he was to receive them honorably in the name of the King of Spain and offer pardon for all past offenses.

This bit of diplomacy worked like a charm. The caciques and the people were impressed by the good treatment their tribesman had received at the hands of the Governor. The Spaniards were not, after all, the cruel and treacherous people they had been supposed. The chief would accept the peace. They came, therefore, to the Captain at San Hipólito and swore friendship to the Spaniards and obedience to the King. Alonzo Ruiz, who for some time had been working with them, helped to confirm this good will. This was in 1607.[6]

These friendly relations lasted for almost three years and all seemed well. The Xiximes came unharassing and unembarrassed into the country of the Acaxées and into the mining camps of the Spaniards. It seemed the beginning of a peaceful penetration. Then on a sudden the peace collapsed like a house of cards. Simultaneously in four different places the newly won savages began to murder both Spaniards and Christian Acaxée Indians. The Acaxées again appealed to the Governor, this time with a threat. If he did not help them, they would flee their pueblos and churches and seek other lands. Indeed, the Xiximes had invited them to an alliance against the Spaniards.[7]

Urdiñola, with seeming weakness, did not even yet resort to arms. Instead, he instructed the captain at San Hipólito again to try the means of diplomacy. The captain prevailed upon a friendly Xixime chief, unpopular with his own because of this friendship, to go with his family and following among the different caciques and try to bring them to reason. But it was the old insolence all over again. They

URDIÑOLA SUBDUES THE XIXIMES

did not want peace with the Spaniards, but war. If this man, friendly with the Spaniards and their church, did not return to his own district close to the Spaniards, he would have to pay for it, for they would know the taste of his flesh. The hostiles then with a force went to the mines called Las Vírgines to destroy them. They came upon the farm of a Spaniard and killed the owner and his son with five of his Indian servants. They disemboweled the victims and carried back their flesh for a cannibalistic repast. At this the whole country rose. Urdiñola sent word to the Viceroy, the Count of Salinas, and the latter ordered the Governor to march upon the rebels, making it possible for him to unite two companies, which made a force of one hundred Spanish soldiers strengthened by a troop of eleven hundred allied Indians. The Governor went forthwith below the Xixime border to the mines of San Hipólito and proceeded to the invasion of the territory, taking two fathers with him, Francisco de Vera and Alonso Gómez. Urdiñola left behind, for the protection of the other fathers and of the Acaxée Indians, a guard of twenty-five soldiers.[8]

The details of this campaign we have from the pen of Father Pedro de Gravina himself, one of the most experienced of the missionaries, and from the eyewitness Alonso Gómez. The Xiximes were in two large groups, one at Guapexuxe, the other at Xoxotilma, which was situated in a deep but lovely vale. Urdiñola chose to march upon the latter first, for he had heard that here was the more numerous of the two divisions. After a very difficult advance the Governor's troops came within sight of the enemy.

The rebels began to weaken before the strength of the Spanish force. They decided to send some caciques to the Governor to arrange for conditions of peace. Urdiñola treated them respectfully; said he did not desire war, nor their own death, but only the punishment of those who had been leaders in the recent atrocities. He told the caciques to give this message to their people, and to have them meet him at Xoxotilma on the day after the Feast of St. Luke, October 18, 1610, that he might speak to them all together.

On the day appointed, the Spanish soldiers put on their armor and advanced deeper into the vale, where they found a hundred and fifty Xiximes in battle array, some with lances and shields, others with daggers, knives, and hatchets. They came up one by one to greet the

Governor, who received them in a friendly manner. But this force was very small, he said, for the number he knew to be in the vicinity. Therefore he would give them two days more to collect all their people for a general meeting with him. It was done. On the morning of the appointed day a great crowd was seen walking to the rendezvous— men, women, and a large number of boys. They all came up respectfully to meet the Governor. Then Captain Suárez of San Hipólito commanded them to lay down their arms and to sit down upon the ground. This they did while the soldiers surrounded them.

Then Urdiñola spoke. He came here, he said, only for their good. In spite of the destruction they had wrought upon Christian people and the murders they had perpetrated, he desired still to come to terms with them. Before this could be, however, they must do two things: go forth to collect still greater numbers of their people, and in the meantime leave with him certain hostages whom he would designate. He began to name the hostages. The first was known for an evildoer and murderer. They put him in chains. The second resisted the handcuffs of the soldiers. This was the match that set fire to the powder. An old man cried out that they would rather all be massacred than allow themselves to be thus manacled. Then the whole crowd of them jumped to their feet, uncovered knives and daggers they had held concealed, and made a dash for liberty, trying to break through the surrounding guard of soldiers and allied Indians. The drawn swords of the soldiers did not deter them. Many fell dead or wounded, many were taken prisoner, some escaped. Others died later of their wounds; and these the padres were able to instruct and then to baptize, that they might die in peace with the God who created them. The Governor ordered withdrawal to a place of greater safety.⁹

Urdiñola upbraided the prisoners for their behavior and for their past murders. He discovered that many of these people were implicated in the recent murder of the Spaniards near San Hipólito and that their intent had been even now only to feign peace, and to lie in wait for the Spaniards as they left the country, falling upon them as they threaded one of the difficult passes. For this only, the Governor discovered, had he been permitted to enter the Xixime country at all. Eleven were therefore condemned to be hanged upon the spot. The fathers instructed these, and they all died repentant Christians after

URDIÑOLA SUBDUES THE XIXIMES 103

baptism, except one old man who remained obdurate to the end. One, because of his youth, was spared through the intercession of Father de Vera.

The Xixime chief, friend of the Spaniards, whose mission of peace had failed, rebuked his tribesmen for what they had done and pointed out the folly of resistance. He asked for baptism here at Xoxotilma, for himself and his wife. The fathers were delighted to accede to his request, for he had picked up enough of Christian doctrine to allow of baptism, and besides, on the march to Guapexuxe, whither the Governor would next go, he might be killed by his infuriated countrymen. Urdiñola stood as godfather. The soldiers shot off their guns and the Indian allies celebrated. The Governor then named the cacique the official head of his pueblo, and his domain was declared a privileged settlement; all who would come to live there would be pardoned and protected. Thus were punishment and reward meted out by Urdiñola in the vale of Xoxotilma.

Before their departure, the soldiers raided the pueblo and its rancherias, finding close to a thousand skulls of the human victims these cannibal Xiximes had devoured.[10]

The way to Guapexuxe proved as perilous as the road to Xoxotilma. A prisoner sent ahead to parley was received with a shower of arrows. Returning, he warned Urdiñola of an ambuscade prepared in a narrow defile. The army advanced warily, and at last arrived at Guapexuxe. Here the Spaniards beheld a sight that made their spirits shudder: they saw human flesh being cooked and a human heart run through on a spit. The victim's eyes had been plucked from their sockets and placed on a leaf of maize. The skull had been stripped of its skin and flesh and placed with the other bones hanging from a pole in the center of the pueblo. The Spaniards thus realized the price of defeat.

Urdiñola again sent ahead a prisoner with a guard to find the enemy, seek out the cacique of Guapexuxe, and treat for peace. The rebels were discovered in a council of war, debating whether they should attack the Spaniards or ask for terms of surrender. This last attempt of Governor Urdiñola at reconciliation met with better success; the Xixime cacique came to see the Governor, who received him with courtesy. The chief had a plausible story. He said that he and his people, including seventeen rancherias, had belonged to the party of peace and had never attacked the Spaniards; but because of what had happened at Xoxotilma his people were in great fear and had all fled their settlements. To confirm the truth of what he said the Xixime cacique of Guapexuxe led Governor Urdiñola to a rancheria which was entirely deserted, its inhabitants having fled to the tallest summits. Another cacique was descried signaling from the brow of a precipice for the Spaniards to come within speaking distance. He confirmed the reports of the cacique of Guapexuxe, averring that should the Spaniards promise not to retaliate, the people would all descend gradually from their hiding places.[11]

The necessary promises were made and Urdiñola awaited developments. The chiefs had not received him. Slowly these savages began moving down into the vale, and after having experience of the good offices of the Governor and of the amiability of the fathers, they evinced a desire to be instructed and received into the Church. An *enramada* or bower of branches was erected and a temporary altar set up surmounted by a cross. Mass was said and for a number of days the Spanish army tarried. Now, the natives of Xoxotilma, hearing of all this through their spies, in their turn came out of hiding, asked pardon, promised good behavior, and begged to be admitted to the rite of baptism.

The fathers now urged Urdiñola that they themselves be allowed to remain behind when the army should depart, that thus they might inaugurate the evangelization of this people. The Governor made a gracious gesture. He freed all the prisoners, saying they owed their liberty to the padres, who were their truest friends. He bade the savages to obey and respect them. The Indians forthwith, especially those released, began to kiss the hands of the missionaries and to embrace them as promoters of their liberty. After this, it was felt safe to leave the fathers behind that they might form here a Christian pueblo. One of the captains with a small guard was left for their protection.[12]

The Black Robes won these people still further by gifts of food. The fathers were able to persuade these Xiximes of Guapexuxe to give up their idols, and, having translated the catechism into their language, they went about the different rancherias every day repeating it publicly. The savages were happy to learn, which they did in large numbers everywhere. Certain superstitions, to be sure, had to be uprooted, such as that of making boys fast on corn and raw meat during harvest time. Instructions, therefore, and corrections prepared the whole nation to be received into the Faith. In a short while thousands of children and adults were baptized, and the dreaded Xiximes were following their old-time enemies of the north into the peacegiving fold of the Church.

The year 1610, therefore, witnessed the Christian birth of a new nation. The Provincial, Rodrigo de Cabredo, meeting with the fathers at Durango in December, 1610, changed the organization of the Topia mission to include the new Xixime Christians. There would be now two units, each with its superior, one for the Acaxées, called the Mission of Topia, and one for the Xiximes, called the mission of San Andrés.[13]

Alarms and affrays and massacres ceased from that time on, and the temporal advantages of the peace were great indeed. The Acaxées could live securely, freed from the dreaded fate of cannibalism. They could now, under instruction from the missionaries, set themselves to cultivate the ground and to sow. Indeed, after a few years, from Guapexuxe to Otatitlán, a distance of thirty miles of formerly barren ground, there was scarcely an acre of land not under cultivation. Calabashes were the product these peaceful Acaxées liked best to raise, and as this was good food both for Indian and Spaniard they both profited abundantly by the peace.[14]

When most of the Xiximes were baptized, there arose the question of building their churches. The padres inspired and supervised the plans, becoming not only architects but likewise laborers in much of the work. Hundreds of Indians, here as elsewhere, employed themselves ardently in the labor of procuring the great crossbeams that would support the roof of their church, going far into the mountains to obtain them from the forests and carry them down on their backs, much as, at a later period in Alta California, the Indians of San Miguel or Santa Inés carried down beams for their mission churches from the not too distant hills. Mud bricks had to be molded and baked in the sun for the walls of these structures; innumerable branches of bush and thicket had to be collected, sorted, and placed with smaller and more pliant osiers to be woven over them. This would form the undersurface of the roof. On top of these osiers straw was placed, mingled with earth. Many of the relics of these earlier churches still rest upon the land, not only in northern Sinaloa and beyond on the banks of the Fuerte and Mayo rivers, but in such places farther south as San Ignacio, Bacubirito, and Atotonilco. Some are now in ruins, as at Mochicahue and San Miguel on the Fuerte; others are practically intact, as at Bamoa and Tesia on the Mayo. Their mud-brick walls are five, sometimes six, feet in thickness and the beams that cross above to hold the roof are as large as those which support the mission of San Luis Rey in Alta California. Some of these first edifices were later replaced by structures of stone.

Here among the Xiximes, in one of the principal pueblos, because of the eagerness of the neophytes to have Mass said in their church of which they were so proud, the Holy Sacrifice was celebrated within its walls before its dedication and before it was quite completed. For the dedication a fiesta was planned, to which Spaniards of the vicinity and Indians from the Acaxée nation were invited. Flowers and paintings adorned the interior, the façade was hung with streamers, and the entrance was embowered with flowers and herbs and foliage. Indian boys trained to play flute and flageolet and to sing, supplied the music, and when the devotions were ended a salvo from Spanish guns concluded the festivities. In the evening there were bonfires and music, song and dance. The Viceroy had sent up 300 pesos for a school for promising Indian boys and for the purchase of bells and ornaments for the church. As a particular mark of favor and encouragement, and because of the infancy of this newborn church, these Indians, like those at Parras, were exempted from the usual tax or tribute to the King.[15]

Trials there were, of course, which inflicted upon the padres a certain kind of soul-suffering which Francis Xavier describes as worse than death and of which only the missionary gazing upon his newly gathered flock feels the dreadful pangs. This visitation was not the ordinary smallpox which took such fatal toll of Indian life. It was another and unknown disease, as dreadful as the smallpox, which raised lumps of blood under the skin of the victims and prostrated them soon in death.[16]

As a counterpoise to trials and sufferings such as these, the padres were immensely consoled by the fervor of the neophytes. Public disci-

URDIÑOLA SUBDUES THE XIXIMES 107

plines were held in the church every Friday, and these took place even when the father was not present in the pueblo. During Holy Week was held the *disciplina a sangre,* or discipline to blood—scourgings during the penitential procession, usually at night. More than once when the missionary, Father Gravina or Alonso Gómez, would arrive at a pueblo, he would find in the plaza a rude hut of the limbs of trees, and within it a cross, and at the foot of the cross a pile of used switches or whips stained with blood.[17] The flagellants had been busy while their father was away. Ribas describes these scourges as used by the Indians farther north on the Sinaloa and Fuerte rivers. They were made sometimes of knotted ropes; sometimes of hemp which the savages obtained from the mescal cactus. Upon the stringy fibers they tied little balls of wax into which they inserted broken needles or thorns of briar or cactus.[18] No wonder there was bleeding! These more modern flagellants were quite as penitential, but not so fanatical, as their European brothers during the years of the Black Death centuries before.

To make assurance doubly sure and to provide as far as possible against a recurrence of rebellion—for with all his Christianity the Indian still retained his savage and fickle nature—a fort was built by the Spanish government at San Hipólito upon the border. Here were designated a captain and sixteen soldiers. The very fact of its presence had a steadying effect upon the converted savage.[19]

Thus by 1610 the Xiximes were Christianized. Santarén and Alonso Gómez came to work permanently among them, this at the request of the Governor. By the end of 1611 they had baptized seven thousand neophytes.[20] Santarén writes in 1613 that there was completed, that year, a copious dictionary of the Acaxée idiom by which a new missionary could readily learn the language—a satisfying experience which was enjoyed by Father Andrés González when he first came to the Xiximes. The dictionary was composed by Father Gravina. Father Pedro Mejía arrived this same year at San Andrés.[21]

Here, then, is the story of how Christianity came to possess a lasting abode among the most savage of the Indians, among cannibals who used to hesitate not at all to devour thousands of their kinsmen, the Acaxées. By the middle of the century, when Pérez de Ribas penned his lines, the mission was in a most flourishing condition, and well might he speak in terms of joy and pride at what his confreres had done many miles south of the scenes of his own labors on the Fuerte and the Yaqui. "There was established in this nation," he says, "formerly so proud and inhuman, a Christianity as fine and as fair as that which was seen among tribes more domesticated and more tractable."[22]

This success had been won by the blood and the sweat of the missionary. Father Rodrigo de Cabredo, Provincial and Visitor between 1609 and 1613, wrote to General Claudius Aquaviva in Rome: "When I read the letters of the fathers of that mission it seems that I behold a perfect imitation of what the Apostle (Paul) writes to the Corinthians concerning hunger, thirst, nakedness, great heats, cold, sickness, persecutions, loneliness, dereliction, and a thousand other trials and sufferings which they bear with extraordinary patience and joy for the greater glory of God and for the good of souls."[23]

It was, then, by means of this sacrifice and missionary virtue and valor that cannibals had been tamed to more human relationships, and savages softened to the pursuits of civilization. Here among the Xiximes was another region added to the frontier of Spain and another people drawn within the embrace of her empire.

Chapter XII

FLOODS, PLAGUES, AND DEVILS

WE HAVE SAID that Santa María de las Parras is set like a gem on the skirts of the sierras; and so it is. To the historian who has read the letters of the missionaries, followed them in their work, and felt their desire not only to gather the Indian of the plain but also to fetch the savage out from his hills and canyons to tame him, these sierras hold a special fascination. The lagoons have dried up long ago, but the blue mountains yet rest upon the land. Looking from Parras south, one beholds tier upon tier of blue and lavender ridge and peak; traveling from Parras west, one passes close to an array of barren and precipitous ridges which cut the blue sky sharply with their lofty, sawlike summits. The whole group, but especially those to the west, are called today the Sierra de las Parras.

After the coming of the four fathers in 1603 or the following year, it was their ambition to bring the Indians of these sierras into the fold either by establishing missions *de visita* in or near the ranges or by attracting their rough inhabitants down into the plain to Santa María. One mountain ridge, says Ribas, was called Quavila. From its description it might well belong to the Sierra de las Parras. The district was excessively dry, beyond even the vast dryness of the great plateau. Since water was entirely wanting, the juice of the maguey was the traveler's only refreshment and when this failed him he perished in the heat of those desert regions. When a Black Robe occasionally visited the sierra the first thing the Indians asked of him was water. One padre going to visit a sick Indian was like to perish in a two days' journey up scorching slopes and along baked arroyos.[1]

The missionaries first got in touch with the Indians of this sierra through their own neophytes of Parras, who at certain seasons of the year communicated with this people. These Christians began by inviting some of the mountain caciques to descend into the valley and to visit Santa María that they might see what a Christian padre was like and what advantages were to be enjoyed by living in the

---

[1] For notes to chapter xii see page 211.

mission. The mountain chiefs came and were well impressed. Presents were given them and every hospitality shown them. But they would not remain. Back to their mountains and canyons they went.

The missionary appetite of the fathers was whetted by reports of a finer morality among these Indians and others of the sierras. They now did the usual thing when they wanted gradually to gain over a group. They asked the caciques if at least they would allow some of their sons to come to the Christian pueblo to live. The missionaries promised that these boys would be well treated and that the parents might come to visit them whenever they liked. As the caciques had already enjoyed certain phases of this treatment, they lent a willing ear to the suggestion and the boys were allowed to go.

The lads proved intelligent. They memorized the catechism readily, and learned to read, to write, to sing, and to play on musical instruments. When, years later, Gonzalo de Hermosillo, the first bishop of the newly created diocese of Durango, visited Parras, he marveled at the aptitude and ability of these *serranillos bárbaros,* or little mountain savages. But the "call of the wild" was upon them and on one occasion three of their number made excuses to run off to their rough mountain home. On the way, two perished of hunger and thirst. Their bodies were later discovered partly devoured by beasts.[2]

In spite of mishaps such as this, the missionaries of Santa María de las Parras began what came to be the complete Christianization of these *serranos,* or distant Indians of the sierras. Encouraged through reports of the parents of those boys who were at Parras, a young cacique called Llepo determined to go down himself to see the mission. He brought fifty of his people, and was so impressed with all he beheld and with the doctrine he was taught that he learned the catechism and was baptized. He took the name of Joseph. This was the very sort of progress the missionaries had in mind when they procured the permission of the caciques to train their sons at Parras. Others followed Chief Llepo's example; by 1612, three hundred and fifty of these serranos had come to live in the mission of Santa María.[3]

But the weight of a heavy cross fell hard upon the Jesuits in 1608. This was a virulent sickness which decimated their flock[4]—a common experience since the coming of the white man. "Among the many misfortunes," says Professor Priestley, "inevitably incident to the clash of two civilizations... none were more destructive than the frequent scourges of epidemic diseases which smote the land with devastating fury."[5] Only two years after Cortés' arrival in Mexico, in 1521, a slave boy introduced mortal sickness among the natives. In 1544 a disease furious among the Indians, called by the Aztecs *matlazahuatl*, probably smallpox, worked havoc with the population. Plague broke out again in 1555, 1575, and 1595. There were many other visitations.[6]

The Jesuit sources often mention *viruelas y serampión,* smallpox and measles. Sometimes only the former is spoken of. Smallpox was the terrible scourge; passing over the missionary, it fell like a bolt upon the Indian and struck him down. Pérez de Ribas, who often had occasion in his history to mention the smallpox, himself saw the ravages of this disease upon the poor savage. Nothing worse had he ever beheld. Great sores would rot into a mass of swarming maggots, and these sometimes would drop from the mouth or nose of the victim, emitting an unbearable stench.[7] Father Martín Pérez, pioneer missionary in Sinaloa, who had seen many such visitations—such for instance as that of 1593 on the banks of the Sinaloa,—describes the horror of the disease with quite the realism of Ribas;[8] and the missionaries living in the mountains of Topia and San Andrés could have written likewise about the plague that broke out there in 1613.

It was a commonplace with the Jesuits to attribute the outbreak of an epidemic to the direct influence of Satan, for they suffered through it a grave setback to their labors. Indeed, besides the human suffering inflicted, these visitations nearly always caused a break-up of the pueblos and the flight of the Indians. Sometimes, as in Sinaloa in 1593, the plague incited to revolt. The hechicero would always say: "You see; I told you. Baptism has caused this sickness." The timid would flee and the superstitious or surly would hatch rebellion.

But there was a perfectly natural explanation for the periodical outbreaks of this plague. As the Indians were proverbially unable to resist the diseases introduced by Europeans, the very fact of their coming together for baptism and gathering into pueblos that they might be near the fathers and the church, would invariably tend to increase the ravages of the disease. It was sad but inevitable. If the Indians were to be Christianized and civilized, it seemed necessary that they be brought together to live in more compact communities than they were accustomed to in their savage state. It was these causes, and neither the Devil nor baptism, that promoted the plague. But the missionaries, like most men of their time, knew little about sanitation or isolation, and were exaggeratedly prone to attribute all ills to the Evil One.

The plague, then, visited the missions of the lagoon country in 1608, soon after the missionaries were first in contact with the tribes of the sierras. It was "a general and mortal sickness," which Ribas calls *cocolitzli* (an Aztec name which came to be applied generally to many diseases), and *viruelas,* which was smallpox. Many children died, but in their sorrow the missionaries were consoled to think that with baptism their souls had been regenerated to everlasting life. Likewise the as yet unbaptized adults, especially the serranos, though they succumbed to the plague, received the saving waters and thus died with the grace of Heaven fresh upon their souls.

The Jesuit missionaries were logical and intellectually consistent in this their spiritual happiness even in the face of death. Both their faith and their philosophy told them that this life is brief and passing, a mere preparation for an existence without end. Therefore, if the everlasting was saved at the expense of the ephemeral (and death will come speedily in any case), these Catholic priests had some reason for consolation, provided it was through no act or negligence of theirs that the temporal life ceased. The parents of the plague-stricken children listened for the most part docilely to the spiritual explanations and consolations of the missionaries, such as in time of trial Christian philosophy holds up to mortal man to give him strength and courage; and in Christian hope the children were taken out to be buried, their bodies garlanded with wild flowers and crowned with roses.[9]

This visitation meant gigantic labor for the Black Robe. He had time to rest neither day nor night, attending the sick or dying not only in the pueblos, but also in the distant settlements *de visita* and in the sierras. He assisted both Christian and pagan. The fathers were able often, to their no small spiritual consolation, to baptize the pagans on the threshold of death. Indeed, the Jesuit was physician to both body and soul. To the sick he brought corn, flour, and beef, this last being a great delicacy for the savage. The missionaries expended thus in alms the salary of 300 pesos they yearly received from the King. They administered medicines, too, for the Indian knew no remedy except cautery and bleeding. The savage cauterized his pustule or his sore with burning rods and bled his feet with arrowpoints. The Jesuit offered the juice of the refreshing orange, and tea made from soothing herbs. Perhaps, too, the fathers administered quinine, which their confreres had discovered in Brazil.

In the meantime the hechiceros were busy with their dances and their incantations to lay the fury of the pest. The demons, they averred, appeared to them during the dances for days on end. Sometimes the spirit would come forth clothed in the form of a stag, a serpent, or a soldier armed *de punta en blanco*. Sometimes the devil would be wrapped in flame, his visage proud and angered, inspiring fear.[10] The wizards spread it about that the demon threatened with the plague all who would receive baptism or listen to the instructions of the padre. Did they keep away from the fathers, the plague would keep away from them. And these spirits were hard masters, too, for they kept the medicine men dancing for days at a stretch about an idol, without a bite to eat or drop to drink, until they dropped with exhaustion or became distracted to madness. But the wiles of the hechiceros had little effect. Both Christians and pagans noticed that they too, in spite of all their mad dancing and vaunted contacts with the spirit world, fell ill themselves; that they too were caught by the plague and were dropped into the grave. Therefore their prestige was dissipated and the Black Robe prevailed.[11]

Nevertheless, the medicine men were able to persuade some pagans to practices, as amusing as they were stupid, which were intended to placate the demon of the cocolitzli: to pile up before the door of their huts mounds of flint arrowpoints and the claws and carcasses of sparrow hawks. One said it was the fathers' purpose to gather the Indians into pueblos just to give the plague to all of them at once. But the Christian idea had been too well sown to allow of its being uprooted by deceivers who themselves fell ill. Many, instead of the claws and carcasses of hawks, used the image of the crucifix in their huts and put rosary beads around their necks to obtain the blessing of the true God. Some said, too, with wise philosophy, that every man had one time to die and they would much prefer to breathe their last in the arms of their padre who had been so kind to them than to expire in the clutches of the fanatical hechicero.[12]

Unfortunately, the plague fell heavily upon the serranos. Most of the three hundred and fifty who had come to Parras caught the disease. Some of them died, others fled back to their hills and mountains. This increased the disaster, for many fell on the road and those who reached the hills carried the infection with them and it ran up along the canyons and arroyos of the sierra. The numbers of those who died in this way were so great that, as during the Black Death of the fourteenth century, the victims were gathered up and buried in heaps by the missionaries. The fathers came into the hills and gullies to baptize the dying after a few words of instruction. Some groups were found perishing of hunger as well as sickness and reduced to live on the snakes and rats they might be able to catch. Parents held their dying sons to the last instructions of the priest.

Down into the creeks and estuaries of the lagoon the plague went. Here, too, the missionary had to labor, where the dry and parched hills gave way to wide shallows and muddy creeks. To reach some of the islands where dying Indians lay, it was necessary to wade through miles of water sometimes breast-deep.[13] The plague was carried even to far-off Mapimí, more than a hundred miles from Santa María— borne by winds that blew like a roaring furnace over the baking land. Here the fathers had a mission near a place where the Spaniards had a mine. Father Diego de Pangua wrote in 1607 about a strange mode these people of Mapimí had of appeasing the god both of plagues and of comets. For this year a comet made its appearance, and the Indians, like the men of the Middle Ages, and even like the scholars of their own times, thought this high glowing object shook disease from its hair.[14]

Here is how the savage children of Mapimí placated this high divinity. They celebrated a mitote, the dance we have alluded to,[15] and put into it certain rites good for the god of plagues and good for the comet god. They marched two by two, male and female, beginning with children of seven and ending with old men of a hundred years, who closed up the rear. A basket of dates or prickly pear in the right hand, they carried an arrow in the left with its head of flint just above the heart. Four old men at the rear, all jeweled and painted, bore each a leather whip. Since the comet had a tail, some thought to please it by imitation and therefore carried the tail of a mountain lion or fox. Be-

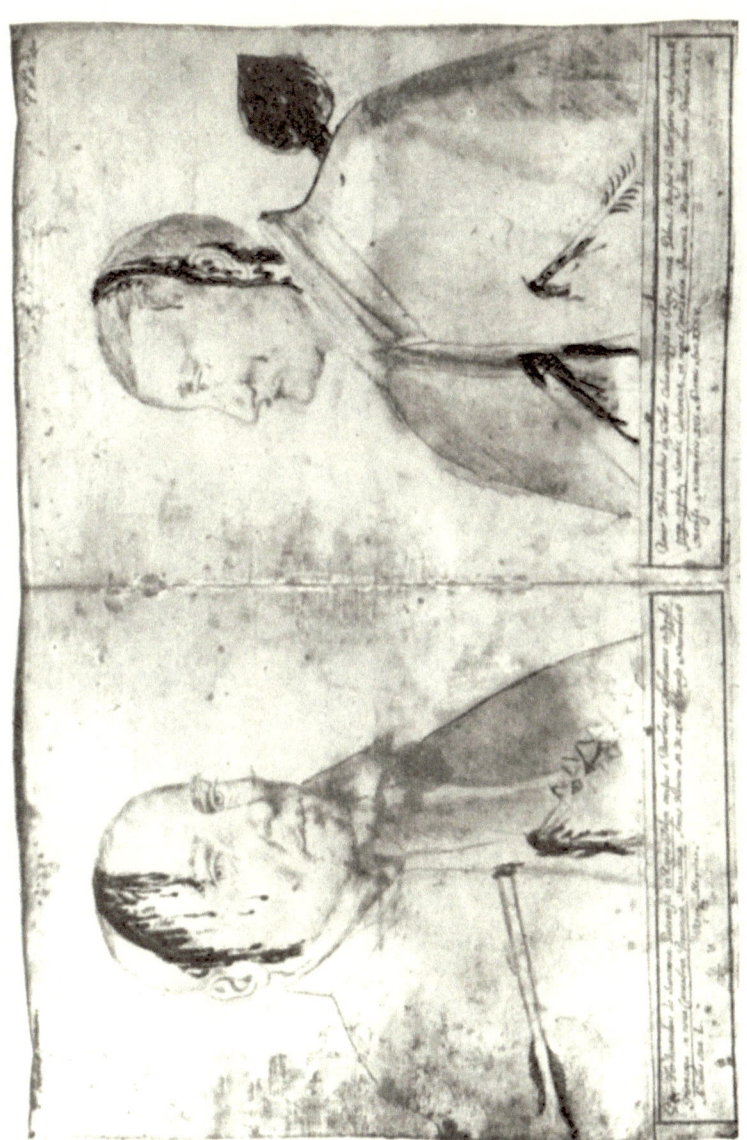

HERNANDO DE SANTARÉN   HERNANDO DE TOVAR

GERÓNIMO DE MORANTA   JUAN FONTE

cause the tail of the comet looked like a feather, some adorned their heads with plumage. Others carried in their baskets, besides fruit, dead mice, rats, rabbits, and snakes.

Thus arrayed and ordered, these people of Mapimí marched to the middle of the plaza of their pueblo. They made a fire, into which they flung all they had in the baskets. It was a sacrifice, but all depended upon the direction of the smoke. If, like that of the sacrifice of Abel, it went straight to heaven, then the comet would be appeased, for it would be able to feed upon the smoke and be satisfied. This explains the use of the whips of the four old men: they began to lay about them so soon as the fruits, mice, snakes, and rats were thrown into the fire, thus by beating the air to force the atmosphere to remain quiet that the smoke might rise direct. Unfortunately, wrote Father de Pangua, at this particular time the air was disobedient, for a wind was blowing and the smoke did not rise. This demanded further propitiation through sacrifice. Six maidens, to their chagrin, had to lose their hair. Then not only the four old men, but all persons in the procession, began to beat, not the air, but their bodies till the blood flowed. They gathered up the gore with switches made from the hair of the maidens, and the old men, emitting horrible cries, flung the besmeared objects into the air. After these rites were over, they burned the switches.

By the time all this ritual had been gone through, the wind had died down, and these poor people dispersed to their rancherias, some going back to Mapimí, satisfied that they had placated the comet and the god of plague. Nevertheless, an epidemic made its visitation. It ravaged the environs of Mapimí and many died.[16]

After the plague, flood scourged the land, pouring its waters in 1612. Rain fell for whole days. The river rose and the lagoon began to swell and spread, creeping over the land for miles. For thirty years, the elder Indians said, they had not seen such high waters. Still the rain continued until the Río de las Nazas, like petulant Tiber of old, rent its banks and poured its flood over the country of the Christian pueblos. Near San Gerónimo the river cut out a new bed for itself, to the danger of the village. At San Ignacio the waters carried down the church and the house of the missionaries, one padre narrowly escaping death from a falling wall. At San Pedro the river carved a channel which destroyed part of the Indian dwellings. Here the danger was greatest. The Indians warned the fathers not to remain. The latter prepared to go. But delayed with trying to carry to safety some of the ornaments of the church, they found themselves with only two Indian boys for guides. After many adventures they came to a small elevation covered with mesquite. Beast and serpent had taken refuge here with man. The rising waters soon enclosed them in a place so narrow that hardly an enramada could be erected to shield them from the ever-pouring rain. The refugees were crowded here for three days. Then the waters began to subside. These people of San Pedro escaped from their island prison through shallows of mud and water and on returning to their pueblo found that although the waters had risen to a third the height of the church, the fabric was still erect.

These ardent Christians found blessings even in calamity. None of the fathers had been harmed by poisonous reptiles, which caused, by their bite, the death of fifty during the flood. Many strange pools were left, as the waters receded, where an abundance of fish was entrapped and easily caught. There was another and a more positive blessing. The Spaniards and the Indians had long desired to dig a canal to a fertile spot in the valley; but the undertaking was too vast for their resources. Now nature had done it, for where the flood broke through at San Gerónimo it scooped out for itself precisely the kind of channel in form and direction which the population had desired.

Flood was followed by drought which drove in the outlying Indians to the lagoon for water and for game and fish. These savages were formerly enemies of the lagoon Indians and the latter used always to fight them off in time of drought that they alone might enjoy the blessings of the water. But Christianity had induced a less selfish spirit and the Laguneros allowed their neighbors peacefully to come up, sharing with them the fish and the wild duck.[17]

Let this chapter conclude with the consecration of an ancient devil-beridden cave. One night, near which pueblo we are not told, the padre heard a clamoring voice as of one crying for help. The Indians told him it was a man possessed by the devil. They followed the cries, which led them over rough and difficult terrain to a place hollowed out into caves and caverns. Soon they came to a capacious hollow where, the padre was informed, the devil was wont to appear in forbidding aspect, clothed at times in the black robe of the Jesuit. Many had died of fright here, they said, and in proof pointed to a pile of skulls and bones, partly covered over with rocks to hide them from view. The Indian guides told the missionary that upon the high vaults of the cave, where certainly no man could reach, marks of human blood stained the rock—blood smeared there by the evil spirit.

The individual whose cries they had heard lay on the ground unconscious. The first efforts to resuscitate the victim were unavailing. Finally, the next morning, he came to his senses. In a precarious state of health he was willing to receive baptism and showed such marks of contentedness that a hundred of the village became willing themselves to be baptized that they be freed from the fearsome apparitions. The padre then organized a religious procession of his new Christians, who carried crosses into the cave. Here an altar was rechristened, and the place was called the Grotto of Santiago because this was done on the Feast of St. James the Apostle. From that moment, avers the Jesuit historian who had the facts from the pen of the padre, the fearful apparitions ceased.[18]

So here in the lagoon country the new faith was sorely tried. But in spite of conflict with sorcerer and devil and the shock of plague and flood, Christianity struck deeper and deeper root. It is true the numbers had been sadly diminished by the epidemic, but the Faith spread in ever-widening circles and after the lapse of a few years the entire country had become entirely Christian. The fathers had succeeded in evangelizing the eastern section of Nueva Vizcaya right up to the valley where the town of Saltillo during these very years was being made into an important center.[19]

Chapter XIII

DISTANT RUMBLINGS

THUS THE MISSIONS east of the Sierra Madre progressed apace. We have watched and followed their development from the first permanent residence in Durango in 1593 and the beginning of the missions *entre infieles* in Cuencamé in 1594 down through twenty years to the middle of the second decade of the seventeenth century. We have seen progress and trials among the Laguneros of the eastern plains from the time that Juan Agustín de Espinosa started work among them in 1596; we have witnessed the beginnings of the mountain missions of Topia and San Andrés, among the Acaxée Indians first and then among the cannibals to the south, the Xiximes, who required to feel the strength of the secular arm before they would willingly submit. The work of Santarén begun at Topia in 1598 was carried splendidly along. In almost twenty years of development, of which he was the pioneer and much of the soul, he saw two numerous nations brought into the fold.

And the Tepehuanes—Father Gerónimo Ramírez had come to them in 1596. His initial success was encouraging in a high degree, and when other Jesuits came to aid him there was recorded a marked progress through the course of the years. It was noted only that this widespread nation of the plains to the north and east of Durango, and of the mountains to the north and west, was not so enthusiastic by nature as were some others; that they were more given to idolatry, superstition, and the leadership of the hechiceros. Three fine Christian pueblos had been organized among them: Santiago Papasquiaro, Santa Catalina, and Zape. There were also the missions of Indé, Guanaceví, Santa Cruz, Sauceda, and Atotonilco, with other mission stations. When the number of fathers had been augmented, especially after Father Juan Fonte arrived, a beginning was made with the Tarahumares far to the north. Habitually warlike, the Tepehuanes, almost Christianized by 1615, consented to live in peace and concord with their neighbors, the Tarahumares north and the Acaxées south.

By the following year eight fathers were working in the Tepehuán

DISTANT RUMBLINGS 119

mission and the reports that came in from each of them had been as encouraging as usual. At Santiago Papasquiaro, for instance, things were as flourishing as in any other mission. The sacraments were frequented, feasts were celebrated. A school for boys educated and Christianized young hearts to grow into well-formed, moral manhood. A church building was erected too, a goodly structure for the place and time. Outside Indians came in to make their residence in Santiago that they might share in the peace and prosperity of the pueblo. Old Christians, the Indians from the south, had for long been residents here, and even some Spaniards made it their home.[1]

Nevertheless, it was among these Tepehuanes that the most serious revolt in the history of the Jesuit missions of Mexico broke out, a revolt which gave from among the clergy ten martyrs to the Faith, eight of them being Jesuits. A Dominican and a Franciscan likewise suffered death. The only other time that there had been such a holocaust of Jesuits was in the mission of Florida when Segura and his seven companions in 1571 were slain by Don Luis, a renegade neophyte, on the banks of the Rappahannock. But the massacres of Chesapeake Bay occurred before the missions had fairly started and before any conversions had been made. Gonzalo de Tapia was martyred on the banks of the Sinaloa in 1594 and Juan Pascual and Manuel Martínez were slain near the Chínipa country in 1632. In Tarahumara in 1650 and 1652, respectively, Cornelius Beudin and Jácome Basilio were killed. In the second Tarahumar uprising in 1690, Fathers Juan Ortiz Foronda and Manuel Sánchez fell, and five years later Father Francisco Xavier Saeta was slain in Pimería Alta. In the following century Tello and Rowen were slain for the Faith in Sonora; and finally, in the uprising of Baja California in 1733 Fathers Lorenzo Carranco and Nicolás Tamaral were murdered. But here among the Tepehuanes in 1616 eight Jesuit missionaries, as it were at one blow, were struck down.

What were the causes of this terrific disaster to the missions east of the mountains, and what were the events which led up to it? There was apparently no reason. All things seemed at peace at the end of 1615. The three principal pueblos were organized in the political manner of civilized communities, with their own Indian officers whom

---
[1] For notes to chapter xiii see pages 211–212.

they had elected, and they lived quietly under the supervision of the fathers. What was far more important for the elimination of any apparent cause of rebellion, these Tepehuanes lived at peace with the Spaniards of the mines and farms in their vicinity. The sources are quite clear that Spanish ill treatment of the Indian, so frequent a cause of revolt, did not at least at this time have influence here. There existed a constant commercial and friendly intercourse between the Spaniards and the Indians, especially at Santiago Papasquiaro, which was excellently situated for the commerce that flowed to and from the mountains.[2] Had cruelty or violence by the Spaniards led to the trouble, the missionaries would have made some mention of it. They say just the contrary.

The anuas of 1614 and 1615 mention no particular difficulty, except it be the rather more frequent presence here of the hechicero than in the other nations. It is true that in 1614 in one pueblo the missionary discovered that four of these wizards or medicine men were misleading the people, who under their influence were in communication with an evil spirit with howls and cries. But this difficulty was met and overcome, and things quieted down. True, there was some trouble at Indé. In another district, when a giant of a fellow threatened to kill the padre for depriving him of his concubine, the missionary, warned of the threat, knew arts of kindness and diplomacy to disarm his irritation. Reports, this year, from a settlement called San Ignacio, representing a group recently converted, speak of the vastly improved and evident Christian spirit of these new children of the Church.[3]

It is much the same for the year 1615. One of the missionaries, Father Juan Pérez de Córdoba, died this year, and it was written of as a great loss to the mission. He was drowned while trying to ford the Río de las Nazas. Guanacevi and Indé mourned publicly his death. The Provincial wrote for 1615: "They tell me that this year there has been no cause for disquietude." The processions, the devotions of the Tepehuanes are lauded. "The Sundays of Lent they marched at night to the church to take the discipline." And when some hechiceros came to Santiago Papasquiaro and gained some measure of success, receiving gifts from a number of the neophytes, they were punished together with those who had favored them. The final effect of this disturbance was a revival of faith and greater assiduity at the spiritual

DISTANT RUMBLINGS

exercises. When an hechicero at Indé told the people their padre was a killer, hurting the health of their children, the neophytes laughed at him and came with filial confidence to tell the father all about it. Fonte writes consolingly from the north that Indians are coming to him from the back country seeking baptism. When a woman lost her child and ran to the wizard for help, the missionary taught her to go to God in prayer, and to His mother, the Blessed Virgin Mary; when blight got into their crops, they were taught the special prayers of the Church against this calamity.[4]

Why was it, then, that by the end of the following year a most destructive rebellion had been hatched and had actually broken out beyond all control? We can reduce the causes to three: the general and well-known fickleness of the Indian nature, the influence of the hechicero, and the particular restlessness of the people of Santa Catalina, which had been apparent from the beginning.

The Indian was only a child, after all: a lovable child sometimes, and a simple one, but withal a child, open to suggestion, swift to change, and, unless sustained by the strengthening presence of the padre or of the captain, weak and shifting of purpose. If ever the sower of cockles had a fertile field for his mischief it was among these savages. Destructive propaganda never elsewhere was able to work so speedily and so tragically. Juan Lautaro, leader of the Ocoroni rebels on the west coast, was able in 1609 to poison the entire Yaqui nation against the Spaniards and to bring about the only defeat that Captain Hurdaide ever suffered.[5] A single hechicero coming up from the Mayo River with the band that accompanied Father Pedro Méndez was able through evil whisperings to prejudice many of the Yaqui women against the sacrament of baptism in spite of long years of waiting and petitioning.[6] When Taxicora, the wizard of the west coast, was removed from the Fuerte, the Suaquis showed themselves amenable to correction. Instances of this weakness in the Indians can be multiplied a hundredfold.

All through this story we have seen that the hechicero was the great thorn in the side of the fathers. These medicine men frightened the people by their magic, they deceived them by their incantations, they harried them with their threats of evil and duped them by their promises of reward. "Bathe in the river and you shall regain your youth," said an hechicero of the Yaqui, through whom a spirit was said to appear first as an old man, then as a youth.[7] This influence came near to starting a most serious revolt among the Yaquis recently baptized. And when they could hear the bellowings of the demon's voice or behold, as at Guasave with Father Clerici, the physical effects of his presence in the violent jostling of objects or persons, then would they be led to run off from their pueblos, frightened of Christianity, and dreading the punishment announced to them by their wizards.[8] So it was here in 1616 with the Tepehuanes. Sorcerers, as we have seen, were numerous and powerful among this nation. Some of the Indians, fleeing justice and the opposition of the padres, had gone over the divide to the west and were taken in by the Cahuemetos on the upper Sinaloa River. Here they stirred up disaffection and revolt, giving no end of trouble to Father Pedro de Velasco and to Captain Hurdaide.[9]

So now an hechicero started an agitation which led to rebellion, murder, and war: a thin wisp of smoke from a tiny spark, hardly perceptible at first, but growing and carefully concealed, broke forth into a devastating conflagration.

Indeed, regarding the Tepehuanes, the early missionaries from Ramírez to Fonte have told us that they were particularly given to their idols and the influence of their hechicero. Neither will it be surprising that the trouble should have started at Santa Catalina. When Gerónimo Ramírez first preached to this group they were cold and held aloof. As we have seen, it was an old woman who, rebuking them for their tepidity and setting them the example, turned the scales in favor of acceptance of the gospel.[10] Ribas says that Santa Catalina was always a difficult place and that the fathers had expended all their energy to tame it. As the years went on, although it enjoyed a church and all in it were baptized and were assiduous at the instructions, from time to time there would be a flare of disturbance, and more than once the fathers had to give warning notice to Governor Urdiñola, and then to his successor, Gaspar de Alvear.[11]

Pérez de Ribas himself passed through the Tepehuán country in the fall of 1616, just a few weeks before the revolt broke out, and he gives us his impressions. His confreres invited him to visit some of their pueblos. He perceived unfavorable signs. First, Ribas missed among these people the same affection for their churches that he had been accustomed to witness on the banks of the Fuerte. Then, the Tepehuanes did not seem to have, for they did not show, that tincture of Christianity and that affability with their padres which the Indians had always manifested elsewhere. "I signified something of my impressions," says Ribas, "to the father who accompanied me, and he replied: 'Who knows what demon of an idol has come into this nation to render it changed and restless! We spare no possible effort to help and quiet these people, I and the other fathers.'" Thus spoke to Ribas Father Bernardo de Cisneros, one of the eight to die.[12]

The Spaniards, too, noticed the growing coolness, which was for them a dangerous sign; for when the Indian has a plot brewing he cannot dissimulate altogether the dark purposes of his heart. Lack of enthusiasm, aloofness, silent goings about were always a sign that trouble was afoot. For some time now this evil wind had been blowing.[13]

The revolt was mostly due to one particular hechicero who had been plotting for some time but had cloaked his movements in deepest secrecy. His name was Quautlatas. He had been baptized, but he only feigned Christianity. He had gone from pueblo to pueblo carrying with him an idol, and he infected by degrees the whole nation with the spirit of revolt. He went to Tunal near Durango and to more distant Tenerape, Santiago Papasquiaro, and Zape. He carried his idol always with him. It was his oracle; through it a spirit spoke.

At Tenerape he caused the image to be adored. He told the Indians that both he and the idol were gods. They were both offended, he said, because the Tepehuanes had allowed the Spaniards to enter their lands and because they had embraced Christianity.[14] All this should be remedied. They must put to the knife all the old Christian Indians from the south, all the Spaniards, and especially the missionaries. If the Tepehuanes would obey him and his idol they would have security for themselves, their wives, and their children forevermore against the oppression of the aliens. It is true, he said, some Tepehuanes would die in the war, but after seven days they would arise from their graves and when victory should crown their efforts all the old would regain their youth. Once the Spaniards should be killed, he and the idol would prevent their ever coming again into the land, for by causing storms at sea he would prevent their passage from Spain. The Indians averred afterward that he gained the ear of many by being able actually to persuade them that a man of Tenerape named Sebastián and a woman at Santiago Papasquiaro named Justina had been swallowed up by the earth for not obeying him; also that the same misfortune happened to one Cacaria, a woman of another pueblo.[15]

Quautlatas likewise asserted that the Indians of other nations were also in revolt against the Spaniards, and he endeavored to persuade the Acaxées and Xiximes to join him and his Tepehuanes. The fathers later heard wild things of how he tried to do this. He whom the Acaxées knew for an old man appeared to them one day as a youth with a crystal like a looking glass over his belly, which, they said, spoke to them correctly and strongly in all languages. The words that came from this object were of such force and did such violence to them that they felt it almost impossible to resist its demands. Word of these phenomena reached the Spaniards, who considered that this hechicero was possessed with a demon, the same that had bellowed about the pallet of the sick old woman at Guasave and knocked the holy water out of the hands of a catechist who went to aid her. We have mentioned this case above. It was Father Alberto Clerici who drove out this demon through the prayers and exorcisms of the Church. As this had happened but a short time before, the Spaniards thought the same demon had entered into this rebel hechicero, for when the evil spirit left the old woman he said he would be heard from elsewhere.[16]

Now the new Governor was apprised of the mischief this fellow was doing. Had he acted more strongly and decisively, like his great subject, Captain Hurdaide in Sinaloa, this whole revolt could easily have been nipped in the bud. Urdiñola, now in Saltillo, had been succeeded by Don Gaspar de Alvear, who seems to have labored under some of Urdiñola's very defects, namely, a certain spirit of procrastination and lack of vigorous action. Governor Alvear looked upon the hechicero as an old but harmless evildoer and ordered the wizard and his companions flogged for the scandal they were giving. The Governor contented himself with this, and, though the misgivings of the fathers led them to send repeated warnings, Alvear did not take action. Hurdaide would have had the man hanged by the neck. So the evil went on unchecked, though no one dreamed that a plot so widespread and so murderous was being hatched by this old and possessed hechicero.[17]

The poisonous brew kept fermenting and spreading from month to month, and the success of old Quautlatas was far greater than Alvear and perhaps even the missionaries suspected. Here was the plan: All the pueblos would take arms and on the same day and at the same hour would fall upon the Spaniards in their farmhouses and their mines. The rebels would slaughter them as well as the fathers. They had set the day and the principal place. The day was the 21st of November in the Roman calendar, the Feast of the Presentation of the Blessed Virgin Mary. The place was to be Zape, for on this feast at Zape a statue of Blessed Mary the Virgin recently brought from Mexico was to be solemnly dedicated. Much preparation had been made for the fiesta and a large crowd of unarmed Spaniards was expected to be present. Some fathers would be there, too. This was the place for the rebels to begin, for here by one strong blow much destruction could be wrought.[18]

Chapter XIV

THE STORM BREAKS

THE SAVAGES could not await the time. Five days before the date fixed they broke out in riot and murder. The place was not Zape as prearranged nor was the victim one of their own missionaries. Hernando de Tovar, a native of Culiacán, after entering the Jesuit novitiate at Tepotzotlán in 1598 had been sent to the missions of Parras after the completion of his tertianship. His mother had in the meantime entered a convent in Mexico City, his father being dead. Now this year she asked that her son might be allowed to travel down to the capital for a visit, and the request was granted. The superior at Parras, however, before letting him go south sent him on a commission to the mines of Topia. By the middle of November, 1616, he was on his way from San Andrés back to Durango through Topia, thence to set out for Mexico City.[1]

Traveling the same mule path over the mountains from Topia was a merchant, Alvaro Crespo, leading a train of animals laden with goods. The same road is used today from Topia to Tepehuanes, which is our Santa Catalina. From Topia the path led, and leads, east through the deep pass of the main cordillera, out into more open but still rugged country, and then down the vale of the Río Tepehuanes to the mission. The two travelers arrived together at Santa Catalina on the evening of November 15. Here was a temptation too great for the Indians of Santa Catalina to resist—a padre and a merchant with his wares. True, it was five days before the concerted attack was to be made, but this chance could not be allowed to slip by.

The travelers seem to have suspected nothing. They passed the night, for aught we know, peacefully. The Indians, dissimulating, had provided food for the visitors and their animals. Tovar may have said his Mass in the morning before setting out. But just as the guests were about to leave, as the father was mounting his mule, a group of savages came running up in a state of excitement. The merchant scented trouble, put spurs to his mule and was off, leaving his wares behind

---

[1] For notes to chapter xiv see page 212.

him, but shouting to Tovar to follow. The padre called out: "If the hour is now come, let us receive what God has sent." The Indians knocked Tovar off his mule with a club, made sport of his prayers and his faith, and as he tried to speak of God, ran him through the chest with a spear. Taunts and jibes against religion at the same time pierced his soul. A friendly Mexican Indian had been shackled by the rebels, but he escaped to bring the news to Durango. The day was Wednesday, November 16, 1616.[2]

In the meantime the merchant raced down the Río Tepehuanes to Atotonilco, situated at the junction of the latter stream with the Río de Santiago. He found the Spanish inhabitants ready to protect themselves, for the other padres had warned them that danger was afoot. At the report of the fugitive, they gathered in a house—more than seventy of them[3]—for protection, possessing, however, only slight provisions of food or powder for their guns. With them was Fray Juan Guttiérez, a Franciscan priest. The savages soon came trooping up and attacked the house. Failing to break in, they fired it. The adobe walls held out, but the roof burned and those within suffocated from the smoke. The men tried to disperse the enemy with their guns, but ammunition gave out. At this juncture Father Guttiérez, holding high a crucifix and accompanied by a boy of fourteen, bravely went out to placate the mad rebels. He was straightway pierced through the stomach with an arrow, and the boy, Pedro Ignatio, fell with him. Both were killed on the spot.

The Indians would not treat and there was nothing for it but to surrender. This was fatal. Except two, every man, woman, and child was slaughtered by the infuriated Indians. Their work done, they made off with their booty up the Río de Santiago to attack Santiago Papasquiaro, where they knew two Jesuits resided. The two who escaped at Atotonilco, one by hiding, the other by the ruse of a friendly Indian, were Lucas Benítez and Cristóbal Martínez de Hurdaide, son of the captain in Sinaloa. They speeded for Durango and told of the gruesome massacre.[4]

At Santiago Papasquiaro were Fathers Bernardo de Cisneros and Diego de Orozco. Scenting danger even before the attack upon Tovar at Santa Catalina, they endeavored at the last moment to stem the tide of rebellion by getting in touch with a friendly chief of great authority,

Don Francisco Campos. At the fathers' request Don Francisco with two companions went to the leaders, whose residence was a pueblo twelve miles distant, and endeavored to placate them. The ambassador of the padres was seized and slain; so was one of his companions. The other escaped. Later, two masked Indians rushed in to tell the fathers and the Spanish alcalde, Juan del Castillo, that all the Tepehuanes were about to rise. Then came the news of Don Francisco's death. The alcalde gave orders that the Spaniards should take refuge in the church, which was of stone, with the fathers' adobe house built up against it. He then rushed off a messenger to Durango to ask for help.

All this was on Tuesday the 15th, the day before the death of Father Tovar. On the evening of the 16th came the dreadful report that two hundred Indians were marching south upon the town. They arrived the morning of Thursday the 17th. The Spaniards, some hundred of them, together with the Jesuit missionaries, closed themselves up in the church. Of the Tepehuán residents of the pueblo, some, remaining faithful, joined the refugees in the church; the rest either became rebels themselves or remained neutral.[5]

All day the siege proceeded while the hostiles, abetted by their women, desecrated such holy objects as they could lay hands on. They sacked a chapel near by, dragged out a statue of Our Lady and had it horsewhipped amid jeers and taunts. They took a crucifix from the fathers' house and dragging it about ignominiously, flung it into a corner with the cry of "robber, drunkard, thief." Another large cross stood in the plaza in front of the church. They knocked it down and proceeded against it on horseback as in a joust, mock umpires standing by. They struck at it till it was broken to pieces. They found some *sedilias* or hand stretchers used for carrying statues with honor in processions. On these they put Indian women holding pieces of the crucifix. To the women they offered mock incense. Thus Thursday passed, the besieged being helpless to stop the profanation, fully occupied as they were in their own defense and killing a few of the enemy with what arquebuses they had.

In the meantime the message of danger sent from Papasquiaro arrived in Durango. "Help, help, help," it read, "for we stand on the threshold of death!" Other alarms were rung in. Steps were at once taken to aid the besieged at Papasquiaro. The arsenal at Durango was opened; twenty-six men were armed with coat of mail and given arquebuses and powder. They left the capital under the leadership of Martín de Olivas, rich land and mine owner of Topia, to rush to the release of their brethren shut up in so dangerous a trap.[8]

In the meantime help did come—but for the rebels. A troop of five hundred appeared, having finished other mischief, to swell the mad army. The enraged Indians now proceeded to tear down every dwelling in the pueblo, including that of the fathers hard by the church. They succeeded, moreover, in setting fire to the roof of the sacred edifice. All the refugees might have perished from the smoke or in the flames. However, the enemy wanted their game alive, and hence deceived the Spaniards. They were Christians, they said. They wanted to return to peace and amity with the Spaniards. The besieged on their part asked only to be allowed to go to Durango. Terms were arranged through a rebel Tepehuán who had been a servant of one of the beleaguered Spaniards. Escape from the burning church was offered if the prisoners would march out quietly and hand over their arms. These were hard conditions, but there was nothing for it but to accept. They were to come out one by one in procession.

It was now Friday, November 18th. The fathers had not consumed the Blessed Sacrament—which was probably a mistake, but a readily understandable mistake, since they expected help from Durango at any time and they desired the consolation which the physical presence of Christ could give them. Therefore Father Diego de Orozco carrying the ciborium which contained the Sacred Species headed the procession. After him came the alcalde carrying a statue of the Blessed Virgin. The others followed. The rebels knelt in feigned adoration of the Host and accompanied the procession to the center of the plaza. Here Orozco, still carrying the ciborium, tried to harangue the savages, reminding them of their faith in Christ and of the benefits innumerable which God had conferred upon them. The Jesuit seemed to be making an impression when a voice cried out, "You lie." With that the ciborium was knocked from his hand, the Hosts were scattered and trampled underfoot, and himself smashed down with the blow of a cudgel and pierced through with an arrow. Before he was dead two rebels held him high in the form of a cross while one of their number hacked his body from head to foot with an ax. The last words of Orozco were: "Do with me, my children, what you desire, for I die for my God." The rebels mocked: *"Dominus vobiscum: Et cum spiritu tuo."* Father Cisneros was run through with a spear. The rest were similarly massacred—all except six who escaped. The statue of the Virgin Mary was smashed to bits. Help from Durango had not come in time.[7]

The six fled, guided by two Indian boys over secret paths. One party went to Durango, the other to Sauceda. This latter group when near Sauceda fell in with the company which Captain Olivas was leading from Durango to the rescue of those who had just been slaughtered. Olivas, with agony in his heart, heard the harrowing story. Too late to save Papasquiaro, the Captain resolved to go to Sauceda and fortify himself there in a house which he knew would answer the purpose. He notified the Governor of the dread calamity and took speedy measures for the safety of the other fathers. The Jesuit superior of Durango, planning for the protection of his sons, likewise arrived at Sauceda and none too soon, for the Spaniards here were immediately surrounded by an army of rebels. Olivas made a sortie and there was a skirmish. None were lost on either side. The Spaniards returned to the stronghold to await reinforcements from the capital. This time, aid from headquarters was effective.

Captain Cordejuela, a landowner near Durango and a frontiersman of large experience in Indian wars, had collected at his own expense a column of soldiers. He led his small army to Sauceda and, dispersing the Indians for the moment by the fire of the arquebuses, was able to force his way into the stronghold occupied by Olivas. Cordejuela's force brought the number of the besieged to four hundred. Four different times they were attacked by the enemy, their numbers now augmented, but the Spaniards were able to repulse the rebels with loss, possessing the tremendous advantage of guns with plenty of ammunition. Here the Spaniards remained for forty-two days. The Indians, swollen with pride in their present success and enriched with loot from the churches and Spanish homes, continued their hostilities for this length of time.

There were frays and skirmishes. There were times when the captains enjoyed a certain success, forcing the enemy to retire. Some of the ringleaders were captured and hanged and a great deal of the

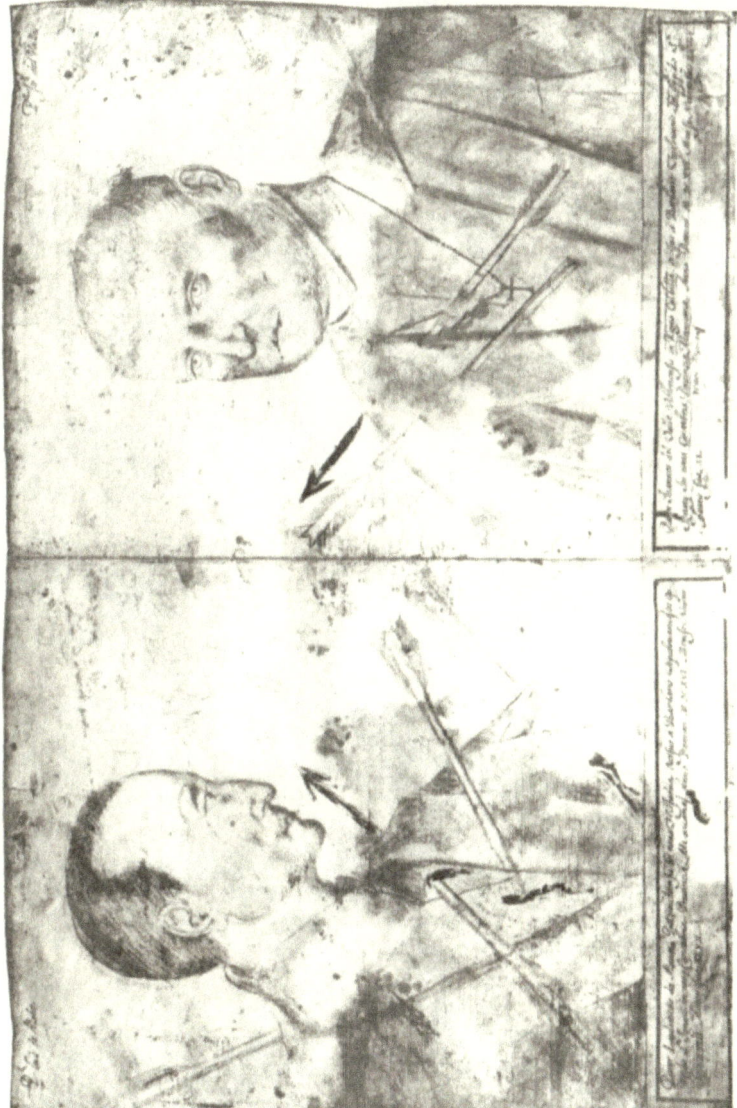

LUIS DE ALABEZ

JUAN DEL VALLE

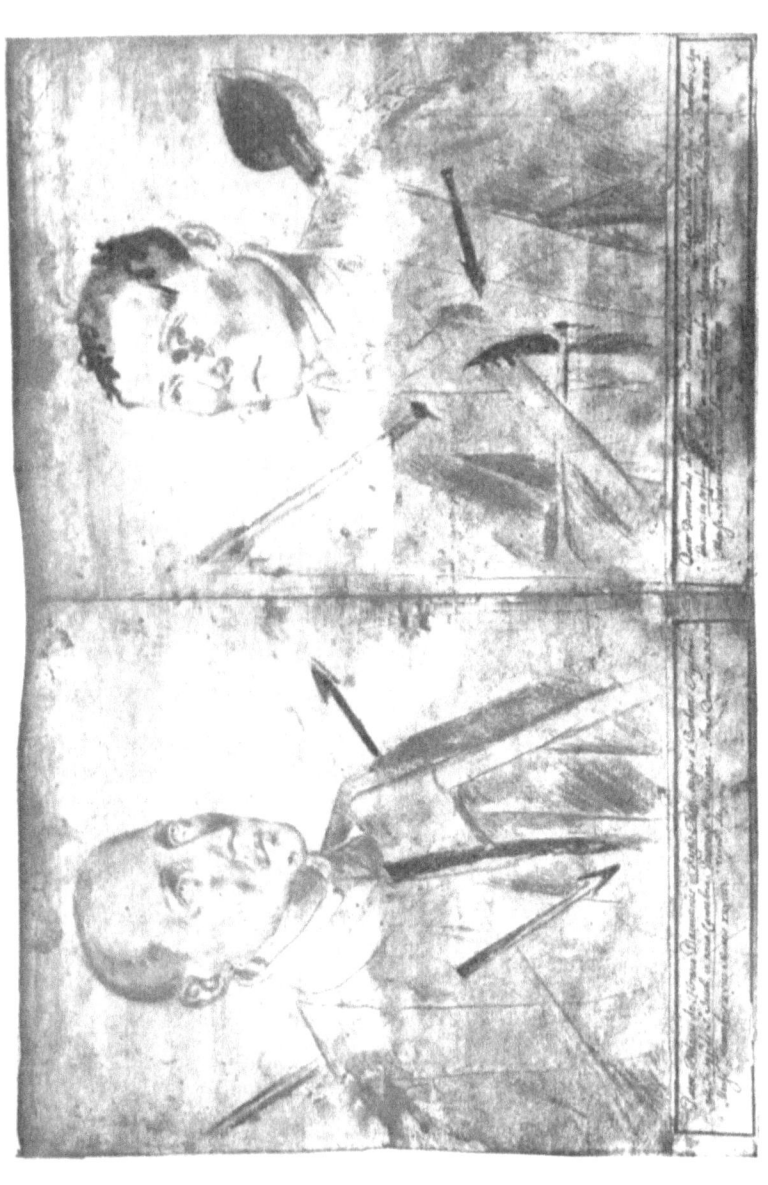

DIEGO DE OROZCO   BERNARDO DE CISNEROS

booty which had been taken at Papasquiaro was recovered—arquebuses, leather jackets, swords, and much church loot: albs, antependiums, vestments. Finally this group of Spaniards was able to fight its way out to a place of greater safety.[8]

While all this horror was being enacted in and about Santiago Papasquiaro, what was taking place in the north, at Zape, sixty miles away? Here, it will be remembered, the first outbreak had been planned for November 21. It was the Feast of the Presentation of Our Lady, and the day fixed for the dedication of her statue which had just been sent up from Mexico City.

No one had warned either the fathers or the Spaniards of the north, so that the preparations for the feast were going forward as usual, and the resident missionaries Juan del Valle and Luis de Alabez were busily happy in the prospect of the coming celebration. They invited in for the occasion Jesuit missionaries from other districts, Juan Fonte from the Tarahumar border with Gerónimo de Moranta, and from the west Hernando de Santarén, who was on his way from the Xiximes to Durango on business. Spanish farmers and miners, too, had been invited in from all about the country, especially from the mining camp of Guanaceví fifteen miles to the north. Many Spaniards with their Negro slaves came from this settlement. A large concourse of people was gathered, intent upon the celebration of the feast.

But, alas, the celebration was destined never to be held. The Indians attacked here and on the same day as at Papasquiaro, Friday, November 18. The blow was sudden and deadly, launched while all were in the church. They were slaughtered, every man of them, namely, twenty-nine Spaniards, seventy of their Negro slaves with other servants, and, along with the rest, the two resident fathers, Del Valle and Alabez. The following day, Fathers Fonte and Moranta, arriving from their northern territory to be in time for the celebration, were cut down unawares near the pueblo. Only a boy escaped. He rushed to Guanaceví to give notice of the blow that had fallen upon Zape.

The alcalde at Guanaceví was Don Juan de Alvear. He pressed twelve soldiers into service and sped to the ruined pueblo. On their way the Spaniards came upon the dead body of one of their own race, his hands cut off and his belly ripped open, presage of what would be seen at Zape. They arrived at night and the horror which the moon disclosed curdled their brave blood. The plaza before the church was strewn with corpses of Spaniards and slaves, naked and mutilated, the snow stained dark with their gore. The interior of the church was a shambles, master and servant prostrate in death in the place where they had knelt in prayer. The padres could not be distinguished from the rest.

Not daring to dismount, Alvear shouted, if perchance a hidden Spaniard, escaped from slaughter, might come forth. His voice rang out over the cold night, but all was still thereafter. Every single body strewn about the holy place was a corpse. The troopers returned horror-struck to Guanaceví, there to fortify themselves against attack.

Nor were they kept waiting long; six miles from the mines the rebels met them. Some of the enemy were on foot, some on horseback; some were arrayed, ridiculously enough, in the black robes and birettas of the murdered Jesuits. The Indian troop was too strong to be attacked and the Spaniards had to retreat from before them, but did so in good order, facing about at intervals to make at them with the guns. Alvear's horse was killed by an arrow; a faithful Mexican Indian servant gave the alcalde his own, he running on foot. But, exhausted from wounds, the servant was left for dead. Later he crawled back to camp and was cared for. Thus Alcalde Alvear, arriving safely at Guanaceví before it was attacked, ordered the entire Spanish population, five hundred persons, into the church to stand a possible siege. Here they awaited help from Durango, which this time did not fail them. But the rebels meanwhile had destroyed the machinery of the mines.'

What of Santarén? Invited to the celebration of Our Lady's feast at Zape and all unsuspecting of any danger, he had set out southwestward from the Xiximes to attend the happy affair. While he was on the road, Father Tutino, companion of his labors at Guapexuxe, got wind of the revolt and understood the danger to his colleague. Therefore Tutino sent message after message of warning to the padre to turn back lest he walk into the mouth of death. None of these warnings reached him, and he arrived one morning at Tenerape, some sixty miles south of Santiago Papasquiaro. Desiring to say Mass, he rang the bell that hung before the church, as was customary for calling the fiscal. No one appeared. He shouted and called, but all was silent. Then he went into the church—and saw the altar disrobed and pro-

THE STORM BREAKS 133

faned, the statuary flung about and broken. He knew immediately his own danger; he was in a country where the Indians had risen.

Hernando de Santarén mounted and rode away with terror in his heart. Indians followed him slyly, as Ribas says, like beasts of prey. In a lonely arroyo they fell upon him and knocked him from his mule. What harm had he done, he asked, that they should kill him thus. He was a padre and that was enough, they jeered. Then they struck him a blow with a war club that split open his head. They scattered his brains about, and inflicted other mutilation. His body lay for months unburied, until, the revolt suppressed, it was found with the skull cracked open. So later did the Spaniards find the corpse of Alabez, garbed in a hairshirt, and the body of Valle forming with one hand a cross with his fingers and with the other trying to cover his nakedness. The spot where these two latter fell, not two miles north of Zape, is marked today by a pile of stones and a cross. Eight Jesuit fathers had been slain, six of whom belonged to the Tepehuán mission, two, Tovar and Santarén, being strangers traveling through the country.[10]

One missionary escaped, Father Andrés López. He wrote a letter to his provincial in Mexico, telling of the tragedy: hearing that the celebration had been postponed, he had not gone to Zape for the feast, and, alas, had missed the martyr's crown. He retired to Indé with some armed Spaniards to wait until the danger passed. Soon he began work among the Negro and Indian laborers who had not risen. He was sending as a relic a portion of the gory tunic of Father Cisneros.

Another and a spectacular escape was made by a body of Spaniards at Guatimapé, which lies forty miles to the east and south of Santiago Papasquiaro in the wide plain of Durango not far from Sauceda. Upon being attacked they had fled to a stockade made of brazilwood in which stood a house. They had been able to get from the mine near by some arrows, hatchets, pieces of iron, and a few arquebuses. Thirty men were thus entrapped. Fortunately, because they had guns and powder, they could hold on for a while, keeping the Indians at a distance by gunfire from the roof of the fort. But, as the ammunition gave out, the enemy gained entrance to the stockade and succeeded in setting fire to the flat straw roof of the little fort. The Spaniards, expecting a rush, feared they were about to be taken, when a thunderous noise was heard and a cloud of dust rose from the ground. The Indians, frightened and considering this the advance of an aiding troop of mounted Spaniards, fled in dismay. The besieged men had been saved by a stampede of galloping colts from one of the near-by corrals.[11]

But the uprising had spread destruction enough. Eight Jesuit missionaries and one Franciscan, and hundreds of other Spaniards, loyal servants, and friendly Indians had been murdered.[12] One lone Dominican too was slain while teaching the rosary to some savages. Approximately three hundred in all had been killed. Added to these massacres, the whole numerous nation of the Tepehuanes was in revolt, endeavoring to influence the neighboring Acaxées and Xiximes and Laguneros to join them in driving the Spaniard from their land. Nay, they went west of the divide and tried to contaminate the Chicoratos, the Ures, and the Yaquis. Here was a fearful muddle for the Governor to clean up; here was destruction threatening the end of the missions, which he had now to take in hand. Had he been more wary and energetic, he and all would have been spared this deep sorrow and this dire calamity.[13]

Chapter XV

THE NATIONS STIR

THE OLD hechicero Quautlatas, wizard of evil among the Tepehuanes, had given out, before the revolt, that all the surrounding nations were about to join the Tepehuanes in their murderous business and kill every Spaniard and padre in all the north. This was a lie spoken to gain adherents. Once, however, the rebellion was begun and the Tepehuanes began to fear Spanish retaliation, they did make various and dangerous efforts for the contamination of the neighboring tribes and nations. Indeed, sparks from the conflagration east of the mountains soon began to fall in the west and, had it not been for the vigorous measures and the high prestige of the strong-handed Diego Martínez de Hurdaide, the fires might have spread over the divide and into the vales and valleys of the Sinaloa, the Ocoroni, and the Fuerte rivers.

Far up the Sinaloa where its banks turn south and then east farther into the mountains, the stream is known today as the Petachán. Here the Tepehuanes had given trouble before, destroying pueblos near Tecuciapa and kidnaping three girls of the northern Acaxées when Father Santarén was in the district. A few miles down the river was the country of the troublesome Cahuemetos, members of the Comanito nation. This group had long been a thorn in the side of the padres of the Sinaloa missions who were working among them. Much worry did they cause Fathers Juan Calvo and Pedro de Velasco, and many marches thither of Captain Hurdaide.[1] These were the people to whom certain obdurate hechiceros of the Tepehuanes had gone, years before the general uprising. Of all the missions administered from Sinaloa this was the closest to the Tepehuanes. Through this sector all the missions of the west might be contaminated.

What did happen in the west? Among the fickle and weak-willed Indians this trouble of the Tepehuanes was sure to spread. Father Diego de Cueto wrote from Las Vegas in the west that the Indians in the mountains of the upper Sinaloa were greatly disquieted, and he

[1] For notes to chapter xv see page 213.

expected danger, for he said, "We do not know where to look." The neophytes of Diego de Azevedo had risen, and there was suspicion on the lower Sinaloa. Father Azevedo considered himself and his companion, Andrés González, to be in immediate danger of death. They were both soon called down to Sinaloa for safety until the storm should blow over. And it was well that they were, for a band of Tepehuanes would have slain them both.[2]

This rebel group and other Tepehuanes now joined themselves to the troublesome Cahuemetos and came down the river to get others of the Comanitos to join them. The cacique Barocopa, for long now the chief of unrest in Sinaloa, led this rebel band. The savages used all their powers of persuasion upon the Chicoratos. They came arrayed in the booty they had taken from the murdered Spaniards on the eastern slopes, and carried with them a shirt covered with blood which had been worn by one of the murdered missionaries. They came to San Ignacio when they knew Velasco was absent. They harangued the people and displayed their loot and the bloody shirt. Let the Chicoratos do what the Tepehuanes had done, kill their padre and make off to real and old-time liberty.[3] But the pueblo of Chicorato held true, steadied by the influence of two caciques, and to them can be given much of the credit of preventing the fires of the east from spreading to the west. Their names were Luis Tutuqui and Pedro Yotoca.[4]

But the rebels vented in violence the rage of their disappointment. One morning as the Chicoratos were about the church waiting for the coming of the father for Mass, a troop of Tepehuanes burst into the pueblo for slaughter and destruction. A skirmish ensued. Fortunately, some Spanish soldiers had been left here by Hurdaide. Their arquebuses wrought execution through ball and fright, the Christians fought with determination, and the enemy was driven off, leaving some dead and wounded.[5]

Captain Hurdaide now acted vigorously. Leaving six soldiers at Chicorato, and fifty allied bowmen, he went in search of the rebels far up the river toward Tecuciapa. Two hostile chiefs were caught and hanged. At Tecuciapa the Captain left likewise six soldiers and seventy of his Indian allies under the *caudillo* Pedro de Torres for the protection of Father Gaspar de Nájera, working in the district of Tecuciapa and Carantapa. The Indians in this district of Carantapa had not risen

THE NATIONS STIR 137

in general, though the Tepehuanes had displayed their loot and the gory shirt; their memory of Santarén kept them loyal.⁶

But the northwestern Tepehuanes of the Ocotlán district soon returned to Tecuciapa. They set fire to the church and attacked the Spanish soldiers and their Indian allies. Now, the Spanish officer of the troop was an old friend of the Tepehuanes. He thought, therefore, to go out to parley with them and bring them to reason. They abused his confidence and friendship and slew him on the spot. The soldiers retired to their little fort while the rebels made off with the horses and cattle. Again they returned, but this time were repulsed with loss.⁷

Hurdaide now displayed his usual energy and aptness of resource. He urged the northern Acaxées to take the offensive, to invade the Tepehuán country themselves and drive the enemy away from the pueblos that were contiguous to their own. The plan worked. A hundred and thirty men of Tecuciapa and Carantapa went on the warpath against the Tepehuanes. The latter were completely surprised. Some were killed and others put to flight, and the border was delivered from danger. The Christians returned with the scalps of their enemies. The Tepehuanes were driven back to their own ranges, and their revolt was kept from spreading to the missions of the Sinaloa River.⁸

Even the far-away Nuris and Yaquis the Tepehuanes tried to corrupt. The Yaquis they tempted with horses, blankets, and fine garments, loot they had got from the Spaniards. They offered the Nuris arrows, plumes, clothes, and sixteen mares and horses if they would join the rebellion. The rebels made a special effort to corrupt the Nuri chief Coyovera, but Captain Hurdaide kept him firm in his refusal. These tribes on this occasion proved the mettle of their loyalty to the Captain and to their padres.⁹

In a letter of March 5, 1617, Hurdaide speaks of the dangerous menace the revolt was continuing to be and of how the rebels were boasting of a great victory over the Spaniards. He tells his superior, Governor Gaspar de Alvear, that there is need of more soldiers and he offers a plan for the pacification of the infected areas. Entradas must be made, he writes, from the west into the Tepehuán country, not only by way of Ocotlán, but likewise through the districts of Yecorato and Cahuemeto. From Tecuciapa, protection must reach Atotonilco, Batoyapa, and the mines called Los Caballeros.¹⁰

As over the divide to the west, so down into the plains to the east did the Tepehuanes endeavor to spread the infection. They were persuaded that could they but succeed in winning over the Laguneros they would possess powerful allies themselves, and deprive the Spaniards of the assistance of these men so skillful with the bow. And this reasoning was correct. The hostiles all but succeeded. They put in jeopardy the entire mission of the lagoons with its many pueblos and thousands of Christians, and endangered the lives of all the fathers working among them.[11] The Superior of the lagoon missions, Father Tomás Domínguez, was greatly worried when, under torture, some of the Laguneros confessed to the existence of a plot to murder the padres.[12]

In the region about Mapimí the Laguneros border upon Tepehuán country. Here a troop of the Tepehuán rebels came and assaulted a mining camp near the town. This was at the very beginning of the rebellion. They here, as elsewhere, worked havoc with the mines and farms of the Spaniards, destroying machinery and stealing provisions and desecrating mission chapels, taking plate and ornaments. In this raid at Mapimí the circumstance which gave grave concern to the Spaniards was that the Tepehuanes were aided by certain of the Laguneros themselves. The officials of Durango, therefore, punished such guilty lagoon Indians as they could lay hands on.

With this, certain unquiet spirits began to stir more restlessly and to spread over the plains the word that they too must rise and slaughter all the Spaniards in their country as the Tepehuanes had done. They even debated in meetings whether all the padres should not be killed along with the rest and the missions ended. They played up two arguments to win over the leaders of their tribes and nations: first they spoke of the enrichment of the Tepehuanes from the loot they had taken from the Spaniards and from the churches; then they pointed out that since the fathers had come and baptized them very large numbers of their people had died, referring to the plague of 1608. Unfortunately, this very year, 1616, the Laguneros felt scarcity, hunger, and sickness. Anxiety, therefore, was felt at Durango; but nothing could be done, for the Governor, his hands full with the Tepehuanes, was unable to send soldiers. As among the rebel Tepehuanes, so also here among the Laguneros, an hechicero went about pronouncing the same bogus prophecies and holding out the same false promises.[13]

Reports came in to the fathers that the Devil had appeared to various hechiceros urging them to revolt and threatening punishment and death did they not kill the missionaries. The famous Quautlatas came now among the Laguneros with his possessed idol and endeavored to inflame the lagoon Indians as he had the Tepehuanes. An Indian girl living near Santa María de las Parras averred that she had heard her father, a cacique, being spoken to by an evil spirit and being scolded because he had allowed himself to be baptized and because he brought others to the sacrament. The spirit urged this man to rise in imitation of the Tepehuanes.

Thus a war party was formed, and all too well did the fathers understand that, should this party prevail, their own lives would be in the balance. But the crown of martyrdom rose before them, and they quailed not; rather were they glad. Still, their fear for the ruin of the missions led them to take every measure of precaution. They worked with might and main to hold the Indian leaders to what they had been taught.

At Parras one evening, at seven o'clock, when one of the more alarming rumors came in, the missionaries consumed the Blessed Sacrament; they remembered the terrible experience of the martyrs of Santiago Papasquiaro. At Parras, too, an influential cacique was so moved by the fatherly exhortations of his missionary that he got all the people together in the plaza of his pueblo and made a speech in favor of loyalty to the Black Robes. Fearing immediate attack, he ordered his people to arms to protect the mission, and throughout a rainy night he had sentinels watching near the church and about the fathers' house.[14]

Both at Mapimí and at San Francisco, called sometimes Las Nazas because it was on the banks of the river, meetings were held by the caciques to decide what measures should be taken in this crisis. Father Juan Ruiz, who labored in this district, brought forth at this time his best diplomacy and his most Christian virtue. He dealt deftly with two of the principal caciques and so influenced them that their loyalty remained true. They influenced their followers and formed a party of peace. Fortunately for all concerned, this peace party prevailed. Recognizing the great benefits that had come to them through the Jesuits, and inspired by the devotion of the fathers which shone resplendently this year of trial and sickness, the majority decided not to slaughter the missionaries nor to rise against them; they would rather protect the missions and the fathers and hold the country to peace. A cacique made a speech warning his people against the Tepehuanes as evil men, and pointing out all the ills that would flow from the imitation of their rashness. Some were so moved at this discourse that they went straight from the meeting to the padres and swore to protect them with their lives. Thus did the Laguneros remain faithful, and when finally, early in 1617, Governor Gaspar de Alvear took the field against the Tepehuanes, the first and bravest of the Indian allies he could call upon were these faithful men of the lagoons.[15]

Things went not so smoothly with the mountain Indians of the south, the Acaxées of Topia and San Andrés and their southern neighbors, just won from cannibalism, the Xiximes. Father Andrés Tutino, who had tried by so many warning letters to reach Santarén before he should arrive at Tenerape to die, had serious difficulty with two caciques at Coapa, the Acaxée pueblo nearest the Tepehuanes. As soon as Tutino heard of the trouble across the divide to the east, he sent letters of warning to all the pueblos of his missions and visited as many of them as he was able, in order to quiet them and hold them to loyalty. Fathers Pedro Gravina and Juan de Mallen, the latter a new arrival, fled from among the Xiximes to the mines of San Hipólito, where was a presidio. Captain Bartolomé Suárez de Villalta girded himself for battle. These three leaders, the Captain, a man of high courage and piety, and the two padres, though aware of their duty to defend the mission and themselves, would have gloried in martyrdom.[16]

There was trouble with two chiefs at Coapa. These men, Don Andrés and Juan Gordo, were old evildoers and though baptized were not to be trusted. When the rebellion became known in these sierras, they did what they could to sow the seeds of trouble. Let the Acaxées rise, too, against the Spaniards and the fathers. They need have no fear of Captain Suárez. Should any Indian die, he would be brought back to life again. Especially did Juan Gordo spin a story to dupe his stupid people. One night, he said, when passing near the church he heard a voice calling him to enter. Through fear he did not at first obey, but at repeated summons he ventured in, only to see an Indian who had recently died, Diego Marido, raised in the air. Diego had a message to give. His wife must be told not to marry again, for her husband was not dead but sleeping and when God should visit the village he, Marido, would come back to her and live in greater happiness than ever. So would all the others who might die in conflict with the Spaniards.[17]

Meetings were held here at Coapa that boded no good. Tutino felt it necessary to summon Captain Suárez. The latter made the difficult journey in a day and a half, accompanied by Father Pedro de Gravina, who with Juan de Mallen had fled from among the Xiximes. Gravina brought the disturbing news that some of his people here had gone over to the revolt. The Captain and the two fathers went to Coapa. They were seemingly well received, with lighted torches, for it was night, and they spoke persuasively in favor of peace, to all appearances with good results. Suárez became convinced, however, that he would have to punish the two caciques, Don Andrés and Juan Gordo. He had them seized at a meeting held after Mass, and ordered those who had listened to them to be surrounded. He would pardon the others, he said, but the two would have to pay the penalty of sowers of sedition, especially as they had earlier been guilty of other misdeeds. He had them hanged; and this seems to have quieted the trouble at this place.[18]

At the mines of Topia, Captain Sebastián de Alvear fortified the plaza and the church with two towers and held seventy armed and mounted soldiers in readiness for an attack, though powder was lacking for a prolonged siege. The precautions were not useless, for on January 6, 1617, two pueblos of Acaxées rose with the intention of killing their padres, Juan Acacio, superior of the mission, and Juan Suárez. The rebels had all the more hopes of success because the leaders of the plot were the Indian governor and the fiscal. The latter the missionaries had reared from a child. The rising here at Topia was fixed for January 6, Feast of the Epiphany. The padres were first to be killed, then the other Spaniards. However, the missionaries had been warned by faithful Indians, and Captain de Alvear was able to secure and execute the ringleaders.[19]

As two pueblos of the Acaxées had done, so a band of Xiximes, urged by the Tepehuanes, rose to disrupt the Christian pueblos and to kill the missionaries, Pedro Gravina and Juan de Mallen. These, warned in time, fled as we have seen to the presidio of San Hipólito. Disappointed of their prizes, the rebels razed three mission chapels and, discovering where the fathers had hidden the ornaments, looted the treasure. It was an idol, a speaking stone, which they kept in a hermitage removed from their pueblo that urged them to this devastation, promising immortality to those who should fall in combat.

The rebels here had it far from easy, for goodly numbers of the Xiximes, especially those of Guapexuxe, where also Santarén had worked, remained loyal. They too, imitating those of Tecuciapa, took up arms against the rebels of their own nation. Their campaign was successful and they had some scalps to bring in to San Hipólito. Only the heavy snows prevented them from gaining a more signal victory. Although these Xiximes fretted and threatened, they were powerless against the stronger party of peace, led by the Guapexuxes, who were able thus to prevent the fires of revolt from taking on alarming proportions, and who saved the town of Culiacán from serious danger.[20]

Father Andrés Tutino wrote of these events to his superior. We have also a letter of Captain Suárez himself, written from Las Vegas, which for the ardent piety of some of its lines deserves to be reported: "Father Andrés González and I remain at this post of Las Vegas awaiting death each day.... If it is the most holy will of Our Savior that we die in this trouble, our own lives will never have been better spent. May the Divine Majesty be served in this our happy readiness to die for His Holy Faith."[21] We have in Captain Suárez a noteworthy example of the Spanish soldier, as brave as he was pious, preserving in the New World the best traditions of Spain in the Old.

Thus everywhere there was trouble following hard upon the revolt of the far-spread Tepehuán nation: anxiety in the lagoon country, corruption of the Cahuemetos, and war in the district of Carantapa; an uprising of two pueblos of the Acaxées and the destruction of three missions among the Xiximes. Although the loyalty of certain groups of Indians and the energy of certain captains had kept the conflagration from becoming general, harm enough had been done to the neighbors of the Tepehuanes to warrant a most watchful eye and the convergence of every available organization for the suppression of so dangerous and so costly an outbreak.

Chapter XVI

THE GOVERNOR RIDES FORTH

THOUGH NEITHER the resident Governor, Gaspar de Alvear, nor any other Spanish inhabitant was aware of it, Durango, the capital of Nueva Vizcaya, had been for a long while in great peril. The Spanish population was not large, only a hundred at this time, with two religious houses, one belonging to the Franciscans, the other to the Jesuits.[1] A pueblo of the Tepehuanes, Tunal by name, lay six miles to the south. This settlement had been corrupted by the rebels months before the outbreak of the revolt, and these Indians had laid up a store of provisions and of arrows, knives, and clubs, in order to join with the hostiles from the hills in an attack upon the capital. The plan was spoiled by the premature rising at Santa Catalina: by the five days' impetuous anticipation of the fixed time, the morning they murdered Father Tovar and left him naked upon the snow. Warning arrived at Durango while the rebels at Tunal knew nothing of the outbreak at Santa Catalina. This was a stroke of luck for the Spaniards which brought the conspirators into the power of the Governor.[2]

It was soon after the report of the revolt had sped to Durango that the Governor had become aware of the complicity of the natives of Tunal and of other villages lying out from the capital. Word came to him that these neighboring Tepehuanes intended to attack at a fixed time. Alvear acted swiftly and vigorously. He summoned into town the caciques of Tunal and of other near-by pueblos under the pretext of fortifying certain government buildings, and at the same time appointed Rafael de Gascue, a trusted and experienced officer, *maestre de campo* or captain-general for Durango and its environs, who might act with authority in the possible future absence of Governor Alvear. Under orders from the Governor, on Monday, November 21, Gascue arrested seventy-five Indian chiefs and governors of pueblos and put them to the torture to force confession. These admitted that indeed they were implicated in the conspiracy of the rest

---

[1] For notes to chapter xvi see pages 213–214.

of their nation and that the following day, the 22d, had been fixed for an assault upon Durango. The confessions were confirmed by what a Franciscan, a visitor from San Juan de Dios, overheard from other Tepehuanes as they were working on the fortifications.

But while the process of examination was going on, at nine o'clock in the evening of the 21st a tumult was heard in the streets, and a shouting that two thousand rebels were approaching the town to murder the Spaniards. With that the guards of the prisoners shouted, "To arms! To arms!" In a flash the soldiers whipped out swords and poniards, slew their prisoners, and rushed into the streets to defend the town.

It was all a mistake! Not a single enemy could be seen! How did it happen? Who raised the alarm? Was it a distant cloud of dust lifted by the wind that had startled the quietness of the little capital, or the stampede of a band of frightened colts, like that which saved the Spaniards at Guatimapé? The historian does not know. But our pious Ribas considers the thing very providential, for several of the prisoners had not been killed but only wounded in the melee which followed the alarm and these made further confessions, probably to save their lives. Their confessions availed them naught. They were hanged the following day, November 22, all having made their peace with the Church except Don Marcos, a ringleader, who remained obdurate. The corpses of all these rebels of Tunal and the vicinity were strung along the roads which led into Durango, that their dangling and rotting carcasses might serve as a warning to all intending rebels against Spanish might.[3]

According to the confessions made, it was the intention of the rebels either to exterminate the Spaniard or to drive him from their land. Thus was the treachery of Tunal and of the district around Durango made known. Moreover, a crown made up of feathers was found in one of the near-by pueblos. This was to be the crown, the Governor learned, of the Tepehuán king of Durango after the country should have got rid of Spanish rule. Some time later—November 27, to be exact—a spy was caught. He confessed that the Indians of Santiago Papasquiaro were in collusion with those in the vicinity of Durango and that they waited two leagues away for a favorable opportunity to attack the town; that their leader was Pablo, he who inspired the betrayal at Santiago where Orozco and Cisneros, with a hundred other Spaniards, had been massacred.[4]

A report arriving that the rebels were marching on the city, Alvear collected whatever available weapons might be had and placed a guard of soldiers in the four quarters of the capital. He was in sore need of manpower, for he must soon march forth himself with what soldiers he could spare to put down the revolt afield. He therefore released all the malefactors in the prisons, Spaniards, mestizos, and Negroes, and offered them a pardon provided they would aid in the defense of the province. He collected the women and children, the *gente menuda,* into the largest of the churches, that of the Jesuits, and when their numbers were found too great for this single asylum, he crowded them into the royal houses, those, namely, of the government officials. This was a temporary arrangement until help should come from Mexico City. Finally, he dispatched arms and ammunition to such places in the north as had been able to hold out, as Guanaceví, or to such as had not yet been attacked, as Indé.[5]

What were the prospects of aid from Mexico? Diego Fernández de Córdova, Marqués de Guadalcázar, had been Viceroy since 1612. It was to him, then, that this disastrous news and these appeals for help came from the wilds of the north. Our historian, Andrés Pérez de Ribas, had been in the capital at the time the revolt broke out, close to official circles. He had been sent down from his mission on the Fuerte River in Sinaloa to get permission to advance the frontier from the Mayo to the Yaqui River and to obtain from the Viceroy and from his Jesuit Provincial the addition of missionaries needed for this project. But Ribas had left the capital shortly before news of the northern disaster came in. When the fearful report finally got to headquarters, the Viceroy, taking counsel with the audiencia and other persons of experience, ordered a levy to be made at Zacatecas and commanded that the royal treasury there and at Durango release the necessary sums for repression of the revolt.[6] But Alvear could not wait for help. Weeks had passed and the rebellion was spreading, as we have seen, to the other nations. He had to take the field at once.

This was to be a difficult, prolonged, and costly campaign, yet one that would have to be a second and even a third time repeated. The Governor could well now regret his lack of wariness and energy when the fathers had warned him in good time of the brewing of trouble. They had told him of the restless state of the Indians and had asked protection. There were some who had approved the Governor's inaction, saying the missionaries were timorous and unduly concerned. The Governor on his part did not wish to cause added expense to the King's treasury, but, as the historian remarks, his inaction did in the end cost the royal exchequer ten times the amount he feared at first to expend.

Nevertheless, Gaspar de Alvear, Caballero del Hábito de Santiago, was a brave man and bravely he took the field. This was December 19, 1616. His troop consisted of about seventy Spaniards, well armed and mounted, and one hundred and twenty Indian allies, mostly from the loyal tribes of the lagoon country and of the Conchos. He drove before him seven hundred head of cattle and carried stores of corn for the posts that had been besieged.[7] There were no illusions about the difficulties ahead: wild and savage terrain, no pitched battle where the soldiers might use their guns to advantage, no fortified places to capture and thus get the enemy at a blow. It would be guerrilla warfare of the most difficult kind.

Alvear in the two months and a half of this his first expedition made a wide circle to the north of Durango, inclining to the east at the outset and then swinging to the west on the return. He went north by way of Sauceda, San Juan del Río, and Indé, and returned by Guanaceví, Zape, Santa Catalina, Santiago Papasquiaro, and Tenerape. The killing of the spy in Durango had discouraged eight hundred rebels ambushed in El Jaral so that this force retired west to the mountains. Arrived at Sauceda, the Governor relieved Captain Cordejuela, who, as we have seen, had marched up to protect the town at the first reports of the revolt in November. Leaving Sauceda December 30, he arrived at Indé by way of San Juan del Río on January 7, whence he marched to Guanaceví, which he reached January 15, to the immense relief and joy of the hundred Spaniards besieged there, who had come to the end of their resources and were driven to devour dogs and cats for food. Governor Alvear now came to their assistance with flour and corn and even with the livestock he had driven from Durango. But the town was in ruins—torn, charred and burned, except for the church which had protected the Spaniards.[8]

During all this march northward the soldiers beheld the ruined farms and homesteads of the Spaniards, and in the churches or chapels still left standing they saw holy objects desecrated and the altars destroyed. They came within sight of the enemy, but because of the cattle they could not pursue them. They were able, however, to slay some of the Tepehuán rebels and to seize five hundred fanegas of corn, besides other stores which they burned to keep them from the hostiles. Threading a narrow defile, they were ambushed and in danger from hurtled stones. But these caused no casualties, and the arrows of the Indians thudded harmlessly against the soldiers' leathern jackets, while the arquebuses of the Spaniards spat death.

Near Guacaceví the Governor's men gained the summit called Del Gato. Here was human wreckage, for it was the site of the labors of a lone Dominican friar come among these people to teach them the devotion of the rosary. They came upon the dead bodies of the layman, Pedro Rendón, Regidor of Durango, and of the friar, Sebastián Montaño, with the bodies of Christian Indians who had been slaughtered with them. The priest's breviary was near him and uninjured, and from the pious and credulous account of the old-time chronicler we read of the usual miracles, namely, that the body of the friar, although he had been dead for two months, exhaled a delicious odor, and that the blood of one foot, of his head, and of the thumb and index finger, which used to hold the Blessed Sacrament, was as fresh as if he had but that moment passed away. The bodies of the Dominican and of the Regidor were taken down from the heights and respectfully borne to Guacaceví. Here in the midst of the desolation the two bodies were given solemn burial.[9]

For the return south to Durango the army was divided. Since it was to be guerrilla warfare, two small bands armed with guns could work faster and more efficiently in these mountains than one large troop. The Governor kept twenty-seven armed and mounted men and thirty Indian allies; to the experienced Captain Montaño aided by Cristóbal de Hontiveros, he gave twenty-five soldiers and seventy Indian allies.[10] Among the orders given the Captain was to repair to Zape and take cognizance of the destruction there wrought. Marching thither, Captain Montaño came upon a band of Tepehuanes. He put them to flight with heavy loss; many fell and others were captured.

Among the latter was one Antonio, son of the cacique of Santa Catalina. He confessed himself a ringleader and said the conspiracy was so general that it included among the guilty, besides many other tribes, the Tarahumares.[11] He also confessed those of Tunal to be allies.

Arrived at Zape January 23, Captain Montaño tied Antonio to a pole and raised him in the air. There he hung dangling until he was dead. The cacique's son died in front of the church at Zape where he had been instrumental in the murder of the fathers and in the universal desecration.[12]

Here at Zape the Captain beheld the saddest of imaginable spectacles.[13] In and about the church he counted some ninety corpses strewn about in various postures, some flat upon their backs staring sightless up to heaven, others crumpled, their mouths to the earth, literally biting the soil. They were Spaniards and their Indian servants, men and women, old and young, Christians all, who had come to honor the Mother of God on the Feast of her Presentation in the Temple, November 21, 1616. In an adjoining dwelling the Captain found thirty Indians burned in the place whither they had fled for safety. Babes of two years had been slaughtered, the church and the house of the fathers had been pillaged. And, among the rest, the bodies of the fathers Del Valle and Alabez, residents in the pueblo, were found a few paces from their house, which adjoined the church. The body of Del Valle, wrote Father Luis de Bonifaz, the superior at Durango, was found well preserved, which astonished them, since more than two months had passed since his death. Juan Fonte and Moranta, who had come late for the celebration, were found where they had fallen, something over a mile north of the town and a few hundred yards from the Río de Zape over the shoulder of a sloping terrain. Some of their sermons and manuscripts were found near by, for snow falling after their murder had preserved them. Four or five small dogs which usually accompanied the fathers on their journeys were found there still guarding the bodies of their dead masters. Corruption, Bonifaz averred, had not set in. Piles of stones and a cross today mark the spot where the martyrs fell. In the church of the little, compact village all four Black Robes are to this day held in honor, and old paintings of the pioneer padres hang from the walls of the ancient fane.

When Governor Alvear arrived at the pueblo, he gave orders that all should be buried where they were slain except the four Jesuits, who should be taken in great reverence to Durango, there to be solemnly laid to rest in the mother house of these missions.[14]

The two sections of the Governor's army were again joined. Thus strengthened, the whole troop, carrying the bodies of the missionaries, made their way south to Santa Catalina. They probably followed the route which is still used, up ridges and down into deep arroyos, the roadbed, sometimes passing over hundreds of yards of solid rock, worn deep with furrows today from the travel of centuries. The troop arrived at the ruined mission on February 12. Here the Governor was attacked by a large force of rebels, but he repulsed them with loss, killing one hundred and thirty and taking among the prisoners the leader Andrés López, who confessed that a rebel force was concentrated at Tenerape.[15]

A search was made for the body of Father Tovar, the first to fall on that fatal 16th of November, but the wild would not yield up its dead. Only a little basket of papers belonging to the Jesuit was found, and bits of sacred ornament! This was all that was left of the mission and pueblo of Santa Catalina, whose Christianity had been active and promising for well-nigh twenty years. The troop, saddened by this further desolation, continued its journey south to Atotonilco and Santiago Papasquiaro. They caught glimpses of bands of Indians who fled before them shouting that they would meet at Santiago.

Upon arrival here, there was no sign of the enemy; but signs aplenty, and monuments, of destruction. Dwellings ripped and torn, the house of the missionaries smashed, the church a shell with its roof lying in charred and half-burnt timbers on the ground—this is what the Governor and his army saw. However, the results of the terrible massacre had been removed and the bodies buried. Alas, the forms of the two Jesuits, Orozco and Cisneros, could not be distinguished from the rest. Neither could Santarén's body at this time be recovered. Thus only the four from San Ignacio del Zape could be taken to Durango for interment.

When the Spanish troop was about to depart, the rebels came out to offer battle. They were led by a cacique, Don Pablo, and Mateo Canelas, a mestizo, notorious for his leadership in the uprising. There was a skirmish. Some of the enemy were killed, others wounded, still others taken prisoner. The rest fled, including Canelas. No casualties for the Spaniards. Later, Canelas himself was caught. He confessed his guilt, but excused himself by saying that he was forced into the conspiracy, for had he not joined it the Tepehuanes would have slain him. He said he had remained with them that he might betray them to the Spaniards. The prisoners, under torture, confessed that at the pueblo of Tenerape, twenty miles up the Río de Santiago, where the talking idol had been kept and which had been the very center of the conspiracy, many of the rebels were at that time gathered.[16]

The Governor held a council of war at Atotonilco, whither he had retired. It was decided to march all night up the river and attack the enemy at daybreak. The Governor set forth lightly armed, with fifty Spanish soldiers, taking with him Captain Cordejuela and seventy Indian allies. Captain Montaño was left with the rest of the troop to guard the camp and the prisoners and the bodies of the missionaries. At early dawn, February 12, Governor Alvear was at Tenerape, but the Indians, warned of his approach, stood ready to meet him. Alvear attacked immediately. Sixty Indians fell, two hundred and twenty women and children were taken prisoners, and the rest fled, led by Canelas, who had this second time escaped.[17] Among the women were two Spanish girls who had been held captive ever since the betrayal and massacre at Santiago Papasquiaro, where their father, the alcalde, Juan del Castillo, had been slain with the rest. Here too were set free some other captives and five Negroes, servants of the Spaniards.[18]

Among the old women captured some had been the leaders in the atrocities and sacrileges that preceded the betrayal at Santiago. Two were those who had been carried in the sedilias in mock procession as if they were the honored statues. Several of these women were hanged by order of the Governor. Some loot was recovered: coats of mail, leathern jackets, and more than one hundred and fifty horses and mules.

This had indeed been a great success, crowning a number of victories over the rebels. Not once had they been able to make a stand against the Spaniards. In every encounter some of them had been slain, others taken, and the rest had fled. It looked now as if the power of the Tepehuanes had been broken and the backbone of the rebellion cracked. Governor Alvear, with a feeling of satisfaction and security, could now march back to Durango with the bodies of the four Jesuits and arrange for their solemn burial as Christian martyrs. The prisoners trudged with him, chained together two by two.

Slowly the army with its precious burden made its way south. When they arrived at Sauceda they learned of a report that a band of rebels stood ready to attack them on their march south to Durango. For this reason the Governor left here the group of women and children who had thus far accompanied him for protection. The Governor heard, however, the encouraging news that during his absence the captain-general, Rafael de Gascue, had repulsed and dispersed a band of two hundred rebels who had come secretly to Tunal to attack the capital in the absence of so many of its defenders.[19]

After a rest the Governor's troop started on the last thirty miles to their destination. It was the beginning of March when Alvear approached Durango and on the 5th of the month, the fourth Sunday in Lent, he came within sight of the capital.[20]

Durango came out to meet the Christian martyrs, headed by the Superior of the Jesuits, Father Luis de Bonifaz. The bodies were carried on four mules belonging to the Governor, and each was covered with a rich mantle on which was embroidered his coat of arms. The soldiers led the march, flanked on either side by a line of Christian Indians. Most of the three hundred of them were on horseback carrying bow and arrow. Following the corpses was the Governor with a group of the clergy, Jesuits and Franciscans. The baggage train drew up the rear. The procession was more than a half a mile long and guarded by soldiers. When they were within a mile of the city the chief official of the royal exchequer, Rafael de Gascue, came out with his carriage. In this the bodies were solemnly placed and the procession entered the town by the Calle de San Francisco, which was lined with the curious but devout inhabitants.

A request of the Franciscan fathers was acceded to, that the bodies of the martyrs be first brought to their own church, there to repose in state until the approaching Feast of St. Thomas Aquinas. Then they could solemnly be interred in the church of the Jesuits. As the procession, therefore, came up to the convent of the Franciscans the soldiers parted the crowds, and through the press, with the salute of guns, the martyrs were borne into the church of St. Francis, headed now by a procession of the friars and their congregation, a raised cross carried in advance. While they thus slowly filed down the center of the church the tones of the organ were caught up by the people and a hymn of praise and triumph resounded through the temple of God.

This was Sunday night. Solemn vespers were sung, led by Juan Gómez, Provincial of the Franciscans, the townspeople now carrying flags which had been distributed to them by De Gascue. Here, then, the martyrs reposed until Tuesday morning, the bier lighted by four torches and guarded by four soldiers. Monday night the solemn office of the dead was chanted.

The ceremonies of transfer and burial were imposing. The procession was led by a hundred and fifty soldiers, who signaled the march with a salute from their guns. They were followed by the chief citizens of Durango and the students of the Jesuit school. A line of vaqueros in gala dress, their hats decorated with flowers, carrying lighted torches, added color to the occasion. The episcopal vicar, holding a white cross and accompanied by the Jesuit fathers, drew up the rear. The Franciscans themselves carried the bodies, which were covered with mantles of rich embroidery. Thus the procession moved a few hundred yards to the Jesuit church, where a throng awaited it.[21]

The High Mass of St. Thomas was sung, for this day, March 7, was his feast. After the Holy Sacrifice, with a sermon by the Franciscan Gerónimo de Rosales, came the blessing of the bodies and the solemn burial. Under the altar of St. Ignatius on the gospel side of the sanctuary a vault nine by fifteen feet had been hollowed out and lined with stone. Herein a large wooden chest had been placed for the reception of the four bodies, each enclosed in a casket. The floor of the vault was carpeted with flowers and its entrance was aflame with lighted candles. Each Jesuit was laid to rest clothed in the priestly chasuble, a paten and a chalice resting on his breast. After the martyrs were reverently placed, verses were read consecrating and celebrating their holy death. The organ was played softly, the clergy filed from the church, and the crowd departed, visibly moved by a spectacle of honor and of devotion.[22] The Tepehuán revolt had taken its toll, the martyrs had been laid to rest, the work of reconstruction would now have to begin.[23]

Chapter XVII

THE DEATH OF COGOXITO

IN SPITE OF the Spanish victories, and of the numbers of Tepehuanes killed or taken prisoner, indications were soon manifest that trouble was still afoot. It was unfortunate that one of the principal chiefs was still at large, Francisco Cogoxito by name—brave, bold, sagacious, and a linguist. He had been a leader in performing public adoration of the possessed idol. He was a leader in the destruction, desecration, and massacre at Santiago Papasquiaro and was one of those who had dragged through the dust statues of St. Francis and of Our Lady.

Until this man was destroyed the pacification of the country could hardly be permanent or secure. Indeed, Governor Alvear, while on his way to Durango to bury the martyrs, after his first campaign, heard reports of continued atrocities in several places, reports not a little disconcerting. Going south to Durango with his troop, the Governor learned at Sauceda, as we have seen, that the rebels were in ambush along the road to fall upon him and snatch away his treasure. The report was true. Soldiers sent ahead discovered and dispersed the enemy, killing two. A report came in that the church at Tunal had recently been sacked. Alvear heard, moreover, that the soldiers whom he had sent to accompany a convoy of goods worth 3,000 pesos to Chiametla on the west coast had been killed by the rebels and the goods looted. A report came in that the Tepehuanes, still on the warpath, had perpetrated further outrages, and that at San Sebastián, thirty miles from Chiametla, the Spaniards had all fled to their church for protection. This was in or near southern Xixime country, southwest of Durango, near the sea.[1]

At this very time, the spring of 1617, Pérez de Ribas, his business in Mexico for the Yaqui mission successfully concluded, was on his way back to the coast with three other fathers, new recruits for the missions of Sinaloa and Sonora. This band of Jesuits arrived at Chiametla only to find the inhabitants in terror of assault from the Tepehuanes. As in the old days of paganism, these rebels were again carrying war over

---
[1] For notes to chapter xvii see pages 214–215.

the border and invading Acaxée and Xixime territory. The anxiety was still greater at San Sebastián, which was closer to the Tepehuán borderline.

The inhabitants of both places, too few to resist the enemy in case of attack, begged the fathers to remain with them in a time of such danger when at any moment the dreaded enemy, headed by Cogoxito, might burst upon them. "The father who acted as superior," says Ribas, "ordered me to go to San Sebastián in that work of Christian charity."[2] Ribas obeyed and offered the few Spaniards of that settlement the consolations of religion which they so much desired in this trying time. He prepared them by exhortation, confession, and Communion, for a possible violent death. Each night, the women and children retired to the church, there to sleep within the strongest wall the settlement possessed, the men watching at sentinel duty. For ten days the four fathers tarried in this district. Then, accompanied by some Spaniards who were traveling in the same direction, they pursued their way to Sinaloa.

Hardly had they departed when San Sebastián and southerly Acaponeta (in the present state of Nayarit) were attacked. A convent of Franciscan fathers in the latter place was sacked and burned and the church destroyed. Fortunately no Spaniards were killed. This was part of the disturbing news that came to the Governor's ear on his return with the martyrs to Durango after his first successful campaign. Besides, the Indians of Zape and Santiago Papasquiaro were still in a ferment.[3] There was nothing for it but to take the field again.

Therefore, after the solemn burial of the martyrs, Governor Alvear again organized his troop. His force was augmented by forty-four soldiers under Captain Sebastián de Oyarzabal sent from Saltillo by the former Governor Urdiñola, and by the arrival of Captain Hernando Díaz with two hundred Indian allies.[4] The Governor had already sent north the trustworthy Captain Suárez to subdue the country about Indé. Alvear himself went far west and south upon another difficult campaign, setting out from Durango on March 22 of that year, 1617.[5] Farther into the mountains, the heights were thickly sheeted up with snow, and it lay deep and dangerous in canyon and defile. Cogoxito was the enemy to be taken dead or alive. He fallen, the backbone of resistance would be broken.

THE DEATH OF COGOXITO 155

The chief had retreated far west to a most rugged part of the mountains, into a treacherous gorge of the Piaxtla called Del Diablo, walled about with such precipitous bastions of rock that the Indians in places descended therein by means of ladders. Here no Spaniard had ever set foot. In this place the rebels guarded their women and children; the men ventured forth for purposes of loot and destruction. Alvear's troop ran short of supplies, and at one time the soldiers were driven to chopping the soles of their shoes into bits and boiling them for meat, and to chewing on boiled clippings of their leather jackets. The Spaniards lay hidden during the day and did most of their searching for the hide-out of the chief at night, crawling sometimes on hands and knees, that the Indians take no alarm.

Some of these fugitives killed themselves rather than fall into the hands of the Spaniards. Others died of hunger. Those driven to bay fought with the fury of desperation. One of them faced five Spaniards and succeeded in killing two before he was overcome. Another killed a Spaniard with a spear and wounded the horses of six others, then killed himself.[6] The Governor, even, descended into the gorge to fall upon the rebels unawares. But the hostiles got away, enjoying the services of a Negro spy who had escaped from the Spaniards while the hechiceros, especially one, Valenzuela, stiffened the rebel resistance. Cogoxito, alas, could not be taken in this second campaign of 1617.[7]

But other and constructive work was done. Alvear continued south of the Río Piaxtla to San Sebastián on the Río del Presidio; and farther south to Chiametla on the Río Balvarte; then onward to Acaponeta in the Nayarit country into the kingdom or province of Nueva Galicia. He frightened away the rebel Tepehuanes who had raided these districts and settled the country in peace. Grateful for this service to their province, the audiencia of Guadalajara officially decreed Governor Alvear a vote of thanks. He then retraced his steps northward and arrived in Durango in August after an absence of five months.[8]

In the meantime the captain-general at Durango, Rafael de Gascue, had been insistent with the Viceroy, Diego Fernández de Córdova, the Marqués de Guadalcázar, that reinforcement of troops be sent north for the complete suppression of the widespread revolt. His plea was successful. On September 22, 1617, three companies of soldiers, already paid for eight months, arrived at Durango.[9]

It was now known that the rebels had separated and were abroad in six groups widely apart, and therefore Governor Alvear, making use of a portion of this fresh force, sent his captains into different parts of the vast Nueva Vizcaya that the various bands of rebels be dispersed or annihilated. Captain Bartolomé Suárez was sent far north to Mesquital and the district of Guazamota. During a six months' campaign he had several brushes with the rebels and on December 8 took some prisoners and hanged twelve. Captain Montaño was ordered west to Tecuciapa, and Captain Mosquera was sent northeast to the fringes of the Salineros, Tobosos, and Conchos.[10]

But Cogoxito, arch rebel and clever fugitive, was still abroad. Until this renegade savage should be taken or slain, trouble was likely at any moment to plague the country. Hence it became necessary for the Governor to set out a third time westward into the mountains, a third time to brave the elements and the ravines in order to run the human quarry down or to trap him in his haunts. The chances of success were greater now because of the reinforcements sent up from Mexico City.

The details of this third and finally successful expedition of the Governor are interesting in the extreme.[11] Governor Gaspar de Alvear marched out of Durango in search of Cogoxito on February 25, 1618, with seventy Spaniards and two hundred Indian allies, accompanied by Father Alonso del Valle as chaplain. After the first day's march the little army, not yet completely assembled, camped four leagues out from the capital, to await a further muster of men and the report of the scouts whom the Governor had sent out. Doing service in this latter capacity were twelve Spaniards and forty Indians—Laguneros, Xiximes, and Acaxées under the command of Alfonso de Uria.

A group of these scouts had the good fortune to come upon two Indians, scouts themselves, sent out by Cogoxito. They were an old man named Antón and a younger called Francisco. The latter the Spaniards killed, but they took Antón back to the Governor for questioning. The old man first said that Cogoxito was at Estelage of the Tepehuanes, but as his story was not consistent he was put to the torture till the blood started from the tips of his fingers. Hot coals were likewise applied to his feet. He did not wince, but seems to have been driven to tell the truth, for he now averred that the rebel leader had indeed been in the parts about Yamoriba, near where the Xiximes

THE DEATH OF COGOXITO

had risen, but that for purposes of food he had come down to the valleys of Texame and Guatimapé. But even these statements were partly lies spoken to divert the Spaniards, for other scouts came in who reported that they had located the rebels still in hiding in the *serranía* of Guarisamey, where was the gorge of the Piaxtla, Del Diablo. The Governor determined to take the road thither, though it was evident he was penetrating into the most difficult defiles of the mountains. It was Monday, March 5, that they began the hazardous penetration.

The Spanish scouts had been correct, because at four in the afternoon they came upon a band of the rebels led by Cogoxito himself far from his hiding place and looking for food. The Spaniards, on the summit of a ridge, saw the Tepehuán rebels defiling in the gulch beneath them. They numbered thirty or forty, four riding on mules, Cogoxito among the mounted and in the lead.

The Indian allies of the Spaniards quietly put themselves in ambush halfway down the declivity. Cogoxito seems to have been aware of their presence, for he proceeded with eyes fixed on the ground to detect some print of the enemy. Suddenly he saw the footprint of one of the Lagunero Indians and gave the order to his men to turn back. The Indian allies had hoped to take the chief alive, but this became now impossible. They fired upon him. One arrow pierced Cogoxito's throat, issuing from the right side of his neck. The wounded chief now threw himself from his mount and tried desperately to reach the summit of a rocky prominence across from the Spaniards, when another arrow wounded him between the shoulders. No sooner had he gained the height than a Xixime Indian pierced him with a third. The Spaniards now came running up. They dared not shoot for fear of hitting their allies, but with Cogoxito's own lance they dispatched him.[12]

Four other rebels fell, among them a chief named Agustinillo, native of Sauceda. The rest escaped across a deep gorge. But the Spaniards took booty of horse and mule and cut off the heads of the five Tepehuanes. When they got down to level ground, Del Valle, as he himself tells us, took into his hands the head of Cogoxito, which was still warm, dropped to his knees, and recited the *Te Deum,* the rest of the Spaniards spontaneously joining in the chant. We can understand this rejoicing, for with the leader slain it was felt the rest could be scared into submission.

Immediately, though night was fast falling, the Governor selected thirty Spaniards and a hundred Indians to take the road to Guarisamey in order to rout out the Tepehuanes who were there and to destroy the rancheria of Cogoxito and of the others. All night they traveled until three in the morning, over country the asperity of which it was impossible to describe. But when they reached the pueblo all the Tepehuanes had fled. Guarisamey lay hidden in that all but inaccessible gorge, Del Diablo. It lay directly west of Durango by almost one hundred miles. Along its rocky bottom in the rainy season roared the waters of the Río Piaxtla. Besides its name Del Diablo, it was called, from the name of its chief pueblo, Guarisamey. Here was the country of the Humi Indians, and in the gorge, besides the chief pueblo, were eight other villages, each with four or five rancherias.

The rebel Tepehuanes had fled hither, forty or fifty of them, under the chief called Hernandilla de Valenzuela, thinking the country inaccessible to the Spaniards. They had rather imposed themselves upon the Humis than been invited or eagerly accepted by them.

Cogoxito had his rancheria hung on the brink of so inaccessible a ravine, one of the shaggy borders of the gorge, that it would have been impossible to surprise him and take him there. He had foreseen all eventualities and had every detail ready for instant flight. Near his hut was a small corral with six mares ready for any emergency. On a horse or mule he could flee for several hundred yards without entering a ravine, and with this start he could let his mount go and clamber over the still rougher places on foot.

He had indeed been safe so long as he remained in his lair. It was hunger that drove him forth. From the valleys of Texame and Guatimapé he had gathered in three hundred head of cattle, of which number a half perished over the crags of that cloven land; the Spaniards saw their bones strewn along the declivities. When this supply ran out, he divided his people, placing some in Sariana and some in Cocorotame. Then he himself with a small band ventured again into the Texame Valley to gather in more cattle. He was on this expedition when he was discovered and killed.

This event, so fortunate for the Spaniards, led to the flight and dispersal of the rest of the Tepehuanes and to the submission of the near-by Humis and Xiximes.

THE DEATH OF COGOXITO

The Spaniards, discovering at Guarisamey no Tepehuanes, spread out to comb the country and, if possible, to get in touch with the Humis who had also fled, fearing vengeance of the Spaniards. A lone Humi was soon descried standing on the point of a crag. He was given a signal to descend. He made known that there were others with him and he would descend for a parley provided only one Spaniard with an interpreter should meet them at an indicated rancheria six miles away. Governor Alvear, however, sent six men of valor and prudence under Captain Tomás García and with them six Indian allies tricked out in brilliant feathers and white breeches. But the Humis said they would not come unless these remained behind. So it was done. Captain García, come to the rendezvous, was asked to lay down his gun; the Indians put down their bows and arrows. Then they began to speak, García on one side of a ravine, they on the other. García in the name of the Governor promised forgiveness. The Governor was then desired. Only he with Father del Valle must come. They made him a great obeisance from their side of the ravine and finally were persuaded to cross it if the father would meet them at the bottom. They were evidently taking great precautions against deceit on the part of the Spaniards.

When the group gathered, all things were amicably settled. The Humis made their excuses for harboring the Tepehuanes, saying they were forced to it through fear and, besides, had been deceived by the lies of these rebels. Alvear said he would pardon them on two conditions: first, that they would never again allow entrance to their country to the enemies of the Spaniards; second, that they would form a group as large as they could muster and guide the Spaniards to Sariana that there the remaining Tepehuanes might be attacked and destroyed.

All was agreed to, but they asked for two or three days to gather up their men from the nine pueblos of the gorge. Instead of two or three, the Spaniards waited eight days in snow by night and rain by day. Their provisions gave out and they were driven to killing horses for food, for they were leagues away from their main camp. Finally on the eighth day the Humis, in what numbers we are not told, arrived with their cacique, a strong young buck of twenty-two named Mehigua. A plan of action was discussed and it was decided that the Governor should march with his whole troop to Zapiuris, a Xixime pueblo, and attack the Tepehuanes who might be there. The Humis would hold the summits and attack from Guarisamey and Sariana. All would finally meet at Yamoriba. The Humis were to have a banner that they might be distinguished from the other Indian allies of the Spaniards and the Governor promised that for each head of a Tepehuán Indian they should bring in, there would be made over to them four hatchets, four knives, four hoes, and a coat. At the same time Alvear delighted the chief and his servants by presents of two cloaks of fine cloth, and of knives and handkerchiefs.

The Spaniards returned to their base, where they found many mules had died from the cold. Resting for a day, which was Saturday, March 16, they set out to do their part in exterminating the Tepehuanes in this wild part of the mountains. But word of the death of Cogoxito had sped over summit and ravine and Tepehuanes were nowhere to be met with. Once, indeed, the Spaniards were hot upon their trail, having come upon two cows too weak to follow the camp. Hastening on, like dogs on the scent, they came upon a hundred head of cattle of the Tepehuanes. This was a great windfall for the Spaniards. But the rebels had taken alarm and fled and could not be caught. It only remained to them, now, to receive the submission of Yamoriba, Zapiuris, and other small Xixime settlements which had lent assistance to the rebels. At Mehigua's intercession the Governor was ready to pardon these Xiximes.

After a most difficult march Spaniards and allies reached Yamoriba. Here the caciques came out to beg forgiveness. Seventy of them arrived with bows, lances, and arrows as if for war. Governor Alvear was seated in a large shelter, and as the caciques came into his presence they dropped their arms and listened to their spokesman, old Mihaykuet, a man of more than seventy years, and then to Maicohueta, the Indian governor of Humase. They were ardent in their promises— they would do everything to please the Governor. They would go to San Hipólito and carry the fathers hither on their shoulders and build churches like their neighbors at Zapiuris and Guapexuxe. Finally, the old chief who had first spoken closed with a showy oration.

Much the same happened at Zapiuris. The people here had been made Christians by Santarén; but during the last two years, after expelling their padre, they had lapsed into paganism. But now they came out to meet the Governor, who was harangued by the two chiefs Huahuapa and Teuchius. They promised to rebuild their churches, to recall their father, who was Pedro Gravina, and to live again in peace as Christians.

At Guarisamey, Mehigua brought about the last reconciliation with the remaining Humis. He prevailed upon the men of Cocorotame to meet the Governor near the very gorge where Cogoxito was killed. Nine o'clock one morning in the early part of April was the time set for this meeting. Mehigua appeared high on a pinnacle of rock and shouted to learn if the Spaniards were there. The Governor's men responded with a volley from their muskets. Then Mehigua requested that only the Governor and Father del Valle climb part of the way to meet him. The Humi chief descended, embraced both of the Spaniards, expressed his great happiness at seeing them again, and said he wanted to leave his people and follow the Governor back to Durango, there to serve him always.

Then he gave a call and at this signal the men of Cocorotame, seventy of them, came tumbling down the steep, carrying their bows and arrows, their hatchets and *macanas* as if for war. These Humis humbled themselves before the Governor and embraced the padre particularly. They asked forgiveness for the past and begged friendship of the Governor. He responded with kindness, and laid down the same provisions as for the others of their nation, which they gladly accepted.

For the return to Durango Governor Alvear divided his army into three parts; his captains might thus lead the several units back by different routes, that the country be more thoroughly covered for stray bands of Tepehuán fugitives. The final meeting place was to be Las Cruces, and the date the last day of April.

The first to arrive was the division led by the Governor himself, accompanied by Father del Valle. Soon came in the other two divisions, led respectively by Captains Tomás García and Gonzalo Martín. The Governor's and Martín's march had been uneventful, but García had come upon a band of eight of the enemy, given chase, killed two and taken the rest prisoner. Among those killed was the well-known leader of revolt Juan Vinagre y Cuscusillo. The prisoners were forced to indicate their rancherias, and eight women and children were thus added to the number caught. The men were summarily hanged by the Governor after Del Valle had been able to prepare them for a Christian death, and their bodies were left dangling from trees that fringed the road leading from Texame to Las Bocas. On the last lap of the return into Durango, the divisions again separating, two more rebels were caught and killed, one being Juan Quequejal of Santiago Papasquiaro, a leader of disorder.[13]

Thus ended a campaign that lasted from February 25 to May 9, and although only seventeen of the rebels had been killed, a great advantage had been gained in the west country. As Father del Valle remarked in his letter, which contains all the foregoing details, had the Xiximes and Humis been determined upon hostile resistance, not all the armies of the King of Spain would have been able to subdue them among those crags and gorges, cliffs and barrancas. As it was, friends were made with the Humis, with their pueblos of Guarisamey, Humase, and Cocorotame; and with the Xiximes, with their pueblos of Zapiuris, Yamoriba, Vasisy, and Guapexuxe. These Xiximes should have been Christians; and the Humis would soon enter the fold. Thus allies of two thousand bowmen were secured to the Spaniards who were bent on scouring the rebel Tepehuanes out of the country. Besides, the roads to Topia, San Andrés, and San Hipólito had again been made safe and the coast provinces of Culiacán, Chiametla, Piaxtla, and Aoya were made secure. Letters from the padres there, from Gravina, Castro Verde, González, Mallen, speak of security and manifest gratitude to Governor Alvear.[14]

This campaign decided finally the fate of the revolt. Now, with most of their leaders killed and with their growing persuasion that it was futile to try a stand against the Spaniards, who possessed infinitely superior weapons, the arquebuses, and whose coats of mail and leathern jackets the arrows could not pierce, the Tepehuanes lost their incentive for continued insubordination and further rebellion. The Indians beheld, too, the determination of the Governor to root out every last rebel. Alvear had ridden some six hundred miles in this campaign, scouring all the Tepehuán country, destroying crops and pueblos and recapturing the animals stolen from the Spaniards. The rebels had been forced to abandon their fields and pueblos and to make out a bleak and precarious existence in the wilds of their summits and ravines, where starvation stared at them menacingly.

THE DEATH OF COGOXITO

Captain Suárez, the year before, had run the rebels down in the north, pursuing them far over hill and dale, far over precipice and gorge. While Alvear was in the west in 1617, Suárez frustrated a proposed attack on Indé, slew a hundred hostiles, and took two hundred prisoners. There were other expeditions, followed by summary executions. A leader among the rebels, a woman called La Tenanchi, was hanged at Indé. Besides Father Del Valle, Father Andrés López accompanied some of these expeditions.[15] The hostiles, thus discouraged, gave up the fight. The Tepehuán must submit to the Spaniard or drag out a wretched and starving existence.

Another consideration broke the spirit of the Tepehuanes. Their hechiceros, especially Quautlatas of the talking idol, had made promises of immortality: the killed should come to life, the old should become young again. But not a single one came back to life, not one old person received back his youth, nay, even the old and the hechiceros were slain together with the rest. Their sorcerers and medicine men had fooled them; it had all been a hoax. The simple and stupid Indian came dully to realize that he had been deceived by his leaders. Hunger and discomfort and danger spoke to him in terms that he could more concretely understand.

The harm done by the revolt was almost beyond exaggeration. Besides the temporary ruin of the entire Tepehuán mission, with the death of the missionaries and the destruction of the churches and the Christian pueblos, a severe damage to the spiritual and ecclesiastical realm, the economic loss to Nueva Vizcaya reached serious proportions.

Before the outbreak, the country was prosperous. There were in the neighborhood of Durango large ranches which sustained some two hundred thousand head of cattle. These herds enriched the country in two ways. They provided meat for the workers in numerous mines strewn through the mountains, which, with the advance of the years, were becoming more numerous, especially to the east, toward Saltillo. Then, droves of heifers were yearly driven to Mexico to be exchanged for silver coin, which in its turn was spent in the purchase of various commodities. Now, the Tepehuanes in revolt killed thousands of head of cattle and stole thousands more, driving them off into their inaccessible mountains to roam wild over the country.

There was the loss to the mines. Those of Indé were abandoned; the others, Guanacevi and Papasquiaro, were ruined, their machinery destroyed, their workers scattered or killed. Moreover, the roads were for months rendered impassable so that all commerce was clogged and industry stagnated. The herds could not be driven south to Mexico City and the constant flow of trade over the mountains from the west coast to the slopes of the eastern divide was brought to a standstill. A few years of this and the country would have returned to its original savagery and wild desolation.

As to the cost of repression, a high-placed officer of the King's fiscal, Don Juan Casaus y Cervantes, gave out that the loss to the King's treasury amounted to 80,000 pesos, besides the financial damage sustained by the King's vassals when the time came to reorganize the mines and to restock their hills and plains. More than two hundred Spaniards died in these troubles, not to mention their servants and laborers, old Mexican Indians and Negroes. Many of them died for the Faith. Of the Tepehuanes, more than a thousand, it was estimated, lost their lives in the revolt.[16] Truly, it had not paid them well to listen to their hechiceros.

One may pause here to reflect upon the historic importance of the mission system. It was the Christianized Indian, loving and loyal to his padre and the Christian Faith, who ceased to be a menace to the Spaniard. Only thus was made feasible the opening up of the country in mines, ranches, and commerce. On the west coast the frontier could not possibly have advanced until the Suaquis on the Fuerte and then the Yaquis on the Yaqui River had given promise of perpetual peace through their acceptance of Christianity. This same reason explains why the ranchers and mine owners of the plains to the east desired so strongly the conversion of the Laguneros; for mining was at that time moving eastward and the Spaniards well knew that progress could not continue until their own personal safety and that of their developments and investments should be rendered secure by the Christian submission of the savage to his padre.

Moreover, it was necessary that Christianity be not only planted; it must be sustained by the continued existence of the missions—this contrary to what Jesuit policy at first had planned. The savage, without the constant presence of his padre and the steadying effect of the or-

THE DEATH OF COGOXITO

ganized pueblo, would most speedily relapse into barbarism. This was a phenomenon witnessed continuously in Mexico, just as it was abundantly illustrated by the effect of the secularization of the missions in Alta California. And although the fathers were generously willing, once the mission was on a secure basis, to leave it for further spiritual conquests, as did the Jesuits in southern Durango in the eighteenth century, and the Franciscans in Alta California in the nineteenth, this was proved by universal experience to be impractical and ruinous, even though some political leaders, holding to a theory but lacking experience, continued to cling to the idea that secularization was practical and desirable.

There is another consideration. The Indian deprived of his padre not only went back to savagery; he became the victim of the frontiersman. The miner, the rancher, the slave owner, the pearl fisher, all united to exploit the native. The professional slave hunter had long been suppressed by law, but, as a deep student of the Indian nations of Sinaloa and Sonora once said to the writer, the Spanish frontiersman had generally in view a frankly selfish motive in his frontier activities, while the missionary had just as generally and just as frankly a selfless and humanitarian and religious motive. The encomendero often cruelly mistreated his Indian servant or worker, and many an army captain or even governor of a province was not always gentle in his handling of the inferior race. There was a rather ugly example of this in Sinaloa in the mid-seventeenth century.[17] The results of the secularization of the California missions remind us again of the same facts.

All the sources agree, however, that this time, at least, the Tepehuán uprising was not the result of ill treatment on the part of the Spaniards, which proves that it would be unjust to generalize too largely on the statements just made. But certain it is that the missions played a most important role in the advance of the frontier of colonies and nations over the world. Seldom, perhaps, has the mission influence been more important than in the Jesuit foundations of northwestern Mexico.

Chapter XVIII

RECONCILIATION AND RECONSTRUCTION

OF ALL THE fathers who worked among the Tepehuanes, only Andrés López escaped with his life. López resided at Indé, a hundred miles north of Durango. He, too, had been invited to the feast at Zape, and had he gone would have been slain with the rest. Word that the celebration at Zape had been postponed deterred him from his journey thither just as he was about to set foot in stirrup. Absent from Indé when the revolt broke out, he was warned in time and fled back to this mining town for safety.[1]

López, then, began the work of reconstruction from the mines of Indé. The destruction had not been so complete that the father had nothing to work upon. It will be remembered that the missionaries at Santiago Papasquiaro sent as a last effort to stem the tide of rebellion a loyal Tepehuán cacique, Don Francisco Campos, to Tenerape to treat with the threatening chiefs of his own nation. He and his companion were taken and slain.[2] Many others of the nation remained loyal in their hearts, but, for lack of heroism in resisting the rising wind of disaffection or through fear of what the personal consequences might be to themselves, either dissembled or remained neutral, like many of the inhabitants of Santiago Papasquiaro when those from Santa Catalina invaded the town to perpetrate the destruction and massacre of November 18. And later, when the worst had been done and when these same loyal but unheroic souls saw the Governor ride over the land and defeat the bands of roving Tepehuanes, they again became filled with the fear of punishment from the Governor and so fled with the rest. It was with these that Father Andrés López could put in the first thin wedge which would open for him the door to reconciliation with all the tribe.[3]

Coöperating with the missionary were the Viceroy and the Governor. Through Father López they offered the Indians peace and

---
[1] For notes to chapter xviii see pages 215–216.

amity should they be willing to live again in pueblos under the supervision of their padre as they had done so happily before. The missionary's first attempts, however, bore no fruit. It was difficult for him to get in touch with individuals of the nation, now scattered, cowed, and distrustful.

The first successful contact was made in a unique manner and through an instrument at once unworthy and despicable, but about to be fully reinstated through a repentance the sincerity of which was proved by services in the cause of religion.

There was at Indé an old Tepehuán woman of immoral life and evil reputation, enfeebled and worn out, it would seem, by her excesses. She was in the town a quasi captive of the Spaniards, too old or for other reasons unwilling to escape and gain her liberty. This woman Father López won over through tact and kindness. The padre would now make use of her as a link by means of which he could come in contact with her people. The captain at Indé was at first unwilling that such a creature be trusted. But López overcame these objections and the diplomatic move was attempted.

The Jesuit instructed her well in the part she was to play. He gave her a written note of the commission which he held of the Viceroy and the Governor so that her people might know that whatever he said or whatever promises he made would be respected by the Spanish officials. As a pledge of even greater security he gave her his diurnal, a portion of his breviary, which would be her signet ring for protection and confidence when she should walk among her tribespeople.

Thus armed she set out upon her journey to reach a group whom the father had especially in mind. She was accompanied for a dozen miles or so by a few others, whether Mexican Indians old in the Faith or friendly Tepehuanes we do not know. These soon abandoned her, persuaded that no possible good could come from so wretched and feeble an ambassador. The woman, nevertheless, persevered alone, and borne up by some kind of enduring strength traveled hundreds of miles over the mountains, from ranchería to ranchería, until she found the group with whom the padre wished her to begin his work of reconciliation.

Although in the different rancherías which she visited many would not listen to her proffered overtures of peace, others did incline a willing ear, especially the group Father López had in mind. These hearkened to the message of peace and made themselves ready to enjoy the security offered by him in the name of the Spanish government. They were willing to come back to their old pueblo, rebuild their chapel, and begin the orderly and peaceful routine of their former Christian lives. Others, seeing that these were not molested, but rather favored by the padre and the Spaniards, gathered enough courage to imitate them. Though many were too timid or distrustful to follow this example, an encouraging beginning had been made and it was necessary now to provide for other missionaries to take the place of those who had fallen. Such was the situation at the end of 1617.[4]

The usual steps were taken: López advised the Governor, the Governor informed the Viceroy, the Viceroy petitioned the Provincial for the needed recruits. López wrote also directly to his provincial. The authorities in Mexico City were in favor of the renewed project and the fathers were unafraid. The Viceroy not only wished the Jesuits to come afresh to the field; he also desired the mine owners to return to their property in order to help the missionaries bring back prosperity to Nueva Vizcaya. The Provincial designated Father José de Lomas, who had worked in the province before and knew the Tepehuán language. With him came a companion, a lay brother. Though Lomas had suffered much here formerly, he was glad to return, and the Indians, hearing that their one-time father was coming back to them, trooped out from the destroyed pueblo of Santiago Papasquiaro to meet him and bid him welcome.

A letter of Father Lomas to his superiors in Mexico City has come down to us. So interesting is a part of its contents in view of the recent revolt that some lines deserve direct quotation. He writes: "I arrived at Papasquiaro February 8 [1618]. The Indians received me with demonstrations of joy, although I found everything destroyed except three small huts. It has snowed three times since my coming and the wind has been furious, giving great cause of merit to myself and my companion. As soon as I arrived, I brought all the pueblo over to the cross that had been outraged and there we chanted the Christian doctrine.... They have all been disillusioned, seeing that at the very place the devil spoke to them they suffered the greatest losses, Captain Suárez taking as prisoners their wives and sons." Father Lomas is

RECONCILIATION—RECONSTRUCTION 169

alluding to Tenerape, which had been the core of the conspiracy and where the speaking idol had been kept and adored. Governor Alvear, as we have seen, had here put to flight the Tepehuán leaders and captured a large number of prisoners. Every day, avers Lomas, they now gathered together at this outraged crucifix at Santiago Papasquiaro for public prayer, and every day, as in the happy time before the revolt, the children came together for instruction.[5]

Indeed, the Tepehuanes, offering another proof of the fickleness of the savage, now performed a complete *volte face*. They themselves delivered a blow to their past spirit of revolt which the Governor for all his past efforts and royal expense had been unable to effect. They themselves executed the infamous hechicero Quautlatas, originator of the revolt, leader of all their trouble, who with the talking and possessed idol went from pueblo to pueblo spreading disaffection among the fickle and stupid people. Lomas calls him "closest to the Devil, great hechicero and sort of high priest of the new religion, who sustained the rebellion and directed the war."[6]

But this was not the only member of their own nation upon whose head the Tepehuanes visited dire retribution. Another, unnamed, cacique who was endeavoring to keep them from the peace they executed also. Still another whom Lomas was going to try to win over fled from the death penalty. Also, Guixiuita, archtraitor, kidnaper of one of the Spanish girls at Santiago Papasquiaro, and one of the leaders of evil in Santa Catalina, fled likewise now from his own reconverted people and went far over to the west to Boyagame close to the borders of the Acaxées. Here he was able to gather together a knot of the disaffected around about Tecuciapa. They looked upon him as their cacique. Guixiuita caused further trouble in the west. This condition, thought Father de Lomas, shows that complete security for the fathers could not be had without the presence of some soldiers.

It is to be remarked that, during the twenty years of labor of the missionaries among the Tepehuanes, Christianity had not struck deep root into the hearts of many. As elsewhere, once the good influence was removed, paganism began to push up in the garden of their hearts its ugly and ill-smelling weed. Even after the padres had returned, a youth killed another at Santa Catalina following a revel and the family of the dead man then killed the murderer. At Navidad a flood lasted eight days. To cause the river to subside the Tepehuanes thought to appease the anger of the river god by the sacrifice to him of a human victim. They seized an infant from the arms of its mother and flung it into the river. They likewise had relapsed into the old superstition of endeavoring to give back vitality and strength to the old by killing the young. The Spaniards reported that some every day at dawn adored the sun and in the evening the moon, with gibberish of their own barbarous concoction. Certain ones came about the fathers' hut at night and by weird howlings tried to frighten them.[7]

In spite, however, of these lapses and of the initial difficulty of Lomas and his companion, continual progress was made, so that it soon became evident that more workers were needed. Four more fathers were sent to the mission in 1620, and a presidio with a captain was provided at Santa Catalina for the special protection of the missionaries.[8] With the help thus afforded, a gradual but sure recuperation was taking place. The old pueblos, Sauceda, Atotonilco, Santiago Papasquiaro, Guanaceví, again gathered in and about them a peaceful population of Indians and Spaniards. San Simón, formerly a ragged settlement of only fourteen families, now became one of the most populous pueblos, its numbers augmented by a colony of Tarahumar Indians who had come down from the valley of San Pablo to live there. The most flourishing of all became Zape, where the greatest slaughter of missionaries had taken place and where a statue of the Blessed Virgin, being dedicated when the revolt broke out, had suffered indignities and been partly disfigured.[9]

When the new fathers arrived, their first desire was to restore again to her former place of honor in the pueblo the memory of the Mother of God under whose protection Zape had been placed. They thought, therefore, of installing solemnly another statue in reparation of the sacrilege. Now, there was a pious captain at Guanaceví, not many miles from Zape, who at the time of the atrocities of the revolt made a vow to the Virgin Mary that should he escape he would reinstate the statue and adorn it with jewels.

As soon as it became evident that the new settlement of peace and progress was going to endure, he took steps to fulfill his vow. He ordered the statue to be carefully repaired in Mexico City and redecorated to be what Ribas calls one of the finest of all the Madonnas of the kingdom of New Spain, "as if the sculptor had been given grace by the Son for the glory of His Mother." When this remade piece was finished and had been shipped safely to Nueva Vizcaya, it was kept for some time at Guanaceví against a fit season for a grand and solemn celebration which in the intention of Spaniards and fathers should far outshine the disastrously interrupted fiesta of 1616. This solemn installation was fixed for the vigil of the Feast of the Assumption, the 14th of August, 1623.[10]

When the time approached, the Indians of three pueblos joined with the Spaniards in preparing for a gala day. There was to be a solemn procession from Guanaceví to Zape in which the statue was to be carried in honor. They made triumphal arches along the way, adorned with flowers and fragrant foliage from the fields and mountains, and about half a league from Zape, at the spot where Fathers Fonte and Moranta were slain on their way to the feast of years ago, the Indians and Spaniards made a comely enramada embowered in flowers. This was to be the first halting place of the procession.[11]

Numerous Spaniards and Indians came to take part in the rites on the afternoon of the 14th. All marched on foot along the way that had been prepared, and some of the more devotional Spaniards marched barefoot. The statue was placed, prayers were offered and hymns chanted. Then followed, in the evening, solemn vespers with torches and the salute of guns. That night there was dance and song with music of oboe and trumpet. The following morning a High Mass was sung in honor of the four martyrs who had fallen there so gloriously seven years ago. Many tears, says the ancient historian, were shed by Spaniard and Indian, of sorrow for the loss of the padres, of devotion at this honor to the Mother of God. That she was reinstated in her former glory at Zape could not but touch these pious people.

The shrine in which the statue was set was called Santa María and it became a famous and much-frequented place of devotion for all the province of Nueva Vizcaya. The spiritual life of the Spaniards was renewed through the presence of this holy spot, so rich in sacred memories, while the Tepehuanes came back to inhabit their old pueblo in greater numbers than ever before. Even materially the country was aided, for shortly after this celebration the richest mine in all New Spain was opened, that of Parral, near the land of the Tepehuanes.[12]

The pious Ribas recounts various and sundry miracles performed here through the invocation of Santa María de los Martires and through drinking the water in which pieces of the old statue had been dipped. The fane was still renowned and still frequented when the Jesuit fathers were ordered from their missions by King Carlos III in 1767. When Bishop Pedro Tamarón of Durango made in 1763 an extensive visitation of his diocese and left, to the delight of historians, a careful and minute record of the whole region, the statue was included among the objects of his inquiry. Witnesses of long standing and old families in the country were examined concerning the tradition connected with the image.

One, Francisco Jaques Gutiérrez, who had a high reputation for reliability, testified that it was a tradition in the country that when this statue had been remade in Mexico City and was being returned to the north, a mule driver at Guadalupe opened the case to look at the image and saw the mark of an ax upon the face. The statue was taken back and repaired; but later the same mark again appeared. This happened a third time, when those who noticed it became persuaded it was the will of Our Lady that the mark remain in perpetuity, a reminder of the calamity and suffering that had come upon the country.

The pious Bishop tells us that the mark remained to his time and that he himself mended it with his own hands. He says: "The holy image which I mended with my own hands is one vara and a third in height and the gash which runs from the middle of the left cheek down through the chin close to the neck is a little more than four fingers' breadth in length. The countenance, beautiful, majestic and pious, inspires devotion, and keeps a white and roseate hue. They call it commonly the Virgin of the Ax, Our Lady of Zape, Our Lady of the Valley, while even the devotion of some has given it the name of Our Lady of the Missionaries."[13] But the memory of the statue is now faded from the land.

While the number of missionaries was being thus augmented in 1620 and after, and while the Black Robe was carrying on his work of reconciliation and reconstruction, the civil authority was doing its share to stabilize the Indians, and with a strong but just and benignant arm to hold the country to security and peace.

The reputation of Governor Gaspar de Alvear had suffered much

RECONCILIATION—RECONSTRUCTION 173

by the Tepehuán revolt, which had cost the kingdom so many hundreds of Spanish lives and the royal exchequer so many thousands of silver pesos. Alvear was succeeded late in 1620 as Governor of Nueva Vizcaya by *El Almirante,* the Admiral, Don Mateo de Vesga. The new governor was strong enough to be energetic for the peace and fair enough to win the Indians through kindness. His official report for the first two years of his incumbency, though perhaps favorably colored for the viceroy in Mexico City, details the progress of conciliation and of renewed prosperity.[14] Just after the death of Cogoxito in 1618, four or five pueblos, with the important cacique Rafael, sent into Durango overtures of peace, and the movement thus begun continued during the years of Alvear's incumbency.[15] The new governor carried on consistently: he confirmed the friendship already begun by receiving renewed promises of good behavior, and he was able to extend farther the frontiers of conciliation by sending messages and pledges of peace throughout all Nueva Vizcaya.

No sooner was Mateo de Vesga in office than leaders of the pueblos came to attest their loyalty. Already in December, 1620, the Indian governor of Zape, Don Juan Torillo, came to Durango with three other caciques and ten tribesmen to renew and confirm with the new governor the covenants of peace and alliance. Thus before this same year was out did Santiago Papasquiaro and Santa Catalina renew their bond of friendship and submission. The following year, deputies came from Tunal, Cocorotame, Las Lajas, and even from the Tarahumar country. In 1622, besides Guarisamey, the northeast country of Mapimí and Toboso sent ambassadors, and caciques like Don Cristóbal who lived on the fringes of Tarahumara did likewise. An old Tepehuán rebel, Xixiculta by name, who with four others had skulked in the mountains for four years, came down to Durango in 1622, led there by a pledge of peace, a banner sent him by Governor Vesga through the good offices of the Tarahumares.[16]

In May, 1621, the new governor made a tour of friendship to the north; he was received everywhere with overtures of loyalty and alliance. At Zape, for instance, when the Governor arrived, the whole pueblo came out to greet him, led by their cacique Don Lucas, and all good pledges were renewed.[17] Farther to the north near Indé, in the district of Tizonazo, further additions of peaceful Indians were made in 1624.[18] It is true that during these years there were some alarms. In the north, where the Tepehuanes and the Tarahumares blend, a few Indians rose in 1621 and murdered some Spaniards. In 1622 a cacique, named Oñate, with the half-breed Canelas, took the field and invited malcontents to join him. Some even left Zape to go to the rebels. But both these minor eruptions were soon covered over. Oñate was caught in Zape and repented in the presence of Fathers Juan de Sanguesa and Martín Larios, some Franciscans, and Captain Gonzalo Martín. He died soon afterward. In spite of these belated sputterings the general peaceful face of the province was maintained.[19]

Durango increased and prospered under this continued regime of peace. When the Governor came in 1620, the capital was still down from the effects of the rebellion, but in 1624 things were looking up encouragingly. Twenty-two new and for that time sumptuous homes were built by important residents, such as our former captain-general, Rafael de Gascue, and by Captain Alonso de Quesada, while eight new shops were opened by merchants. The Augustinian fathers were introduced into the city, and a new pueblo, called San Antonio, was organized for Indians from the sierra. This was half a league distant from the city. New farms were started in the wide valleys of the capital and the machinery of the mines was gradually reinstated.[20]

Thus progress continued. The pueblos all picked up and became more populous than before, even though the general number of Tepehuanes had been diminished because of the wars. However, Santiago Papasquiaro, where a beautiful new church was built in 1626, seems to have been the only place where some Spaniards took up, as before, their residence. The country, rid of the hechiceros and the consequent troubles and deceits of evil spirits, became more quiet than before. The progress was shown particularly in the manner in which the Indians kept the Lent of each year, with the devotions of the Stations of the Cross, penitential processions, confession, and communion.[21]

A very interesting and beautiful thing was done for the Tepehuanes by the far-off Indians of Culiacán, old Christians and very ardent Catholics. During the revolt the rebels had carried about their idol from pueblo to pueblo. Now the Indians of Culiacán carried over the mountains from their city in the west into the country of the Tepehuanes a statue of Blessed Mary the Virgin which they considered to

RECONCILIATION—RECONSTRUCTION 175

be miraculous. These pious Tahues of Culiacán, in reparation of the sacrileges of the revolt, carried this statue likewise from pueblo to pueblo of the former hostiles. The latter received well these their brethren from the west coast and were happy to join in the devotion of honoring the Mother of God through veneration of her image. Where the idol had been carried and listened to, here the statue was honored, staying from two to three days in each pueblo.[22]

Another statue of the Blessed Virgin, desecrated by the Tepehuanes, came into the hands of a devout and wealthy Spaniard who traded between Mexico City and Durango. He carried it to his estate within a few miles of the capital of New Spain. Here he built a fine chapel for its repose and adorned it with gold and jewels. It became a place of pilgrimage and devotion, so that the intention of the pious man, one of reparation for the indignities of the Tepehuanes, was well fulfilled.[23]

This chapter could not better conclude than with an event which occurred the year before the solemn dedication at Zape. Durango was made an episcopal see in 1621, the diocese being made from portions of the bishopric of Guadalajara to the south and of indefinite territory to the north. The first Bishop of Guadiana, as the diocese was then called, was the Augustinian Gonzalo de Hermosillo. He made an official visitation of his new diocese in 1622 and began it with a journey to the missions of Parras and of the Tepehuanes. He wrote enthusiastically to the Provincial in Mexico City: "I am able to offer a thousand congratulations to Your Paternity for the happy results which the fathers of the Society have achieved in these parts where religion does so well and promises so abundantly. I give thanks to Our Lord for the rich favors He does me and for the good results which during my time take place among that nation [the Tepehuanes]. I am very affectionately grateful to Your Paternity and to all the other fathers for the great benefits they confer upon these Indians and for my part I offer myself with all my energy to help them and to serve them in these missions."[24] It is very clear, therefore, that within a few years after the terrible revolt things had been well reinstated. Six fathers were now in the mission. The Tepehuanes had redeemed themselves, Christianity was advancing apace, and if the nation had been reduced in quantity by the wars, it is quite evident their quality had been refined.

Chapter XIX

NEW NATIONS

THE RÍO PIAXTLA, like all the other streams of the west coast, drops into what the Spaniards called the Mar del Sur, and we, the Pacific Ocean. The Piaxtla is nearly a hundred miles south of Culiacán, the capital of Sinaloa, and separated from it by the Río San Lorenzo. The rivers north of Río Culiacán fall into the Gulf of California, those south into the Pacific proper. Up the Piaxtla into the Sierra Madre is the gorge of the Piaxtla, the famous Del Diablo, hideout of Cogoxito, down which in the rainy season the boiling waters are poured from the mountains to the valleys and then to the sea. Up this gorge lived the Hina nation, and still higher near the headwaters of the stream dwelt the Humis, closely akin, both of them, to the Xiximes. The Hinas and the Humis had many of the same customs as the Xiximes, though the Hinas differed from them in speech.[1] For twenty-four years the Spaniards had lived and mined near these nations, but had never set foot in their territory, "the roughness of the mountains having closed the gate to Spanish arms as to missionary fathers; but for seventy years old Christians of the Tahue nation, in the environs of Culiacán, dwelt contiguous."[2]

It was our first Bishop of Durango who gave the impulse to the *entrada* of the fathers into this wild and steep country. We have just seen what an ardent admirer Bishop Gonzalo de Hermosillo was of the missionary ability of the Jesuit Fathers, his enthusiasm raised to a high pitch after his visitation of the Tepehuán missions in 1622. It was after this visitation that he placed these southern mountain nations under the charge of the Black Robes. The Bishop asked the Father Visitor, Luis de Bonifaz, to send a skillful missionary into these parts that the conversion of the tribes might be set on foot. Bonifaz designated for the difficult assignment Father Diego Gonzales Cueto.[3]

The man was well chosen. Having labored in these missions since 1605, first at San Gregorio and then among the Xiximes, he knew both languages better than the savages themselves and, for the help of those

---

[1] For notes to chapter xix see pages 216–217.

who might come after him, he had made a grammar and dictionary of the Xixime idiom. He was abstemious in food and austere with his floggings and hairshirt. He had been long a personal friend of Captain Bartolomé Suárez of San Hipólito; thus was understanding and cooperation with the secular arm assured.[4]

Cueto was glad to go and, like an obedient son of Loyola, he set out with alacrity. On his journey south the missionary fell in with the churchman Francisco de la Osa, Canon of Cogotá. This dignitary tried to dissuade the Jesuit from the hazardous entrada, representing the fierceness of the natives and the cliffy ruggedness of their country. The padre had discouraging talk even from some of his confreres. However, "nothing in the devoted religious man could prevail over his love of obedience; the recital of the expectant risks and hardships did but whet his desire to be on."[5] He arrived, then, at Huaimino, the lowest of the pueblos of the Hinas at the beginning of the higher sierra. From this meager settlement he sent word upstream, telling of his presence and inviting the Indians to come down to meet him, for he had orders to do just this and to proceed no farther.[6]

Only six came down. But these he treated so well that they were willing to go back to the mountains and tell their brethren of the kindly dispositions of the Black Robe and of the message of the Bishop of Durango. However, they told him they would not descend all the way to Huaimino, offering as excuse their fear of the Spaniards. They would listen to his message only if he should consent to advance twelve miles up the river to a spot called Iztlán.

This placed the padre in a quandary. He did not want to overstep the restrictions placed upon him by obedience, and yet the mission would be a complete failure should he not continue on. Besides, his life was in as great danger here as it would be there. Interpreting his orders like an intelligent soldier, he decided to proceed to Iztlán (since called San Francisco Javier). Here, to his disappointment, he saw only two natives, the others being farther up the gorge. At this, Cueto took a piece of silken altar covering which he used for Mass, tore it into three parts, and wrapped in each a sacred article: a rosary, a relic of a saint, and a small statue of Blessed Mary the Virgin. These he gave to the two Indians at Iztlán and bade them take the holy objects up the river to their brethren, inviting them at the same time to come down to him. Alas, they sent back the same discouraging message: let the padre come farther up, to Quilitlán, which the Spaniards called Quebos (later Santiago), and there doubtless they would await him. Cueto's companion said that at this fresh disappointment the padre cried out: "Oh, help me God! How much patience is necessary to do great things, especially among a nation so barbarous." Cueto, seeing that his danger could not become greater than it was, sent word that he would soon meet them where they wished.[7]

He traveled in the evening and at a late hour reached a small settlement. When his presence had become known, there came to the river's bank some three hundred rough and sturdy fellows without their women and children and armed for war. Cueto realized that now he would have to put all his trust in the Almighty. He spoke to them with what diplomacy he could muster, considering in his mind just what plan he had best follow. He resolved to continue on to Quilitlán since these men seemed not bent on violence. The next morning he started out with this shaggy escort and as he turned a bend of the river he saw fixed in the sand three spears and hanging from each was one of the holy objects he had sent on to the Indians. Not a soul was near and this aroused his further apprehension. He kissed the objects, stirred by a double emotion: a sense of impending danger, and joy at the privilege of suffering for souls and for Christ.

The missionary's suspense was soon relieved. He beheld Indians coming toward him. They had held aloof to see whether he were accompanied by soldiers. They kept coming down the stream until about a thousand, men, women, and children, stood about him.

He was able now at long last to give them the Bishop's message, that is, to invite them to become Christians and to promise them good treatment and the protection of the King of Spain. Cueto remained three days and preached to them the Catholic Faith. Here the padre enjoyed a goodly measure of success. He formed a pueblo and was able to baptize a hundred and fifty children. Then he returned the way he had come and pursued his journey back to Otatitlán, his former field of labor. He sent an account to Durango to his superior, Luis de Bonifaz, of what success he had enjoyed. Before leaving he promised the Indians he would soon return.[8]

Alas, Father Cueto was not able to keep this promise. He was delayed year after year. Then the Bishop of Durango died some years later while returning from a visitation of the Sinaloa missions, and Cueto's former superior, Father Luis de Bonifaz, was recalled to Mexico City to be placed in positions of trust. The two, therefore, who had been the principals in this entrada to the Hinas were both removed from the scene.[9]

The removal of Bonifaz was unfortunate for the Hinas, who year after year waited for the return of their padre whom they esteemed so highly. They finally did what was for savages a very remarkable thing—they sent a message to the Jesuit Superior of San Andrés begging him to let them have their father back. But this superior had been opposed from the start to the Hina mission and would therefore give no heed to the request. On the other hand, the provincial, Gerónimo Díez, was thinking very seriously of sending Cueto back to Mexico City to employ his talents for the pulpits of the capital. This move would have spelled the ruin of the Hina mission.

The tribe now became bolder in pressing their suit and, represented by some of their caciques, went all the way to Durango to interview the provincial, Gerónimo Díaz, who was at that time visiting the mission. The Provincial could not resist the determined sincerity of such a request and consented to change his mind with regard to the definite removal of Cueto. He would make it possible for the father to reënter the Hina nation. After some further delays the order was given and the padre went south for his second entrada to the Hinas.

During the time that all of this was taking place—death of the Bishop, change of superior of the missions, two delegations sent by the Hinas—many years had passed. It was 1622 when Cueto made his first entrada; it was 1630 or even later when he finally made his second.[10]

By that time things had changed even among the Hinas. The two delegations sent first to the superior of San Andrés, then to the Provincial, were an earnest of the constancy of their purpose. But not all the nation were of the same mind. The caciques who made the petitions were the ones who held firm, they and their party; but the delays were too long for many others and they gradually fell away from their initial good desires. Therefore, when Cueto returned to their country he discovered a coolness among many of his former admirers and had difficulty in coaxing them down from their peaks and summits. Trouble, moreover, was stirred up by an apostate Tepehuán Indian from Tunal north of Durango. This man tried to gather about him a knot of conspirators to kill the padre. He overshot his mark, however, bringing into the secret some loyal tribesmen of Tepuxtla, who informed the captain of the new presidio at what was then called San Sebastián de Huaimino. The Captain warned Cueto and arrested the Tepehuán, keeping him in chains at San Sebastián. Then the Captain himself entered with a few soldiers and, seconding Cueto's efforts, aided in the formation of several pueblos. Success was now afoot. The numbers of Christians increasing, Cueto asked for an assistant, who came in the person of Father Pedro Ximenes.[11]

Now that there were two fathers working among the Hinas a promise of more rapid advance stood above the horizon. However, there came one of those droughts and famines which periodically desolated the Indians in their savage state. Food was not at hand; they must leave their pueblos and go to seek it in the fastnesses of their mountains. They must hunt for roots and berries which grew in far-off vales and valleys. Now it was manifest again that many could not long be away from the influence of the padre without relapsing into barbarism and savagery. Only a few returned to their pueblos, a general coolness was noted, and it looked as if stormclouds were gathering which might burst in fury upon the mission. As a matter of fact, another plot was hatched among a large portion of the nation to murder the two missionaries in order that the tribes might be able to enjoy untrammeled the former liberty of their paganism.

In this crisis Cueto considered it necessary to send a warning message to the governor, now Gonzalo Gómez de Cervantes. Father Ximenes was dispatched for this purpose, traveling all the way to Durango. The Governor gave orders to the captain at San Andrés, our old acquaintance Bartolomé Suárez de Villalta, who for twenty years had shown himself so fine a soldier. He was to enter the country with a force and to see to the definite ending of the troubles.

There was some delay in the execution, and in the meantime so energetic had Cueto been that in spite of a spirit of rebellion he was able to form another, the sixth, pueblo at Quilitlán, which he called Santiago. The Captain marched down with some thirty soldiers accompanied by Father Ximenes and some Indian allies, having sent notice to the heads of the tribe to meet him at Yamoriba. November 18, 1633, was the date of the Captain's arrival, but no caciques were there. While he waited, he was disturbed by a letter from Father Juan Mallen, superior at San Andrés, saying the older men of the nation were all in disfavor of the conference. Captain Suárez remained till the 20th; still no chiefs. But a letter came from Cueto saying they would be there the following day. The Hinas did arrive, to the number of about two thousand, and were received by the allied Indians. The Spaniards shot off their guns to awe the chiefs and thus the Captain was able to do his work.[12]

Captain Suárez rebuked the savages in grave terms for their abandonment of their pueblos and for their treachery toward the missionaries and made them take an oath of fidelity to the King. The caciques were willing to do so, and as a sign of their sincerity they presented him with a bunch of arrows. The Captain gave them in turn bullets used for the Spanish arquebuses. He then made over to them a document in juridic form accepting their alliance. Spaniards and Indians then marched in procession to the church, the latter singing the prayers they had been taught. Father Ximenes delivered a sermon to the chiefs. The service over, Captain Suárez gave to the leaders as gifts of the King of Spain a good measure of corn and a quantity of beef, which went far to confirm the tribe in peace. Suárez showed his piety by depositing his arms before a statue of the Virgin and smashing to pieces an idol. He again exhorted the Indians to show the utmost loyalty to the fathers, while, to give an example of what this devotion ought to be, the Captain himself got down before the whole company and kissed the feet of Father Ximenes and brushed them, says the padre in a letter, with his venerable hair![13] A dance at night set a seal upon these overtures of peace.

This meeting in November, 1633, had been a perfect success. The Captain on his return to San Hipólito visited many of the pueblos lower down and still further confirmed the peace that had been sworn to. His meeting with Cueto was touching in its affectionate embrace, and Suárez was met everywhere in good spirit by the Indians, who came out to greet him with raised crosses and with the chanting of hymns. Six pueblos along the Piaxtla were now settled in a quiet condition of peace and the whole Hina nation was in a short while gathered into the Faith. A church was soon built, and when one of the chiefs of highest prestige was baptized and named Don Luis and appointed governor of a new pueblo named after him, the Hinas were thereby finally won to Christianity.[14]

Upstream from the Hinas and in the great gorge were the Humis. Father Alonso del Valle came to know this nation well during the Tepehuán revolt, and, as we have seen, was partly instrumental in making them staunch allies of the Spaniards.

The padre esteemed these people and described minutely their customs. They had some political organization and obeyed a central chief or governor. They were industrious and in spite of the savagery of their land were able to raise good crops of corn. They cultivated also beans, chili, squashes, and sage and they enjoyed the fruit of the sugar cane, the sapota tree, and the guava. They wore gowns of variegated colors gathered by a belt, and on their heads diadems of the richly colored plumage of the parrot or the macaw and sometimes even leaves of pounded silver. The tails of various animals completed their decoration and to these they tied rattles made of empty gourds. Their arrows were made of brazilwood and they carried no macanas, but iron hatchets instead. They had skill and some measure of taste, for their adobe houses were well made and even painted with colored mud. These dwellings had, however, but one small door and no other opening. This was more like a window and, since it was raised from the ground, one had to crawl through it and tumble in: this as a protection against their enemies the Tepehuanes, the Xiximes, and the Hinas.

Each of the nine pueblos of this people, the first being our familiar Guarisamey, consisted of four or five rancherias, and each rancheria of six or seven families. The houses of each rancheria were built so closely together that the inmates could speak softly from one to the other. The rancherias themselves were perched so precariously on the edge of rocky ravines or steep barrancas that for the Spaniards to go from one to another required three or four hours of dangerous climbing on hands and knees, though the natives seemed to fly or to leap up like deer. The houses were ranged around a little plaza.[15]

The Humis were not a numerous tribe, being only a little over three

NEW NATIONS 183

hundred families in all. They began thirty miles up from Santiago and were so close to the divide that before the conversion of the Hinas they had come in contact with the fathers at Durango. There they had been well treated. They had seen the Black Robes working among the Tepehuanes at Papasquiaro and had been well impressed. They showed themselves to be stuff out of which good Christians could be made. Father Santarén had been among them years before, so that through different channels they had become acquainted with the fathers. It is true that at the time of the Tepehuán revolt the chief and archrebel Cogoxito had taken refuge, as we have seen, in their defiles whither he had driven cattle and sheep stolen from the Spaniards. Although some of the Humis harbored Cogoxito, it does not appear that the Humi nation in general favored the revolt. Indeed, although the Tepehuán chiefs tried to corrupt these people, they met with no success, the Humis remaining loyal in their friendship for the fathers. Repulsed here, certain rebel Tepehuanes, fleeing the wrath of Governor de Alvear, migrated as far south as the Nayarit country, here to seek shelter in the natural fortresses of this last stronghold of paganism. Captain Bartolomé de Arisbaba was sent after them by the Governor.[16]

As the Humis' desire for Christianity continued to increase, they did of their own accord what they knew would hasten the coming of fathers among them: they descended from their summits and formed two pueblos, called Humase and Guarisamey. Then in 1627 or a little later they took the very direct step of sending a delegation to Father Nicolás de Estrada, Superior at Durango, and to the Provincial, Father Gerónimo Díaz, who was visiting the capital. They begged that missionaries might now enter their country because of the settlements they had made where the padres might easily reach them and instruct them. Their wishes were partly fulfilled in 1630 when Father Estrada was able, taking time from his duties as rector at Durango, to pay them temporary visits and baptize a few of their infants. When Floriano de Ayerve, former missionary in Topia, became Provincial in 1633, he ordered the well-tried Pedro de Gravina to go permanently among them.[17]

Gravina had been working among the Xiximes at the pueblo called Santa María de Otaés, where he had built a church. He left at the call of obedience, his place filled by Diego Ximenes, and, traveling over most difficult country, came to the land of the Humis. The padre began his labors with baptizing many of the children of the nation. But the fatigue was too great for his aging years. He fell ill and died in the high country of the Humis on January 17, 1634. His dying request was that his body be taken across the mountains, a journey of two and a half days, to his old pueblo of Santa María de Otaés, that there, under the protecting eye of God's Mother, to whom during life he had shown so great a devotion, his bones might quietly be laid to rest.[18]

Ximenes was now sent to the Humis, Francisco Serrano succeeding him at Santa María. The new missionary followed in the footsteps of his illustrious predecessor and, not satisfied with the baptism of those already gathered into pueblos, sought out the scattered sheep in the declivities and defiles of their mountains. After renaming the old pueblos of Humase and Guarisamey, San Bartolomé and San Pedro respectively, and polishing off the work of Gravina, he went over some rough country south to the headwaters of the Río del Presidio, which drops into the Pacific near Mazatlán. Here he was able to gather two hundred and fifty savages, many of them not of the Humi nation, and begin with these the work of evangelization. Six or seven months were spent in making a path to this sequestered spot, and when it was completed there were places difficult even for the sure foot of a mule. A pueblo was formed, and the padre called it San Pablo because it was thirty miles from San Pedro Guarisamey. Among these mountains Father Ximenes had a long and indeed an isolated career; his was the most southerly position during this whole century of all the Jesuit mission system. In 1644 he was still laboring among his Humis and their isolated and ragged neighbors.[19]

Thus were the mountain missions to the south rounded out among the Hinas and the Humis, cognate to the Xixime nation. There had been some trouble with the Hinas, and near-rebellion; even among the seemingly milder and more friendly Humis an old spark from the former fires to the north still glimmered. A Tepehuán tried to corrupt these Humis, as one of this difficult tribe had endeavored to corrupt the Hinas, and Father Ximenes was for a while troubled. But the danger passed and his continued success was as great as the earlier friendliness of the Humis had given promise.

EPILOGUE

Thus was the Jesuit mission system of Northwestern Mexico rounded out east of the Sierra Madre and in the mountains themselves to the north of Durango and to the west. With Durango as the hub and center, what we may call a mother house, the Indian pueblos were organized into four missions: that of Parras, taking care of the Laguneros assembled in five main pueblos and many *visitas;* that of the Tepehuanes, in five chief pueblos; that of Topia, taking care of the Acaxée Indians; and that of San Andrés, engaged with the Xiximes. While all the missions had many visitas, the main pueblos of these last two missions do not stand out so distinctly in these early decades of their history. Among the Acaxées may be mentioned chiefly Topia, Tamazula, and Otatitlán; among the Xiximes south were Santa María de Otaés, Guarisamey, and Yamoriba. The Jesuits were aided in Topia, and in certain towns of the valley of Durango like San Juan del Río, by Franciscan missionaries, whose great system extended north and east of the Jesuit territory.[1] Later the missions became more closely organized into *partidos* consisting of pueblos and visitas, each unit designated with the name of a saint.

As the decades passed, the missions grew in personnel as they expanded in extent. Parras early had the largest number of missionaries, possessing in 1604 six fathers, while at this time Topia and San Andrés together (they were counted as one this early date) had only four, and the Tepehuanes had four.[2] Parras maintained her six until 1612, when she lost one while the others were augmented. Topia and San Andrés had six the following year. The Tepehuanes had five in 1610, and Topia and San Andrés each six. When the revolt broke out in 1616, the Tepehuanes were enjoying seven, and at the end of that year only one!—But revival was speedy and by 1624 the Tepehuán mission had again seven missionaries.[3]

The missions of the lagoons, however, were destined to suffer a diminution. Under the Benedictine, Fray Francisco de Quintanilla Evía y Valdés, third of the long line of the bishops of Durango, the missions of the Laguneros, all except Parras, were taken from the Jesuits in 1646 and given over to the diocesan clergy. The successors to the Black

---

[1] For notes to Epilogue see page 217.

Robe were not so skillful nor so energetic, and there was grief among the fathers still resident in Parras to see along the broad plains of the lagoon the work of half a century dissipate and slowly disappear. But the Jesuits remained at Parras and the Indians here were cared for and a college in the forming city took care of the Spanish youth.⁴ A college did the same in Durango.

The Tepehuán mission continued advancing northward on the eastern slope of the Sierra Madre up to the edge of the Tepehuán nation, the Valle de San Pablo, and beyond. Father Juan de Sanguessa paid a brief visit to the Valle shortly after 1616. He returned in 1630, and, following Juan Fonte's example, he made contact with the Tarahumares who were asking for Black Robe missionaries.⁵ San Miguel de las Bocas was founded, and Tepehuán mission history begins to blend with Tarahumar. When mines were opened up in 1631 at Parral and the town sprang up as the result of another gold rush, the spiritual advance northward was facilitated and speeded. By 1632 the Jesuit missionary was laboring in and about Parral. Juan de Heredia and Gabriel Díaz came to the pleasant banks of the Río Florido, and in 1639 the lower Tarahumar mission was formally organized by Andrés Pérez de Ribas, then Provincial in Mexico City.⁶ The Tarahumar missions would continue to advance north and northwest through all the Tarahumar country up to the Jovas and the Opatas near Kino's land, where the mountains straggle and lose their altitude. Here the eastern missions will blend at the end of the seventeenth century with the West Coast system begun on the Sinaloa by Gonzalo de Tapia in 1591. Kino will carry them farther north to the Colorado and the Gila, to the very gates of Alta California.

APPENDIX

A PARTIAL LIST of Jesuits laboring in the missions of Durango in 1625, with the number of baptized to which they ministered, according to a contemporary report,* follows:

Topia

Guillermo de San Clemente 300
Bartolomé Toledano 381

Indé

Nicolás de Estrada
Guillermo de Solier . . . . 514 (for both)

Santa Catalina

Andrés López
Padre Burgos . . . . 634 (for both)

Guanaceví

Martín Larios
José de Lomas . . . . 264 (for both)

Parras y La Laguna

Alonso Gómez de Cervantes
Mateo de Castro Verde
Martín de Egurrola
Diego de Quellar
Miguel Vernon
Martín Brizuela . . . . 1,569 (for all)

San Andrés y San Hipólito

Diego de Cueto
Juan de Mallen
Pedro Gravina
Juan del Castillo . . . . 5,380 (for all)

Two Franciscans were working likewise in Topia with 384 neophytes, in the Valle de San Bartolomé with 1,003, in Sauceda with 317, and also in Cuencamé, San Juan del Río, San Francisco de Mezquital, Guazamota, and in Durango itself.

---

* *Razon y minuta de los Yndios que se administran en las provincias de la nueba Vizcaia Por los Vicarios Veneficiados y relixiosos de San Francisco y compañia de Jesus que hoy estan bautizados* (1625). Cf. Bandelier-Hackett, *Historical Documents* . . . , II, 152 ff.

ESSAY ON SOURCES

THE CHIEF SOURCES for the history of the Jesuit missions of the west coast of North America are, as would be expected, the annual letters which were written by the missionaries each year to their superiors. Not only did each missionary, living miles out by himself or with a companion, write in to his local superior, but also the local superior each year wrote in to the general superior of all the Province of New Spain, the Father Provincial resident in Mexico City. The local superior would make a summary of the reports sent in to him by his men dispersed far and wide, or quite often, if the report was interesting or important enough, he would make a transcript of the entire letter. The Provincial, in his turn, would make and send to Rome a digest of all of this—a digest, that is, not only of the mission reports, but also of the reports coming in to the capital of Mexico from all the Jesuit houses of New Spain. Sometimes long individual letters from the superior or a member of a particular urban community or from a missionary would be incorporated into these final reports. A copy, of course, would be kept in Mexico City. The result for history is that there are two large collections of these annual letters, called in Latin *litterae annuae,* in Spanish *cartas anuas,* and ordinarily referred to simply as the *anuas.* One collection is now in the Archivo General de la Nación in Mexico City and the other, far more complete, is in the Roman archives in Europe. Included among the documents in Mexico City are volumes labeled *MS. ant.* (i.e., *Manuscritos antiguos*). There is also, in Berkeley, the rich Bolton collection of manuscript and printed sources.

Of the cartas anuas various manuscript copies have for long been in the possession of the Bancroft Library of the University of California, while a few have been printed and published and are likewise in the possession of the University. The most important collection at the Bancroft Library is of the Roman archives, for they are more complete both with respect to the years reported and the fullness of the reports. The photostats were acquired by Dr. Bolton for his collection through personal research in the archives of Europe. For our story of the pioneer Jesuits in northern Mexico we have in this collection the anuas from 1594 to 1628, except the years 1607, 1608, 1613, 1619–1621, 1623, 1626, and 1627. Most of these anuas contain something about the missions east of the Sierra Madre, and many of them contain very much. The advantage of having the whole anua is that the introduction to each, after that of 1600, indicates the number of missionaries at each mission.

Manuscript copies from the Mexican archives of those parts of the anuas which relate to the missions are contained in the *Memorias para la historia de la Provincia Sinaloa;* but those relating to the Durango missions are far from complete. There are those from 1595 to 1598; then only those of 1601, 1607, and 1618. In the *Archivo General y Público de la Nación, Misiones,* Vol. 25, are contained excerpts from the anuas of those portions touching the missions. Here may be found material for the eastern missions in the anuas continuously from 1622 to 1631.

That part of the Jesuit Archives of the Province of New Spain which is now in Ysleta, Texas, contains some valuable material, including a collection of letters of the Fathers-General from Aquaviva to Nickel, and other letters and notices of missionaries. A few notices have been taken from the *Archivo General de Indias,* from the Bancroft Library transcripts.

The printed sources are almost equally important. The first is, of course, Andrés Pérez de Ribas' *Los triumphos de nuestra Santa Fee,* published in Madrid, 1645. The second part of his monumental work, chapters viii to xi, deals with the missions having their center of administration at Durango. Ribas was not an eyewitness to the events here related, as he was to many of the happenings in the missions of the west coast; but he was a contemporary, indeed he was working just over the mountains during a large part of the time included in our story. He passed through the eastern section just before the revolt, and again soon after the trouble had started. When in 1638 he became Provincial of the whole Province of New Spain he enjoyed an unrivaled opportunity of getting at past and contemporary documents. This explains the abundance of actual sources he incorporated into his chapters: letters, namely, of the missionaries themselves. Without Ribas at hand this present volume would have lost much of its substance and entertainment.

Francisco Javier Alegre with his three volumes entitled *Historia de la Compañía de Jesús en Nueva España* comes next in importance, though he must be considered only as a secondary source. He was one of the *expulsos* of 1767 and was at that time engaged in his duties. He wrote therefore a century and a half after the events narrated in these pages. But he had handled and checked most of the documents, and, like Ribas, he often includes entire letters or parts of letters of missionaries in his pages. He has been able here and there to compare Ribas and correct him.

An exceedingly interesting printed source is a book in German published in Augsburg in 1611 by Chrysostomo Dabertzhofer. Its main title is *Drey neue Relationes,* or Three New Narratives, and it concerns the activities of the Jesuit missionaries in different parts of the world. The narratives are made up of letters of the missionaries themselves written from

ESSAY ON SOURCES 191

Japan, Mexico, and India, and this gives the book its value. The publisher, Dabertzhofer, after a long and stately dedication in the preface to the Cathedral Chapter of Augsburg, explains earnestly how these letters of missionaries have been carefully translated into German by scholarly and reliable gentlemen from letters originally written in Latin, Spanish, and Portuguese. These published letters remind one strongly of the *Lettres édifiantes* coming some years later from the French missionaries in Canada and published in Paris by Cramoisy. The Dabertzhofer publication attests the universal interest existing in the Old World in the spread of the Faith in the New.

It is the second part of the *Drey neue Relationes* which is of importance for the Durango missions. The title to this part is as follows: *Andere von Missionibus oder Reisen so etliche Priester der Societet Jesu im Jar 1607, in das Königreich Mexico angestelt.* These letters cover all the Durango missions for the year 1607, for there is a report about conditions in the Parras missions written certainly by the superior which includes a letter of Diego de Pangua; there is a report concerning the northern Tepehuanes in a letter of Juan Fonte. But the larger part of these narratives concerns the missions of Topia and San Andrés. It includes a long narrative from the superior Alonzo Ruiz and three most interesting and informative letters written to him by his subjects dispersed far and wide in this rugged field: Gonzales Cueto writes from the Sobaibos, Gerónimo de San Clemente from Tamazula, and Floriano de Ayerve from Baimoa and Carantapa. This printed source, therefore, is rich indeed and the best we have for the year 1607.

Of capital importance for the revolt itself and of its immediate results is a portion of the Bandelier Documents: Bandelier, Adolph F. A. and Fanny R., *Historical Documents Relating to New Mexico, Nueva Vizcaya and Approaches Thereto, to 1773*, 3 vols., edited by Charles Wilson Hackett, Washington, D. C., Carnegie Institution of Washington, 1923 et seqq. Of the five pieces pertinent to our present story contained in Vol. II of this work the chief is the following: *Relacion breve y succinta de los sucesos que ha tenido la guerra de los Tepehuanes de la gubernacion de la Nueva Vizcaya desde 15 de Noviembre de 1616 hasta 16 de Mayo de 1618.* This is the best and most detailed account we have of the developments in and about Durango during the rebellion. It confirms and completes Ribas and the anuas. Its author is not known. Of the remaining documents, three are official reports of the state of Durango and of the province of Nueva Vizcaya under the regime of the new governor of Nueva Vizcaya, the *Almirante* Mateo de Vesga, who succeeded Gaspar de Alvear late in 1620. The last of the five offers lists and statistics of missions and missionaries. The full titles of these latter documents will be found in the notes to chapter xviii of the present work.

With regard to the Franciscans and their early foundations in the Durango and Parras country, José Arlegui in his *Crónica de la Provincia de N. S. P. S. Francisco de Zacatecas* (Mexico, 1851) holds even a more singular importance than Alegre does for the Jesuits; the sources of early Franciscan history being more scarce, Arlegui becomes indispensable for some of the earlier details of Franciscan mission founding.

Finally there are the *Documentos para la historia de Mexico* in four series, each except the third containing several small volumes. Of these, several volumes of the fourth series contain some excellent source material, including many anuas, which, however, may be found in the other collections. The *Documentos para la historia ecclesiastica y civil de la Nueva Vizcaya* repeats many of the sources contained in the *Documentos para la historia de Mexico,* but offers also some new material, which, however, is mostly after our period.

Snatches of information may be found in Ribas' *Corónica* and in Florencia's *Menologio,* as also in Tanner's *Societas Jesu* and Neumann's *Historia Seditionum.* In short, the biography of the Tepehuán martyrs is multiplied as well in the secondary as in the primary sources, but one account adds little to another, and a large part is often of little historical value, being taken up with their religious virtues, the miracles alleged to have been worked at their intercession, and with similar notices of edification according to the pietistic and often uncritical methods of seventeenth-century hagiography.

BIBLIOGRAPHY

Manuscript Sources

Letters and anuas from 1593 to 1650 in six main collections:
The Roman Archives of Europe.
Archivo General y Público de la Nación, Misiones, Vols. 25 and 26.
Memorias para la historia de la Provincia de Sinaloa.
The Bancroft Library.
The Edward E. Ayer Collection, Newberry Library, Chicago.
The W. B. Stephens Collection, Mexico.

Printed Sources and Early Treatises

Alegre, Francisco Javier, S.J. *Historia de la Compañía de Jesús en Nueva España,* 3 vols., México, 1841.

Arlegui, José. *Crónica de la Provincia de N. S. P. S. Francisco de Zacatecas,* México, 1851.

Bandelier, A. F. and Fanny R. *Historical Documents Relating to New Mexico, Nueva Vizcaya and Approaches Thereto, to 1773,* 3 vols., ed. Charles Wilson Hackett, Carnegie Institution, Washington, 1923 et seqq.

Dabertzhofer, Chrysostomo. *Drey neue Relationes,* Augsburg, 1611.

Documentos para de la historia de México, 20 vols., México, 1853–1857.

Drews, Joannes, S.J. *Fasti Societatis Jesu,* Pragae, 1750.

Florencia, Francisco de, S.J.: *Historia de la Provincia de la Compañía de Jesús de Nueva España,* México, 1694.

Neumann, Joseph, S.J. *Historia Seditionum quas Adversus Societatis Jesu Missionarios eorum. Auxiliares Moverunt Nationes Indicae ac Potissimum Tarahumara in America Septentrionali Regnoque Novae Cantabriae,* Pragae, 1730.

Pérez de Ribas, Andrés. *Historia de los triumphos de nuestra Santa Fee entre gentes los mas barbaros y fieras del Nuevo Orbe,* Madrid, 1645.

———. *Corónica y historia religiosa de la Provincia de la Compañía de Jesús de México en la Nueva España,* México, 1896.

Recopilación de leyes de los reynos de las Indias, 3 vols., Madrid, 1791.

Tanner, Mathias. *Societas Jesu usque ad Sanguinis et Vitae Profusionem Militans in Europa, Asia, Africa et America contra Gentiles Mahometanos, Judaeos, Haereticos, Impios pro Deo, Ecclesia, Pietate,* Pragae, 1675.

Thwaites, Reuben Gold. *The Jesuit Relations and Allied Documents,* 71 vols., Cleveland, 1896.

Urdiñola, Francisco de. *Información hecha por el Gobernador Urdiñola cerca del estado de la Provincia de Sinaloa,* ed. J. Lloyd Mecham, in *New Spain and the Anglo-American West,* 2 vols., ed. George P. Hammond, privately printed, 1932.

SECONDARY WORKS

Astrain, Antonio, S.J. *Historia de la Compañía de Jesús en la Asistencia de España,* 7 vols., Madrid, 1902.

Bancroft, Hubert Howe. *History of Mexico,* 5 vols., San Francisco, 1883.

———. *The North Mexican States and Texas,* 3 vols., San Francisco, 1884.

Bandelier, A. F. *Final Reports of Investigations among the Indians of the Southwestern United States,* 2 vols., *Papers of the Archeological Institute of America, American Series,* Cambridge, 1890.

Barlow, R. H., and George T. Smisor, *Nombre de Dios, Durango: Two Documents in Náhuatl Concerning Its Foundation,* The House of Tlaloc, Sacramento, 1943.

Bennett, Wendell C., and Robert M. Zingg. *The Tarahumara, an Indian Tribe of Northern Mexico,* University of Chicago Press, 1935.

Bishop, Morris. *The Odyssey of Cabeza de Vaca,* The Century Co., New York, 1933.

Bogan, Phebe M. *Yaqui Indian Dances of Tucson, Arizona,* The Archeological Society, Tucson, 1925.

Bolton, Herbert Eugene. *Guide to the Materials for the History of the United States in the Principal Archives of Mexico,* Carnegie Institution, Washington, 1913.

———. *The Spanish Borderlands,* Yale University Press, New Haven, 1921.

———. *Rim of Christendom,* The Macmillan Co., New York, 1936.

Bolton, Herbert Eugene, and Thomas Maitland Marshall. *The Colonization of North America, 1492-1783,* The Macmillan Co., New York, 1925.

Campbell, Thomas J., S.J. *The Jesuits,* Encyclopedia Press, New York, 1921.

Chapman, Charles Edward. *Colonial Hispanic America: A History,* The Macmillan Co., New York, 1933.

———. *The Founding of Spanish California,* The Macmillan Co., New York, 1916.

BIBLIOGRAPHY 195

Chapman, Charles Edward. *A History of California: The Spanish Period*, The Macmillan Co., New York, 1930.

Cook, S. F. *The Extent and Significance of Disease among the Indians of Baja California, 1697–1773, Ibero-Americana:* 12, University of California Press, Berkeley, 1937.

Crétineau-Joly, J. *Histoire religieuse, politique et littéraire de la Compagnie de Jésus*, 3 vols., Paris, 1844–1845.

Cuevas, Mariano, S.J. *Historia de la Iglesia en México*, 5 vols., Revista Catolica Press, El Paso, Texas, 1928.

Cunningham, Charles H. *The Audiencia in the Spanish Colonies as Illustrated by the Audiencia of Manila*, University of California Press, Berkeley, 1919.

De Anda, F. Ibarra. *Geonimia indígena mexicana*, México, 1932.

Decorme, Gerardo, S.J. *La obra de los Jesuitas mexicanos durante la época colonial, 1572–1767*, 2 vols., México, 1941.

Fisher, Lillian E. *The Intendant System in Spanish America*, University of California Press, Berkeley, 1929.

Flores, Francisco A. *Historia de la medicina en México desde la época de los Indios hasta la presente*, 3 vols., México, 1886–1888.

Huonder, Anton. *Deutsche Jesuitenmissionäre des 17. und 18. Jahrhunderts*, Freiburg-im-Breisgau, 1899.

Jacobsen, Jerome V. *Educational Foundations of the Jesuits in Sixteenth-Century New Spain*, University of California Press, Berkeley, 1938.

Kenny, Michael, S.J. *The Romance of the Floridas*, Bruce Publishing Co., Milwaukee, 1934.

Kenton, Edna. *The Jesuit Relations and Allied Documents*, Albert and Charles Boni, New York, 1925.

Kroeber, A. L. *Uto-Aztecan Languages of Mexico*, University of California Press, Berkeley, 1934.

Lanning, John Tate. *The Spanish Missions of Georgia*, University of North Carolina Press, Chapel Hill, 1935.

Mecham, J. Lloyd. *Francisco de Ibarra and Nueva Vizcaya*, Duke University Press, Durham, North Carolina, 1927.

Mendoza y Herrera, Francisco. *Constitutiones del M. I. y V. Cabildo Metropolitano de Durango*, Durango, 1920.

Merriman, Roger Bigelow. *The Rise of the Spanish Empire in the Old World and in the New*, 4 vols., The Macmillan Co., New York, 1913 , et seqq.

Moses, Bernard. *The Spanish Dependencies in South America,* 2 vols., Harper and Bros., New York, 1914.

Orozco y Berra, Manuel. *Apuntes para la historia de la geografía en México,* México, 1881.

Paxson, Frederic L. *History of the American Frontier,* Houghton Mifflin Co., Boston, 1924.

Pierson, William Whatley, Jr. *Hispanic-American History: A Syllabus,* University of North Carolina Press, Chapel Hill, 1926.

Priestley, Herbert Ingram. *The Coming of the White Man, 1492–1848,* The Macmillan Co., New York, 1929.

———. *The Mexican Nation: A History,* The Macmillan Co., New York, 1930.

Rippy, J. Fred. *Historical Evolution of Hispanic America,* F. S. Crofts and Co., New York, 1932.

Robles, Vito Alessio. *Francisco de Urdiñola y el Norte de la Nueva España,* México, 1931.

Saravia, Atansio G., *Apuntes para la historia de la Nueva Vizcaya,* México, 1941.

Sauer, Carl. *The Distribution of Aboriginal Tribes and Languages in Northwestern Mexico,* University of California Press, Berkeley, 1934.

Sauer, Carl, and Donald Brand. *Aztatlán: Prehistoric Mexican Frontier on the Pacific Coast,* University of California Press, Berkeley, 1932.

Schmitt, Ludovicus, S.J. *Synopsis Historiae Societatis Jesu,* Ratisbonae, 1914.

Shea, John Gilmary. *History of the Catholic Missions among the Indian Tribes of the United States,* J. P. Kenedy, New York, 1881.

Shiels, W. Eugene, S.J. *Gonzalo de Tapia,* United States Catholic Historical Society, New York, 1934.

Simpson, Lesley B. *Encomienda in New Spain in the Sixteenth Century,* University of California Press, Berkeley, 1929.

Smith, Donald E. *The Viceroy of New Spain,* University of California Press, Berkeley, 1913.

Sommervogel, Carlos, S.J. *Bibliothèque de la Compagnie de Jésus,* 11 vols., Paris, 1890.

Stephens, H. Morse, and Herbert E. Bolton. *The Pacific Ocean in History,* The Macmillan Co., New York, 1917.

Tannenbaum, Frank. *Peace by Revolution*, Columbia University Press, New York, 1933.

Thurston, Herbert, S.J. *The Church and Spiritualism*, Bruce Publishing Co., Milwaukee, 1933.

Valle, Rafael Heliodoro. *El Convento de Tepotzotlán*, México, 1924.

Winsor, Justin. *Narrative and Critical History of America*, 8 vols., Houghton Mifflin and Co., Boston, 1889.

Wyllys, Rufus Kay. *Pioneer Padre: The Life and Times of Francisco Eusebio Kino*, Southwestern Press, Dallas, 1935.

Zambrano, F., S.J. *La Companía de Jésus en México: Compendio histórico*, México, 1939.

RECENT MANUSCRIPTS

McShane, Catherine M. *Hernando de Santarén*. University of California Library, Berkeley.

Treutlein, Theodore Edward. *Jesuit Travel to America, 1678-1756*. University of California Library, Berkeley.

NOTES

Abbreviations Used in the Notes

Archiv. Gen. Hist.—	*Archivo General, Historia*
Archiv. Gen. Mis.—	*Archivo General, Misiones*
Archiv. S.J. Roman.—	*Archivum Societatis Jesu Romanum*
Decorme—	*La obra de los Jesuítas . . .*
Doc. Hist. Mex.—	*Documentos para la historia de México*
Memorias—	*Memorias para la historia de la Provincia de Sinaloa*
MS. ant.—	*Manuscritos antiguos*
Ribas—	*Historia de los triumphos . . .*
Alegre—	*Historia de la Compañía de Jesús en la Nueva España*

Ribas has been cited according to book and chapter; Alegre according to volume and page, and so with the other authors generally, unless otherwise indicated.

CHAPTER I: THE COMING OF THE BLACK ROBE

[1] Chapman, *Colonial Hispanic America*, pp. 77 ff.
[2] Astrain, II, 305 ff.
[3] Alegre, I, 4.
[4] Cf. Michael Kenny, S.J., *The Romance of the Floridas*, and John Tate Lanning, *The Spanish Missions of Georgia*.
[5] Kenny, *op. cit.*, chap. xvi.
[6] Alegre, I, 44.
[7] *Ibid.*, p. 45.
[8] *Ibid.*
[9] Neumann, *Historia Seditionum*. . . , chap. ii; Wyllys, *Pioneer Padre*, pp. 16 ff.; Bolton, *Rim of Christendom*, pp. 21 ff.
[10] Alegre, I, 48.
[11] Jacobsen, *Educational Foundations of the Jesuits in Sixteenth-Century New Spain*, chaps. v ff.

CHAPTER II: THE PERMANENT MISSIONS

[1] Also called Jacques de Sores. Cf. James A. Williamson, *Sir John Hawkins: The Time and the Man*, Oxford, Clarendon Press, 1927.
[2] Kenny, *The Romance of the Floridas*, pp. 263 f.
[3] Schmitt, *Synopsis Historiae Societatis Jesu*, col. 65.
[4] *Anua* of 1595 in MS. ant., II.
[5] Schmitt, *op. cit.*, col. 89.
[6] *Ibid.*, col. 105.
[7] *Ibid.*
[8] *Ibid.*
[9] Shiels, *Gonzalo de Tapia*.
[10] *Ibid.*, chap. v.
[11] Not to be confounded with the Chichimecos farther north.
[12] The final year of a Jesuit's formation, devoted entirely to his spiritual completion.
[13] Shiels, *op. cit.*, chap. vi.
[14] *Ibid.*
[15] *Ibid.*, chaps. vii and viii.
[16] Dunne, *Pioneer Black Robes on the West Coast*.
[17] *Anua* of 1625, *Memorias*, p. 710.
[18] *Archiv. Gen. Mis.*, t. 25, p. 270.
[19] Ribas, *Corónica*, epilogue.
[20] Shiels, *op. cit.*, and Dunne, *op. cit.*
[21] *The Missions and Missionaries of California*, Vol. I.
[22] *Rim of Christendom*.

CHAPTER III: EAST OF THE MOUNTAINS

[1] Bancroft, *North Mexican States and Texas*, I, 99 ff.
[2] Mecham, *Francisco de Ibarra and Nueva Vizcaya*, p. 123.
[3] *Ibid.*, chap. iv.
[4] Hammond and Rey, *Obregon's History*, pp. 58 f.

[5] Arlegui, *Crónica de la Provincia de N. S. P. S. Francisco de Zacatecas*, p. 33; *Doc. Hist. Mex.*, 3d ser., p. 344.
[6] Mecham, *op. cit.*, p. 184.
[7] *Ibid.*, p. 235.
[8] Bancroft, *op. cit.*, I, 116 and n. 45.
[9] *Doc. Hist. Mex.*, 3d ser., p. 344.
[10] *Anua* of 1599, *Memorias*, p. 157; *anua* of 1601, *Memorias*, p. 342.
[11] Arlegui, *op. cit.*, pp. 59 and 72.
[12] Ribas, IX, 1.
[13] Bancroft, *op. cit.*, I, 118.
[14] Arlegui, *op. cit.*, p. 211.
[15] Alegre, I, 268; *Memorias*, p. 817, which contains the introduction for that part of the anuas which pertains to Guadiana or Durango. This latter is evidently copied, sometimes word for word, from Alegre. Alegre, or his publisher, here falls into a curious error. He twice mentions Martín Pérez instead of Martín Peláez. Pérez was in Sinaloa and made no visit to Durango in 1593, though Tapia the year before visited Topia. The mistake becomes evident when Alegre finally gives the name of Peláez. The *Memorias* copies Alegre's blunder.
[16] Alegre, *loc. cit.*
[17] *Ibid.*
[18] *Anua* of 1595, *Memorias*, p. 821.

CHAPTER IV: THE MISSIONS OF THE LAGOON

[1] *Constitutiones del M. I. y V. Cabildo Metropolitano de Durango*, p. 22.
[2] Durango never became a great city. As late as 1777 only 6,590 persons were living within its limits and 12,774 in its vicinity. Cf. *Doc. Hist. Mex.*, 3d ser., p. 344.
[3] Mecham, *Francisco de Ibarra and Nueva Vizcaya*, pp. 230 f.
[4] Alegre, I, 226 f.
[5] Mecham, *op. cit.*, pp. 62 f., referring to Bernardino de Sahagún, *Historia general de las cosas de Nueva España*, III, 133.
[6] Arlegui, *Crónica*, p. 72.
[7] Ribas, XI, 3; Decorme, II, 17. Bancroft, *North Mexican States and Texas*, I, 125 and 311, says that the Ramírez working among the Laguneros was Francisco, but the sources refer consistently to Gerónimo.
[8] Ribas, XI, chap. i.
[9] The letter is to be found in Ribas, XI, 3, and in Alegre, I, 284 f. Alegre had the document either from the *anua* of that year or from Ribas.
[10] Ribas, XI, 4; Alegre, I, 285 f.
[11] Decorme, II, 20, note, correctly confutes a local tradition according to which the first Mass was supposed to have been said on August 15 at Parras in a cave named Texcalco.
[12] Alegre, I, 286.
[13] Ribas, XI, 4; Alegre, *loc. cit.*
[14] *Anua* of 1593, *Memorias*, p. 29.
[15] *Archiv. Gen. Mis.*, t. 25, p. 385, where the terms "blandura y affabilidad" are used.
[16] Bishop, *The Odyssey of Cabeza de Vaca*, Part I, chap. xi.
[17] *Apuntes para la historia de la geografía en México*, map.
[18] *Anua* of 1595, *Memorias*, p. 821.

[19] Ribas, XI, 5.
[20] Ribas, XI, 1. The traditional date of the first Franciscan mission is April 1, 1578. "La cueva de Texcalco" (Cave of Texcalco), where the first Mass is supposed to have been celebrated by the Jesuits on August 15, 1594, pierces a rough cliff of rock which rises about a mile south of Parras. The cave is still honored as the place where Parras was born, and a cross, decorated with shrubs and flowers, hallows the interior.
[21] *Ibid.* But our historian is manifestly mistaken when he gives the distance as only thirty leagues.
[22] *Memorias,* p. 823.
[23] Ribas, XI, 2.
[24] *Ibid.*
[25] *Anua* of 1595, *Memorias,* p. 822.
[26] *Anua* of 1596, *Memorias,* pp. 842 f.
[27] *Doc. Hist. Mex.,* 3d ser., pp. 390 ff.
[28] Alegre, I, 371; Decorme, II, 20.
[29] Decorme, II, 24. Dabertzhofer, *Drey neue Relationes,* Parras relation, pp. 82 ff.
[30] Ribas, XI, 10.
[31] Ribas, *loc. cit.,* insists that these ought to be called nations because of differences in language and habit. Another narrative (*Doc. Hist. Mex.,* 3d ser., pp. 390 ff.) gives the tribes of the lagoon country as follows: Auritilas, Mamazorras, Neguales, Salineros, Baxameros, Laguneros, and Cabezos.
[32] *Anua* of 1598, *Memorias,* pp. 862 ff., where the long letter of Juan Agustín is given. Ribas, XI, 10, mentions this dance, but gives it as of 1607.
[33] Cf. *Recopilación de leyes de los reynos de las Indias,* Madrid, 1791, t. 2, lib. vi, tit. vii, "De los caciques," pp. 245 ff.
[34] *Anua* of 1598, *Memorias,* p. 882.
[35] *Ibid.,* p. 883.
[36] *Ibid.,* and Ribas, XI, 24; Alegre, I, 371 f.

CHAPTER V: THE TEPEHUANES

[1] Ribas, X, 1. Cf. also the maps of Orozco y Berra, *Apuntes para la historia de la geografía de México,* and of Sauer, *The Distribution of Aboriginal Tribes in Northwestern Mexico.*
[2] Dabertzhofer, *Drey neue Relationes,* Tepehuán relation.
[3] Ribas, X, 1; *anua* of 1596, *Memorias,* p. 823.
[4] *Anua* of 1596, *Memorias, loc. cit.*
[5] Bancroft, *North Mexican States and Texas,* I, 311, speaks of a Francisco Ramírez at Parras and of a Gerónimo Ramírez among the Tepehuanes as if they were two different men. But this is a mistake. Gerónimo, at first among the Laguneros with Juan Agustín de Espinosa, was later sent to the Tepehuanes, leaving Juan Agustín alone at Parras. Cf. n. 7 to chap. iv, above.
[6] Alegre, I, 320.
[7] *Anua* of 1596, *Memorias,* p. 824.
[8] Alegre, *loc. cit.;* Ribas, X, 2; *anua* of 1596, *Memorias,* p. 823. Ribas gives the name without the date, the *anua* gives the date without the name. Both the one and the other are found in Alegre.
[9] "Mexicanos" was the name given to the Indians of south-central Mexico, their language being one of the Aztec dialects. Cf. Sauer, *op. cit.,* pp. 1 f. and 5 f.

[10] Alegre, *loc. cit.;* Ribas, X, 2.
[11] *Anua* of 1596, *Memorias,* p. 830.
[12] Alegre, *loc. cit.*
[13] Alegre, I, 321.
[14] Ribas, X, 2.
[15] *Ibid.*
[16] Cf. Herbert Thurston, S.J., *Spiritualism and the Church, passim.*
[17] Cf. *Rituale romanum,* ed. Pustet, Ratisbonae, 1888, tit. x, ch. i, "De exorcizandis obsessis a daemonio."
[18] *Psychic Phenomena of Jamaica, passim.*
[19] Celestine Capsner, O.S.B., *Begone Satan! A Soul-stirring Account of Diabolical Possession,* published by the author at St. John's Abbey, Collegeville, Minn.
[20] Ribas, II, 27.
[21] Ribas, II, 30.
[22] Ribas, V, 18.
[23] Cf. Carlos Sommervogel, *Bibliothèque de la Compagnie de Jésus,* II, 1894 ff. The first edition of Delrío's work appeared in 1599, entitled *Disquisitionum magicarum libri sex in tres tomos partiti,* Louvain, 1599. Edition after edition appeared: 1601, 1603, 1606, etc.
[24] Cf. H. C. Lea, *Materials towards a History of Witchcraft,* II, 640 ff.
[25] This is the story as given in our primary source, the annual letters. It is found in the *anua* of 1596, *Memorias,* pp. 825 ff. But the *anua* mentions no miracle in connection with the conversion of the hechicero, whereas both Ribas and Alegre mention a marvelous happening, each telling a different story! Ribas, X, 2, says the wizard came to ask for baptism because he was struck with a sudden fever at night; Alegre, I, 323, says he was attacked by a wild beast and appeared the next day covered with blood. But possibly Ribas and Alegre are speaking of another occurrence; indeed, it even appears as if Ribas were making two stories out of one. In X, 2, Ribas writes of a sudden conversion following a sudden fever; in X, 4, he gives the story of the speaking stone as in the *anua.* Both his hechiceros are old and fearsomely respected. As for the details of the wizard's story as given to the missionary, there can be no check upon it. It is very possible that the man drew generously upon his imagination, for reasons that are obvious: the common human inclination toward the marvelous, and the Indians' desire to impress or to please the padre. It is evident that the missionaries took such tales at their face value, and often without that pinch of wisdom which scientific criticism would have given them. For the evils of an experience similar to this hechicero's, cf. J. Godfrey Raupert, *The Dangers of Spiritualism,* London, Kegan Paul, Trench, Trubner and Co., 1906.
[26] *Anua* of 1596, *Memorias,* p. 825.
[27] *Ibid.,* p. 823.
[28] *Ibid.,* p. 838; Ribas, X, 3.
[29] *Anua* of 1597, *Memorias,* pp. 845 ff.
[30] *Ibid.,* p. 848; Alegre, I, pp. 354 ff.
[31] *Anua* of 1597, *Memorias,* p. 851; Ribas, *loc. cit.;* Alegre, *loc. cit.*
[32] *Anua* of 1597, *Memorias,* p. 852.
[33] Ribas, *loc. cit.;* Alegre, *loc. cit.*
[34] *Anua* of 1597, *Memorias,* p. 849. This seems obscure. The Spanish text of the *anua* is the following: "Otros salieron vestidos como demonios tocando cuernos roncos y excribiendo en sus libros con unas hastas de ciervo lo que sirvio de doctrina."
[35] *Anua* of 1597, *Memorias,* pp. 853 ff.; Ribas, *loc. cit.;* Alegre, I, 356.

NOTES

[36] *Archiv. Gen. Mis.*, t. 26, p. 243.
[37] *Anua* of 1596, *Memorias*, p. 838.
[38] Ribas, X, 3.
[39] *Anua* of 1597, *Memorias*, p. 854; *Archiv. Gen. Mis.*, t. 26, p. 243.
[40] *Archiv. Gen. Mis., loc. cit.*
[41] *Anua* of 1597, *Memorias*, p. 856; Alegre, *loc. cit.;* Ribas, *loc. cit.,* where he gives supposedly word for word the speech of the old woman.
[42] *Anua* of 1597, *Memorias*, p. 857; Alegre, *loc. cit.* There is some confusion and obscurity in the sources concerning this celebration. Alegre speaks as if this public celebration were at Santa Catalina, but the *anua* seems clear for Guanaceví. Ribas makes no mention of the northern town in this connection.
[43] *Anua* of 1597, *loc. cit.;* Alegre, *loc. cit.*

CHAPTER VI: THE HEART OF THE SIERRA

[1] Hammond and Rey, *Obregon's History*, p. 59.
[2] Arlegui, *Crónica* ..., pp. 59 and 468. Arlegui here gives the same year for Topia as for Nombre de Dios. Bancroft seems to have confused two dates: when Topia was first started by the Franciscans, and when the house later was given the official status of a convent. Cf. *North Mexican States and Texas*, I, 116 f.
[3] Shiels, *Gonzalo de Tapia*, chap. xiii.
[4] *Ibid.*, and the sources there indicated. Alegre gives a very summary account of this visit. Albizuri, chap. xiii, is more detailed.
[5] Albizuri, MS p. 47. Whether the Franciscans came over from their first foundation of San Pedro y San Pablo, or whether the latter had been abandoned and they came now afresh, we have no means of saying. The available sources are silent on the point.
[6] Ribas, VIII, 2; *anua* of 1610, *Archiv. S.J. Roman.*, fol. 584.
[7] Hammond and Rey, *op. cit.*, p. 67.
[8] Bishop, *The Odyssey of Cabeza de Vaca*, Part II, chap. iii.
[9] Alegre, I, 397.
[10] *Anua* of 1601, *Memorias*, p. 887.
[11] Ribas, VIII, 3; Alegre, I, 398. The *anua* of 1602 and that of 1604 give long accounts of the habits of the Acaxées. Cf. *Archiv. S.J. Roman., Mex.* 14, fols. 31 f. and fols. 381-385.
[12] Ribas, VIII, 18.
[13] Ribas, II, 9.
[14] Alegre, I, 307 f.
[15] Ribas, VIII, 18.
[16] Alegre, I, 354.
[17] *Anua* of 1601, *Memorias*, p. 888, where Nicolás de Arnaya says Santarén had been three years in the mountains of Topia. Decorme, II, 90, says he arrived in 1592.
[18] Ribas, VIII, 4.
[19] *Ibid.*
[20] *Ibid.*
[21] *Doc. Hist. Mex.*, 4th ser., IV, 172-267. The same official account with some slight variations of text may be found in the *Memorias*, pp. 160-340. A fine account of this pueblo founding is given in Catherine M. McShane, "Pueblo Founding in Early Mexico," *Mid-America*, XX (New Ser., IX), No. 1, Jan., 1938, pp. 3 ff. Cf. also, McShane, *Hernando de Santaren*, MS, chap. vii.

[22] *Doc. Hist. Mex., loc. cit.*, pp. 174 ff.
[23] *Ibid.*, pp. 177 ff.
[24] Ribas, VIII, 5.
[25] Decorme, II, 98.
[26] Ribas, VIII, 18.
[27] *Anua* of 1601, *Memorias,* p. 890.
[28] Alegre, I, 393; Ribas, VIII, 6; *anua* of 1601, *Memorias,* p. 885. Alegre is evidently mistaken in saying that they both came in 1602, for the *anua* of 1601 speaks of Ruiz as already working with Santarén. Ribas likewise says Ruiz was the first to come.
[29] Alegre, I, 400.

CHAPTER VII: A MOUNTAIN REVOLT

[1] *Recopilación de Leyes*, t. 2, lib. vi, tit. ii, ley 1; tit. xv, ley 21.
[2] Ribas, VIII, 8; Alegre, I, 403. The latter says concerning the cause of the revolt: "Fifty Indians, either fleeing from maltreatment by the Spaniards, or chafing under the subjection and discipline of the pueblos, fled to different places and stirred up 5,000 to rebellion." The *anua* of 1602 emphasizes the fact that the pride and cruelty of the Spaniards were the cause of the revolt. Cf. *Archiv. S.J. Roman., Mex.* 14, fols. 33 and 349.
[3] *Anua* of 1602, *Archiv. S.J. Roman., Mex.* 14, fol. 33; Alegre, I, 419.
[4] Cf. the more detailed account of this rebellion given by McShane, *Hernando de Santarén*, MS, chap. viii, which has been followed in part.
[5] *Ibid.*
[6] *Anua* of 1600–1602, *Archiv. S.J. Roman., Mex.* 14, fol. 272.
[7] Ribas, IX, 1.
[8] *Anua* of 1600–1602. Three sets of *anuas* tell the story of this attack on the mines. Two of the accounts are the same, one copied from the other with slight change. The original of these may be found in the *anua* of 1602, *Archiv. S.J. Roman., Mex.* 14, fols. 33 ff., which is the fullest account. The other is found *ibid.*, fols. 249 ff. The third narration, the only one which mentions the episode of Ruiz with the crucifix, but which otherwise is shorter, is in the *anua* of 1600–1602, *ibid.*, fols. 292 f. The discrepancies are slight. Ribas, VIII, 8, and Alegre, I, 418 f., are more general, but give a better picture of the whole development. One of the narratives hints that Ruiz' escape was miraculous. We read in the *anua* of 1604: "It was a wonderful thing that though many arrows were aimed at him not a one struck him."—*Archiv. S.J. Roman., Mex.* 14, fol. 385.
[9] *Anua* of 1600–1602, *loc. cit.*, fol. 293; Alegre, I, 420.
[10] McShane, MS, pp. 153 ff.
[11] Ribas, VIII, 9; Alegre, I, 421.
[12] *Anua* of 1600, *Archiv. S.J. Roman., Mex.* 14, fol. 34; *anua* of 1602, *ibid.*, fol. 295; Alegre, I, 422; Ribas, VIII, 9. Ribas and Alegre seem inexact concerning some of the details of the story. Fonte in a letter of May 13 gives the story of the peñol. Cf. Ysleta archives.
[13] *Anua* of 1602, *loc. cit.*, fol. 34.
[14] Alegre, I, 422; Ribas, VIII, 8. Ribas speaks as if this bogus bishop were the sole cause of the rebellion.
[15] Alegre, *loc. cit.*
[16] McShane, MS, p. 164.
[17] *Recopilación*, t. 2, lib. vi, tit. vi, leyes 1, 10, and 14. Titulo vi is entitled: "De los protectores de los Indios."

NOTES 207

[18] Robles, *Francisco de Urdiñola y el Norte de la Nueva España*, p. 284. Alegre, I, 422 f.; Ribas, VIII, 10.
[19] *Archiv. Gen. de Indias*, 66-6-17.
[20] Robles, *op. cit.*, p. 284. The Bishop before returning to Guadalajara paid a visit to the young missions of the Tepehuanes. Cf. Fonte, letter of May 13 from Santiago Papasquiaro, Ysleta archives.

CHAPTER VIII: SUCCESS AMID HARDSHIPS

[1] Alegre, I, 423 f.; Ribas, VIII, 11. Ribas gives the letter word for word; Alegre condenses it. There is a discrepancy, however, in the figures. Alegre gives only 600 as the number of the couples married, while he avers that 1,200 of the baptized received the sacrament before the revolt was over.
[2] *Archiv. Gen. de Indias*, 66-6-17; McShane, *Hernando de Santarén*, MS, p. 200.
[3] Ribas, *loc. cit.; anua* of 1606, *Archiv. S.J. Roman., Mex.* 14, fols. 480 ff., where the letters of Santarén and Ayerve are given.
[4] Alegre, I, 454; Ribas, VIII, 12; Dabertzhofer, *Drey neue Relationes*, pp. 98 ff. Ribas says there were only eight in the mission. Dabertzhofer is an excellent source here, giving letters of Alonzo Ruiz, Cueto, San Clemente, and Ayerve. Both he and Alegre agree on nine.
[5] Alegre, I, 455; Dabertzhofer, *op. cit.,* pp. 99 ff., where Ruiz' letter is given.
[6] Dabertzhofer, pp. 101 ff.
[7] *Anua* of 1606, *Archiv. S.J. Roman., Mex.* 14, fol. 480, where Santarén's letter is given.
[8] *Ibid.*, fols. 482 f., where Ayerve's letter is given.
[9] McShane, MS, p. 201.
[10] Dabertzhofer, pp. 113 ff.
[11] Ribas, VIII, 6, gives part of Ayerve's letter; Dabertzhofer, pp. 113 ff., gives all of it. Cf. also Alegre, I, 458 f. Ayerve was seven years in this mission. He became Provincial in 1632.
[12] Ribas, VIII, 12.
[13] Dabertzhofer, pp. 116 ff.
[14] Ribas, VIII, 15 and 16.
[15] Alegre, I, 460.
[16] *Anua* of 1606, *Archiv. S.J. Roman., Mex.* 14, fol. 484, where Santarén's letter is given.
[17] Ribas, VIII, 13, where Cueto's letter is given. A modern example of this phenomenon of seeming death is narrated by the recent convert to Catholicism, Johann Jörgensen, Danish writer and publicist, as happening to himself; cf. *Jörgensen: An Autobiography,* Longmans, Green, New York, 1929, II, 116 f. St. Catherine of Siena underwent a seeming death, but instead of death and judgment, as with Jörgensen, her vision was of Heaven, and her return to earth was like a nightmare. Cf. Edmund Gardner, *St. Catherine of Siena,* Dutton, New York, 1907, p. 83.
[18] Ribas, chap. 15. Besides the letter in Ribas, Dabertzhofer, pp. 105 ff., gives another long letter of Cueto. This is followed by a brief and unimportant communication of San Clemente written from Tamazula, December 5, 1607. The missionary here speaks of 2,500 Indians come together, 500 of them in a flagellant procession. Cf. Dabertzhofer, pp. 111 f.
[19] Ribas, chap. 12.
[20] *Ibid.*

NOTES

[21] Ribas, chap. 16.
[22] Dabertzhofer, p. 108.
[23] Ribas, VIII, 17.

CHAPTER IX: THE LAGUNEROS WON OVER

[1] *Anua* of 1598, *Memorias*, p. 873.
[2] See pp. 30–31 above.
[3] Ribas, XI, 5.
[4] *Memorias*, p. 885; *Synopsis Historiae Societatis Jesu*, col. 555.
[5] Ribas, *loc. cit.*
[6] Alegre, I, 380 f., where the letter is given.
[7] *Anua* of 1601, *Memorias*, pp. 891 f., in letter dated Dec. 11.
[8] Ribas, XI, 6, where the letter is given in full.
[9] *Ibid.*
[10] *Anua* of 1598, *Memorias*, pp. 873 f.; Ribas, *loc. cit.*
[11] *Anua* of 1598, *Memorias*, p. 875.
[12] *Ibid.*, pp. 875 ff.
[13] Ribas, XI, 6, quoting letter of Arista.
[14] Herbert E. Bolton, "The Mission as a Frontier Institution in the Spanish American Colonies," *American Historical Review*, Vol. XXIII, No. 1, October, 1917, p. 61.
[15] This became in time a rich and thriving mission not far from the ancient hacienda of Hornos, formerly owned by the Jesuits. Santa Ana was near the upwash of the smaller lagoon, called now Laguna de Viesca, formed by the Río de las Nieves or Aguanaval.
[16] This is the site of the modern San Pedro.
[17] Alegre, I, 381 f., where Arista's letter is given in full. As time went on, smaller settlements or *visitas*, so called because visited by the padre, who did not live there, were attached to the main missions. Later annexed to Santa María were the pueblos of Noria del Pozo, La Peña, and Santa Bárbara. San Pedro came to have a visita called Concepción. Santa Ana later lost its importance in favor of San Lorenzo, and joined to these two was Los Hornos. One of the five centers was called San Sebastián, with San Gerónimo attached. Another was San Ignacio, with San Juan de la Costa, San José de las Abas, and Baicuco as visitas. Cf. *Doc. Hist. Mex.*, 3d ser., pp. 390 f. Arista's report was originally to be found in the *anua* of 1599; cf. *Archiv. S.J. Roman., Mex.* 14, fols. 237 ff.
[18] Alegre, *loc. cit.*
[19] *Anua* of 1601, *Memorias*, p. 898.
[20] Alegre, I, 416; *anua* of 1604, *Archiv. S.J. Roman., Mex.* 14, fol. 378. The latter may mean only that the 1,500 baptized this year brought the number to 4,000.
[21] *Anua* of 1602, *Archiv. S.J. Roman., Mex.* 14, fol. 351; Alegre, I, 408, who gives April 29 as the date of Espinosa's death.
[22] Robles, *Francisco de Urdiñola y el Norte de la Nueva Vizcaya*, chap. iv.
[23] Ribas, XI, 8.
[24] Ribas, *loc. cit.*, gives as usual no date, and the *anuas* for these years are silent on the matter. Alegre does not mention the fathers' arrival, but he says speaking of the year 1607 that six missionaries were working among the Laguneros. Cf. I, 448. Seemingly Dabertzhofer, p. 79, gives the entrance of the missionaries as of 1607, but the *anua* of 1604 gives the number as already six. Cf. *Archiv. S.J. Roman., Mex.* 14, fol. 378.
[25] *Anua* of 1607, *Memorias*, pp. 922 and 928.
[26] Ribas, XI, 10 and 11; *anua* of 1604, *Archiv. S.J. Roman., Mex.* 14, fols. 378 ff. Here we read of six pueblos on the Río de las Nazas. Tlaxcaltecos were Indians from Tlaxcala

from over the mountains to the east of Mexico City. The Mexicanos covered a wide area including the present-day states of Michoacán and Jalisco. Cf. Orozco y Berra, *Apuntes para la historia de la geografía de México*, map.

[27] Dabertzhofer, *Drey neue Relationes*, Parras relation, pp. 82 ff.
[28] *Anua* of 1607, *Memorias*, p. 918.
[29] *Anua* of 1601, *Memorias*, p. 896.
[30] Ribas, XI, 8.
[31] *Ibid.*, XI, 10.
[32] *Ibid.*, XI, 9; Alegre, I, 417 f.
[33] Alegre, *loc. cit.*
[34] Ribas, XI, 9.
[35] *Ibid.*, III, 3.
[36] *Ibid.*, XI, 9; *anua* of 1598, *Memorias*, p. 878, which gives a long letter of Espinosa's.
[37] Ribas, *loc. cit.*
[38] Alegre, *loc. cit.*
[39] Ribas, *loc. cit.*; *anua* of 1607, *Memorias*, p. 921; Dabertzhofer, p. 84.
[40] Ribas, *loc. cit.*
[41] The Christian character thus impressed upon the Indian dances remained, so that for example the famous Yaqui Indian dances and those of the Tarahumares retain today the Christian symbolism given them by the Jesuits. Cf. Phebe M. Bogan: *Yaqui Indian Dances of Tucson, Arizona*, and Wendell C. Bennett and Robert M. Zingg, *The Tarahumara, An Indian Tribe of Northwestern Mexico*.

CHAPTER X: NORTH INTO THE MOUNTAINS

[1] *Anua* of 1601, *Memorias*, p. 885, where we have the following: "Carta del padre Nicolas de Arnaya dirigida al Padre Provincial Váez el año de 1601." These annual reports were usually turned in during the spring of the following year. For Alonso Gómez cf. *anua* of 1600, *Archiv. S.J. Roman., Mex.* 14, fol. 257.
[2] *Anua* of 1597, *Memorias*, p. 853.
[3] *Anua* of 1600–1602, *Archiv. S.J. Roman., Mex.* 14, fols. 295 f.
[4] *Anua* of 1604, *Archiv. S.J. Roman., Mex.* 14, fols. 377 and 393; Alegre, I, 415. Fonte, letter of May 13 from Santiago Papasquiaro, asks for more men. Cf. Ysleta archives.
[5] Alegre, 415 f.; Ribas, X, 5. Alegre speaks as if Ramírez had a companion. Judging from statements in Alegre and in the *anua*, it appears that two smaller settlements, called San Ignacio and Los Reyes, were united with the pueblo of Zape.
[6] Ribas, X, 7.
[7] For instance, in 1614, during his first year on the Mayo, Father Pedro Méndez baptized no fewer than 5,420 souls. Cf. *Archiv. Gen. Mis.*, t. 25, p. 270. Also Peter M. Dunne, S.J., *Pioneer Black Robes on the West Coast, passim*.
[8] Ribas, X, 7.
[9] *Ibid.*, VIII, 15.
[10] *Ibid.*, X, 4. Cf. n. 25 to chap. v, above.
[11] *Ibid.*, X, 7.
[12] *Anua* of 1605, *Archiv. S.J. Roman., Mex.* 14, fol. 346.
[13] *Anua* of 1606, *loc. cit.*, fol. 469.
[14] Dabertzhofer, *Drey neue Relationes*, Tepehuán relation, pp. 90 ff. This is a precious document which has been preserved by the press of Chrysostomo Dabertzhofer, the

Augsburg publisher, in the year 1611. This Tepehuán relation is evidently a part of the *anua* of 1607 which has been lost, for it is contained neither in the Roman Archives of Europe, nor in the *Memorias,* nor in any of the volumes of the *Archivo General* of Mexico City. But both Ribas and Alegre saw this portion of the *anua,* or the original letter, most probably, of Father Juan Fonte, from which it was taken, as may be seen by comparing Dabertzhofer, *loc. cit.,* with Ribas X, 11, and Alegre, I, 452 f. This account in Dabertzhofer was written, almost certainly, by the Jesuit who was, early in 1608, superior of the missions along the eastern slope of the Sierra Madre and who resided in Durango. This is an example of how the early European press preserved details of history that otherwise would have perished.

[15] *Anua* of 1676, *Archiv. Gen. Mis.,* t. 26, p. 244.
[16] Alegre, I, 452 ff.; Dabertzhofer, *op. cit.,* pp. 93 f.
[17] Alegre, *loc. cit.*
[18] Ribas, X, 11, where the letter of Father Fonte is given; Alegre, II, 6. A copy of Fonte's letter is in the Jesuit archives, Ysleta, Texas.
[19] Ribas, X, 10. This same story is in the *anua* of 1610, *Archiv. S.J. Roman., Mex.* 14, fols. 577 f., which confirms again the authenticity of Ribas.
[20] *Archiv. S.J. Roman., Mex.* 14, fol. 576.
[21] Alegre, II, 44. Alegre here says it was the provincial Peláez who was in Durango at this time, but from the *anua* of 1610 it becomes obvious that this is an error.
[22] Decorme, II, 249.
[23] Alegre, II, 44.
[24] Ribas, X, 11, quoting Fonte's lengthy epistle.
[25] *Ibid.*
[26] *Ibid.*
[27] *Ibid.*

CHAPTER XI: URDIÑOLA SUBDUES THE XIXIMES

[1] Carl Sauer, *The Distribution of Aboriginal Tribes in Northwestern Mexico,* p. 16.
[2] Ribas, IX, 5.
[3] The *anua* of 1610 reports that when the Spaniards first went into their country a partial count of skulls reached a total of 1,724. Cf. *Archiv. S.J. Roman., Mex.* 14, fol. 584.
[4] *Anua* of 1610, *Archiv. S.J. Roman., Mex.* 14, fol. 584, where a good description of the habits of the Xiximes is given.
[5] Vito Alessio Robles in his biography, *Francisco de Urdiñola y el Norte de la Nueva España,* omits this campaign against the Xiximes.
[6] Alegre, II, 38.
[7] *Anua* of 1610, *loc. cit.,* fols. 581 ff.
[8] *Ibid.,* fol. 582; Alegre, *loc. cit.;* Ribas, IX, 5. The *anua* says that Urdiñola took with him the superior of the residence in Durango. But this was Francisco de Contreras, which seems a mistake.
[9] *Anua* of 1610, *loc. cit.,* fol. 582; Ribas, IX, 6. The *anua* contains a letter of Alonso Gómez detailing these events.
[10] Ribas, IX, 6; *anua* of 1610, *loc. cit.,* fol. 583.
[11] *Anua* of 1610, *loc. cit.*
[12] Ribas, IX, 7.
[13] *Anua* of 1610, *loc. cit.,* fol. 584.
[14] Ribas, IX, 7 ff.

NOTES

[15] *Ibid.*, IX, 10.
[16] *Ibid.*, IX, 13.
[17] *Ibid.*
[18] Ribas, IV, 3.
[19] *Ibid.*, IX, 13.
[20] Alegre, II, 40; *anua* of 1610, *loc. cit.*
[21] Alegre, II, 63.
[22] Ribas, IX, 11.
[23] Alegre, II, 40.

CHAPTER XII: FLOODS, PLAGUES, AND DEVILS

[1] Ribas, XI, 16. Parras had two visitas, San Gerónimo and San Tomás (formerly assigned to San Pedro). Cf. *anua* of 1604, *Archiv. S.J. Roman., Mex.* 14, fol. 379.
[2] Ribas, XI, 16.
[3] *Ibid.*, XI, 17.
[4] *Anua* of 1608, *Memorias*, pp. 930 f.
[5] *The Mexican Nation: A History*, p. 64.
[6] Flores, *Historia de la Medicina*, I, 112 f.
[7] Ribas, II, 6.
[8] *Archiv. Gen. Mis.*, t. 25, pp. 346 f.: report of Martín Pérez.
[9] Ribas, XI, 12. In Parras as elsewhere the plague was recurrent.
[10] Cf. Loyola's description in parable of what the demon would look like: "Seated ... on a lofty throne of fire and smoke in aspect horrible and fearful." *The Text of the Spiritual Exercises of St. Ignatius*, 4th ed., London, 1908, p. 45.
[11] Ribas, *loc. cit.*
[12] Ribas, XI, 13.
[13] *Ibid.*, XI, 18.
[14] *Anua* of 1607, *Memorias*, p. 926.
[15] Cf. above, pp. 28–29.
[16] *Anua* of 1607, *Memorias, loc. cit.*; Ribas, XI, 14; Dabertzhofer, *Drey neue Relationes*, Parras relation.
[17] Alegre, II, 56 f.; Ribas, XI, 21.
[18] Ribas, XI, 9; *anua* of 1604, *Archiv. S.J. Roman., Mex.* 14, fol. 378. Here the account is slightly different and speaks as if the letters and marks had been painted high on a lofty cliff.
[19] Ribas, XI, 20.

CHAPTER XIII: DISTANT RUMBLINGS

[1] Ribas, X, 12.
[2] *Ibid.*; Alegre, II, 82.
[3] *Anua* of 1614, *Archiv. S.J. Roman., Mex.* 14, fols. 658 ff.
[4] *Anua* of 1615, *Archiv. S.J. Roman., Mex.* 15, fols. 31 ff., and Ayer Collection, pp. 24 ff.
[5] Ribas, V, 2; Alegre, II, 32.
[6] Ribas, V, 9.
[7] *Ibid.*, V, 18.
[8] *Ibid.*, II, 35.

[9] Alegre, II, 82; *Archiv. Gen. Hist.*, t. 316, pp. 93, 95, 100 and *passim*, where the letters of Hurdaide are given.
[10] Cf. above, chap. v.
[11] Alegre, *loc. cit.*; Ribas, X, 12.
[12] Ribas, *loc. cit.*
[13] *Ibid.*
[14] *Anua* of 1616, Ayer Collection, p. 71.
[15] Ribas, X, 13; *anua* of 1616, *loc. cit.*
[16] Ribas, X, 14; Alegre, II, 82.
[17] Ribas, *loc. cit.*; *anua* of 1616, *loc. cit.*
[18] Ribas, *loc. cit.*; *anua* of 1616, *loc. cit.*, p. 72.

CHAPTER XIV: THE STORM BREAKS

[1] *Anua* of 1616, p. 72. Cf. Ayer Collection, Newberry Library, Chicago. Mariano Cuevas, S.J., *Historia de la Iglesia en México*, III, 359 ff., gives a long account of the actual uprising, quoting a large portion of the *anua* of 1616.
[2] *Anua* of 1616, *loc. cit.*, pp. 72 and 88; Ribas, VIII, 19, and X, 15. Ribas in both places gives the very wording of the taunts then uttered: "He who is holy, let us see if his God will bring him back to life." "Do those men think there is nothing to do but to teach 'Our Father Who art in Heaven' . . . 'Hail Mary full of grace'?" The *anua* does not mention these details and they have all the earmarks of legend, imitative of the taunts flung against Christ at the Crucifixion.
[3] Ribas, X, 15, says the number was 200; the *anua* says, more than 70.
[4] *Anua* of 1616, *loc. cit.*, p. 73; Ribas, *loc. cit.* The *anua* calls him Juan incorrectly.
[5] Tanner, pp. 470 ff., gives a running account of these events.
[6] *Anua* of 1616, *loc. cit.*, p. 74.
[7] *Ibid.*, p. 75.
[8] *Ibid.*, p. 76; Ribas, X, 19. Cf. also *Archiv. S.J. Roman., Mex.* 15, *anua* of 1616, synopsis, fol. 365.
[9] *Anua* of 1616, *loc. cit.*; Ribas, X, 20. Cf. also *Archiv. S.J. Roman., Mex.* 15, fol. 366.
[10] Ribas, X, 21; *anua* of 1616, Ayer Collection, pp. 75-76, and 87. This account says Santarén was killed at Yoracaya.
[11] Ribas, X, 21.
[12] Some of these Jesuit martyrs belonged to high-placed families. Tovar's mother, whose name he bore, was Isabel de Guzmán de Tovar, closely related to the Cardinal Duke of Lerma. The family mansion at Culiacán had been always open in hospitality to the fathers. Orozco, born in Placencia, Spain, in 1587, was the nephew of Rodrigo de Orozco, the Marqués de Mortara. Alabez was of the nobility of Oaxaca in Mexico. Moranta, born in Majorca in 1575, was nephew to the great Jesuit, Jerome Nadal, secretary to Ignatius Loyola and important in the organization of the early society. Santarén was likewise of the nobility. Cf. Tanner, pp. 468 ff. Most of these men were quite young when they met their death. Moranta was forty-one, Del Valle forty, Tovar thirty-five, Cisneros thirty-four, and Orozco only twenty-nine. The oldest was Santarén, who died at fifty-one. Fonte's age is not known. Cf. Tanner, *loc. cit.* Like St. Peter Claver, apostle of the Negroes in Cartagena, Gerónimo de Moranta had been encouraged to go as a missionary to the New World by the Jesuit saint and brother Alfonso Rodríguez. Cf. letter of Wlodimir Ledochowski, General of the Society of Jesus, Sept. 9, 1917, in *Renovation Reading*, Woodstock College, 1931, p. 212. Cf. also Tanner, *op. cit.*, p. 475.
[13] *Anua* of 1616, *loc. cit.*, p. 73; Ribas, X, 16.

NOTES

CHAPTER XV: THE NATIONS STIR

[1] *Anua* of 1616, *Memorias*, p. 556, where Pedro de Velasco's letter is given. *Archiv. Gen. Hist.*, t. 316, p. 156, where Hurdaide's letter is given; Alegre, II, 78.
[2] *Anua* of 1616, pp. 101 f. Cf. Ayer Collection, Newberry Library, Chicago.
[3] Velasco's letter containing these details can be found in the Ribas MSS, III, 13, and in the *anua* of 1617 in the Ayer Collection.
[4] *Anua* of 1617, Ayer Collection, p, 141; Ribas, II, 32; Ribas MSS, III, 13; Faría, ch. 2.
[5] Ribas, II, 32.
[6] *Archiv. Gen. Hist.*, *loc. cit.*, p. 102; *anua* of 1617, *loc. cit.*, pp. 140 f.
[7] *Anua* of 1617, Ayer Collection, p. 146.
[8] Ribas, X, 24; *anua* of 1616, *loc. cit.*, p. 84.
[9] *Archiv. Gen. Hist.*, *loc. cit.*, p. 96.
[10] *Ibid.*, p. 102.
[11] Ribas, XI, 22.
[12] *Anua* of 1616, *loc. cit.*, p. 80.
[13] *Ibid.*
[14] *Anua* of 1616, *loc. cit.*, p. 82.
[15] Ribas, XI, 22; *anua* of 1617, *loc. cit.*, p. 147.
[16] Ribas, X, 23, where a letter of Captain Suárez is given.
[17] *Anua* of 1616, *loc. cit.*, p. 82.
[18] Ribas, X, 22; *anua* of 1616, *loc. cit.*, p. 82.
[19] *Anua* of 1616, *loc. cit.*, p. 102, where Acacio's letter is given.
[20] *Ibid.*
[21] Ribas, X, 23.

CHAPTER XVI: THE GOVERNOR RIDES FORTH

[1] *Relacion breve y succinta de los sucesos que ha tenido la guerra de los Tepehuanes de la gubernacion de la Nueva Vizcaya* ... , Bandelier-Hackett, II, 102.
[2] *Anua* of 1616, Ayer Collection, p. 77; Ribas, X, 25.
[3] *Relacion breve*, *loc. cit.*; Ribas, *loc. cit.* These two narratives differ in minor details.
[4] *Relacion breve*, *loc. cit.*; *anua* of 1616, *loc. cit.*; Ribas, *loc. cit.*
[5] Ribas, *loc. cit.*
[6] *Ibid.*
[7] *Relacion breve*, *loc. cit.*; *anua* of 1616, Ayer collection, p. 78; Ribas, X, 26, who gives the date of the Governor's departure as January.
[8] *Relacion breve*, *loc. cit.*, p. 104; Ribas, *loc. cit.*; *anua* of 1616, *loc. cit.*, p. 78.
[9] Alegre, II, 89; Ribas, X, 26, where he gives the date of the arrival at Guanacevi as February 14.
[10] The *anua* of 1616 says sixty Indian allies.
[11] The *anua* of 1616, *loc. cit.*, p. 78, names in this connection the Tarahumares and the Indians of Ocotlán, of the Valle de San Pablo, of Piaxtla, of Mangarito, of San Xavier de Mesquital, of Parras and the Lagoon country, besides the Conchos, the Acaxées, and the Xiximes.
[12] Ribas, X, 26 and 27. At the end of the former chapter and beginning of the latter there is a slight obscurity of detail which the writer has endeavored to clarify. The *Relacion breve*, p. 106, does not mention the division of forces, but simply indicates that the Governor left Guanacevi for San Ignacio del Zape on January 22.

[13] "Uno de los mas tristos espectáculos que se pudiera imaginar." Ribas, X, 27.
[14] Ribas, X, 27; Alegre, II, 89.
[15] *Relacion breve, loc. cit.,* p. 106.
[16] Ribas, *loc. cit.;* Alegre, II, 90. The latter's story here differs slightly from that of Ribas.
[17] *Relacion breve, loc. cit.,* p. 106; Ribas, X, 27; *anua* of 1616, *loc. cit.,* p. 98, which here incorporates a letter of Father Luis de Bonifaz, superior at Durango. This document gives the number of women and children captured as 130. Ribas says 30 were slain and 200 captured. The *Relacion breve* indicates nothing about the brush at Papasquiaro, but says that the troop arriving at Atotonilco at 9 o'clock at night made a forced march to surprise the enemy at Tenerape.
[18] *Anua* of 1616, *loc. cit.;* Ribas, X, 27; Alegre, II, 90.
[19] *Relacion breve, loc. cit.,* p. 108.
[20] Alegre II, 90, says that Alvear did not accompany the bodies all the way to Durango; that, receiving reinforcements, he left from Sauceda to reduce those who had fled far west to the roughest part of the mountain country. But Ribas, X, 27, and the *anua* of 1616, *loc. cit.,* p. 98, make it clear that the Governor accompanied the bodies of the martyrs through to the capital.
[21] *Anua* of 1616, *loc. cit.,* p. 99; Ribas, X, 28; Alegre, II, 91.
[22] Ribas, *loc. cit.* Ribas devotes chap. xxix of this tenth book to a refutation of the errors which have crept into history concerning the Tepehuán revolt, assuring the reader that he had carefully authenticated every fact which he set down. And certainly, no historian was better able than himself to do so, for from Governor Alvear and from the thirty witnesses examined at Durango after the tragedy he was able to get first-hand information. Ribas says the author of *Las grandezas de Madrid* errs when he states that the Tlaxcaltec Indians gave the occasion for the revolt; that all the eight Jesuits were together when killed; that the murderers were Chichimecos, etc. The errors of other authors are likewise refuted.
[23] The General of the Society, Father Mutius Vitelleschi, wrote on March 16, 1625, to the Provincial of New Spain, Juan Laurencio, for an account of the Tepehuán martyrs. Later he thanks the Provincial for having received these together with their portraits. The accounts, says the General, are being read in the refectory "to the universal consolation of everybody in the possession of eight brothers who are already in Heaven." *Colección de cartas inéditas de los Padres Generales de la Compañía de Jesús a los Padres Provinciales de la Provincia de Nueva España, 1583–1659,* Ysleta College, El Paso, Texas.

CHAPTER XVII: THE DEATH OF COGOXITO

[1] *Anua* of 1616, Ayer Collection, p. 102; Ribas, X, 30; Alegre, II, 91.
[2] Ribas, *loc. cit.*
[3] *Anua* of 1617, *loc. cit.,* pp. 135 ff.
[4] Alegre, II, 90.
[5] *Relacion breve y succinta* . . . , Bandelier-Hackett, II, 108.
[6] *Anua* of 1617, *loc. cit.,* p. 135; *Relacion breve, loc. cit.* With regard to certain details the sources confuse Alvear's second and third expeditions. The gorge Del Diablo seems sometimes to be called the Rincón de Zamora. Or was this perhaps another gorge?
[7] *Doc. Hist. Mex.,* 4th ser., III, 95, Alonso del Valle's letter.
[8] *Relacion breve, loc. cit.*
[9] *Ibid.,* p. 110.

NOTES 215

[10] *Ibid.*

[11] The following account of the killing of Cogoxito and the pacification of the west is given in a most prolix and partly confused letter of Father Alonso del Valle. The letter was written to his superior from El Llanos de Guatimapé, May 9, 1618, immediately after the expedition, and it may be found in *Doc. Hist. Mex.*, 4th ser., III, 90–129. Del Valle accompanied the expedition as chaplain and was therefore eyewitness of most of the detailed events he recounts. Both Ribas and Alegre speak as if there were only one expedition to the extreme west and that in 1617, but Del Valle's letter makes it clear that there were two made by Alvear to the mountains of the west, one in 1617 after the burial of the martyrs and the other in 1618, for he says, *loc. cit.*, p. 95, that the year before the Governor had come to the famous gorge of the Piaxtla, and had descended therein. There were, therefore, three expeditions in all made by the Governor: the first north in December, 1616; the second far southwest in March, 1617; and the third west in February, 1618. Bancroft, *North Mexican States and Texas*, I, 327, n. 40, thinks there were only two expeditions. Every shred of doubt, however, is cleared up by the important narrative *Relacion breve, loc. cit.*, pp. 102–115. Besides, the *anua* for 1618 mentions the expedition for this year. Cf. *Archiv. S.J. Roman., Mex.* 15, fol. 101.

[12] Here we have an interesting example of the growth of legend. Father del Valle, the eyewitness, mentions no miracle in his account of the death of Cogoxito. Ribas, however, X, 31, and Alegre, II, 91, both say that though the rebel was struck in different parts of the body, the three arrows came out at his mouth in punishment of the blasphemies he had uttered!

[13] The *Relacion breve, loc. cit.*, p. 115, differing from Del Valle, says the Spaniards returned in four divisions.

[14] *Doc. Hist. Mex.*, 4th ser., III, 128 f., Del Valle's letter.

[15] *Anua* of 1617, *loc. cit.*, pp. 136 f., where two letters of López are given.

[16] Ribas, X, 32.

[17] Cf. Francisco Xavier Faria, *Apologetico defensorio y puntual manifiesto* ..., MS, *Archiv. Gen. Mis.*, t. 25, pp. 313 ff.

CHAPTER XVIII: RECONCILIATION AND RECONSTRUCTION

[1] Alegre, II, 86.

[2] Cf. chap. xiii above.

[3] Ribas, X, 34.

[4] *Ibid.*; Alegre, II, 92.

[5] Ribas, X, 35, where Lomas' letter is given; Alegre, II, 144.

[6] Ribas, *loc. cit.*

[7] *Ibid.*

[8] The anua of 1617 says that this year there was only one missionary among the Tepehuanes. This is Andrés López. Of the other missions each had several—Topia 6, San Andrés 6, Parras 6—while three fathers and two brothers were resident in Durango. Cf. Ayer Collection, p. 104. The *anua* of 1618 indicates that two fathers were among the Tepehuanes this year. They were of course Gómez and Lomas. The other missions retained the same number of workers, but two more fathers had come to Durango. Cf. *Archiv S.J. Roman., Mex.* 15, fol. 93. Alegre, II, 144, says that four additional fathers came to the Tepehuanes in 1620.

[9] Alegre, II, 144.

[10] Ribas, X, 36, says an entirely new statue was made. Alegre, II, 145, disagrees with him and cites an excellent authority, the *anua* of 1623, and he is correct. Cf. *Archiv. Gen. Mis.*, t. 25, p. 91.
[11] *Anua* of 1623, *loc. cit.;* Ribas, X, 36.
[12] Ribas, X, 37; Alegre, II, 144 f.
[13] Alegre, II, 145 f.
[14] *Papeles del Almirante Mateo de Vesga Governador y capitan general de la provincia de Nueva Vizcaya, 14 de Deciembre de 1620 hasta 19 de Mayo de 1622:* Bandelier-Hackett, II, 120 ff.
[15] *Relacion breve y succinta* . . . , Bandelier-Hackett, II, 112.
[16] *Papeles del Almirante, loc. cit.*, pp. 120 ff.
[17] *Ibid.*, p. 124.
[18] *Ibid.*, p. 122; *Del legajo de papeles tocantes a asuntos de los Indios revelados en Nueva Vizcaya. Governador Mateo de Vesga (Mayo de 1624):* Bandelier-Hackett, II, 136 ff.
[19] *Anua* of 1623, *Archiv. Gen. Mis.*, t. 25, p. 93.
[20] *Estada en que estaba Durango y la tierra, los edificios, que han hecho yglesias y monasterior el gran crezimiento que tuvo la provyncia y govierno (de Nueva Vizcaya, 1624).* Cf. Bandelier-Hackett, II, 144 f. This document is signed by Mateo de Vesga and several witnesses.
[21] *Anua* of 1626, *Archiv. Gen. Mis.*, t. 25, p. 164.
[22] Ribas, X, 38.
[23] *Ibid.*
[24] *Anua* of 1623, *Archiv. Gen. Mis.*, t. 25, p. 93; Ribas X, 38; Alegre, II, 153.

CHAPTER XIX: NEW NATIONS

[1] Ribas, IX, 14; Alegre, II, 195; Alonso del Valle, letter of May 9, 1618, in *Doc. Hist. Mex.*, 4th ser., III, 96 ff.; Carl Sauer, *The Distribution of Aboriginal Tribes in Northwestern Mexico*, pp. 19 f.—Sauer seems mistaken when he differs from these Jesuit authorities on the location of the Hinas and Humis, respectively. He refers to the Hinas as living near the headwaters of the Piaxtla and the Humis lower down the gorge. Both Ribas and Alegre have it just the opposite, while Del Valle makes it quite clear that it was the Humis who lived at the headwaters in the most savage part of the gorge. Sauer states that those lower down were a tribe distinct from the Xiximes, but of the same speech; Alegre asserts that they had many of the same customs, but differed in speech. Del Valle says that the Humis differed from the Xiximes, though they had the same speech!
[2] Ribas, *loc. cit.*
[3] *Ibid.;* Alegre, II, 196. Ribas says the Bishop asked particularly that Father Cueto be sent among these tribes.
[4] Ribas, IX, 21.
[5] Alegre, *loc. cit.*
[6] Ribas, IX, 14.
[7] *Ibid.;* Alegre, *loc. cit.*
[8] Ribas, IX, 15; Alegre, II, 196 f.
[9] Alegre, II, 197. The exact date of the Bishop's death is nowhere given in the sources. Bolton in his *Guide*, p. 472, puts it at 1631. According to Ribas, IX, 16, Cueto's second entrada was made in 1630. This, according to Alegre, II, 197, was after the Bishop's

NOTES

death. Ribas elsewhere, III, 16, speaks as if the Bishop died some years before. However, the *Constituciones* of the Archdiocese of Durango, p. 5, puts the death at January 25, 1631.

[10] Ribas, IX, 16.
[11] *Ibid.*, IX, 17; Alegre, *loc. cit.*
[12] Alegre, II, 198.
[13] Ribas, *loc. cit.*; Alegre, II, 199.
[14] Ribas, IX, 19, where a detailed but prolix letter of Father Ximenes is given.
[15] *Doc. Hist. Mex.*, 4th ser., III, 96 ff., letter of Del Valle.
[16] Ortega, *Historia del Nayarit*..., pp. 35 f.
[17] Ribas, IX, 20; Alegre, II, 200. However, a list of the Provincials of New Spain gives 1632 as the date of Ayerve's entrance upon the duties of his office. Cf. Schmitt, *Synopsis*, col. 555.
[18] Alegre, *loc. cit.*, where he corrects a mistake of Ribas concerning the date of Gravina's death and points out its source. Ribas, IX, 21, gives January 15, 1635, as the date.
[19] Alegre, II, 200, where he says that the letter of the prolix Ximenes is too long to give. Ribas, however, IX, 20, quotes the whole of it.

EPILOGUE

[1] *Razon y minuto de los Yndios*..., Bandelier-Hackett, *Historical Documents*, II, 152 ff.
[2] *Anua* of 1604, *Archiv. S.J. Roman., Mex.* 14, fol. 393.
[3] *Anua* of 1624, *Archiv. S.J. Roman., Mex.* 15, fol. 127.
[4] *Carta del Padre Gaspar de Contreras al Padre Provincial Francisco Calderon*, Parras, May 1, 1653; *Doc. Hist. Mex.*, 4th ser., III, 210 ff. Alegre, II, 427, mistakenly gives the date of the cession of the Lagunero missions as 1652. Cf. *anua* of 1646-1647, *Archiv. S.J. Roman., Mex.*, fol. 172, which gives only two as the number of fathers in the Parras mission.
[5] *Relación de José Pascual*, Jesuit Archives, Ysleta, Texas.
[6] *Noticias de las misiones sacadas de la anua del Padre José Pascual año de 1651*, *Doc. Hist. Mex.*, 4th ser., III, 179.

INDEX

(Pages 1–187, text and appendix; pages 189–197, sources.)

Acacio, Juan, 141
Acaponeta, 154, 155
Acaxées, tribe, 32, 47–49, 51, 83, 90, 97, 99, 100, 105, 107, 118, 137, 156; attempted corruption of, 124, 134, 140–141; harassed by Tepehuanes, 90, 135–136, 153–154; missions to, 12, 46–47, 51–55, 65–73 *passim*, 90, 105, 118, 185; revolt of, 56–61 *passim*, 63–64, 141–142; victims of Xiximes, 97, 99–100, 107
Aguanaval, river, chap ix n. 15. *See* Río de las Nieves
Águila, valley. *See* Valle del Águila
Agustinillo, 157
Ahomames, tribe, 29
Ahomes, tribe, 84, 99
Ahoreados, river, 43. *See* Río Tepehuanes
Alabez, Luis de, 131, 133, 148, chap. xiv n. 12
Alegre, Francisco Javier, 34, 190, 192. *See also* notes to chaps. i, iii–xiii, xv–xix
Alicamac, 72
Almanza, Martín Enríques de, 4
Alvear, Gaspar de, 122, 124, 137, 140, 143, 145, 146, 149, 150, 172–173, 191–192; expedition against Tepehuanes, 140, 146–151, 153, 154–162, 169, 183
Alvear, Juan de, 131, 132
Alvear, Sebastián de, 141
Andrés, Don, 140, 141
Antón, 156
Antonio, 148
Anuas, 189–190
Aoya, 162
Aquaviva, Claudius, 7, 11, 108
Archivo General de la Nación, 189, 190
Arisbaba, Bartolomé de, 183
Arista, Francisco de, 26, 74–80, 82, 87
Arlegui, José, 192, chap. iii nn. 5, 6, 11, 14, chap. iv n. 6, chap. vi n. 2
Arnaya, Nicolás de, 11, 18, 74–75, 78, 87, 88, chap. vi n. 17
Arteaga, Juan de, 3–4
Atotonilco (Durango), 66, 118, 127, 137, 149, 150, 170

Atotonilco (Sinaloa), 66, 68, 69, 70, 106
Atotonilco, valley, 39, 41, 42
Augustinians, 174. *See also* Coruña and Hermosillo
Auritilas, tribe, chap. iv n. 31
Avellaneda, Diego de, 11, 21
Ávila, Alonso de, 52
Ávila, Diego de, 51, 52
Ayepa, 52
Ayerve, Floriano de, 183, chap. viii n. 11; mission to Acaxées, 66, 68, 69, 70, 71, 183, 191
Azevedo, Diego de, 136
Azevedo, Ignatius, 7
Azevedo, Pablo, 16
Aztecs, tribe, 111, 112, chap. v n. 9
Aztla, 78, 80

Bacapa, 71. *See* San Pedro y San Pablo de Bacapa
Bacubirito, 106
Baimoa, 54, 66, 68, 73, 191
Balvarte, river. *See* Río Balvarte
Bamoa, 106
Bañuelos, Baltásar Temiño de, 14
Baptisms, 1, 8, 12, 22, 23, 24, 28, 30, 34, 35, 36, 38, 39, 40, 43, 44, 52, 53, 54, 65, 68–71 *passim*, 73, 77, 80, 81, 82, 88, 89, 91–95 *passim*, 102, 103, 105, 107, 110–114 *passim*, 117, 122, 138, 139, 178, 182, 184, 187. *See also* Indians, requests of, for baptism
Barocopa, 136
Basilio, Jácome, 119
Batocomito, 69
Baxameros, tribe, chap. iv n. 31
Benedictines. *See* Evía y Valdés, Fray Francisco de Quintanilla
Benítez, Lucas, 127
Berra. *See* Orozco y Berra
Beudin, Cornelius, 119
Bonifaz, Luis de, 148, 151, 176, 178–179, chap. xvi n. 17
Borgia, Francis, 2, 3, 4, 8, 17
Boyagame, 169

[219]

Brizuela, Martín, 187
Burgos, Padre, 187
Cabeza de Vaca, 24
Cabezos, tribe, chap. iv n. 31
Cabredo, Rodrigo de, 94, 108
Cadeña, Diego de, 16
Cagina, Juan de la, 21
Cáhitas, tribe, 12, 24
Cahuemetos, tribe, 122, 135, 136, 142
California, Alta, 9, 12, 28, 165, 186
California, Baja, 13, 28, 119
Calvo, Juan, 135
Campaña Grande, 54
Campos, Francisco, 128, 166
Canatlán (formerly Sauceda), 34
Canelas, Captain Mateo, 61
Canelas, Mateo, rebel, 149–150, 174
Cannibalism, 48, 70, 97, 101, 103, 105, 107, 108, 118, 140
Cano, Agustín, 21
Carantapa, region, 70, 72, 136–137, 142, 191
Carantapa, Sierra de. See Sierra de Carantapa
Carranco, Lorenzo, 119
Casas Grandes. See Paquimé
Casaus y Cervantes, Juan, 164
Castañeda, Juan de, 63
Castillo, Juan del, alcalde, 128, 150
Castillo, Father Juan del, 187
Castro Verde, Mateo de, 162, 187
Caviseras, tribe, 29
Cervantes, Alonso Gómez de, 187
Cervantes, Gonzalo Gómez de, 180
Chacala, 62
Chamuscado, Captain, 17
Chanmayo, 69
Chiametla, 153, 155, 162
Chichimecos, tribe, 10–11, chap. ii n. 11, chap. xvi n. 22
Chicorato, pueblo, 136
Chicoratos, tribe, 134, 136
Chínipas, tribe, 119
Cintos, Padre, 17
Cisneros, Bernardo de, 94, 123, 127, 130, 133, 145, 149, chap. xiv n. 12
Clerici, Alberto, 122, 124
Coapa, 53, 140, 141

Cocorotame, 158, 161, 162, 173
Cogotá, 177
Cogoxito, Francisco, 153–158 passim, 160, 161, 173, 176, 183
Comanitos, nation, 135, 136
Comets, 114–115
Concha, Hernando Suárez de la, 6
Conchos, tribe, 146, 156, chap. xvi n. 11
Conimeto, 72
Contreras, Gaspar de, epilogue n. 4
Contreras, Pedro Moya de, 4
Cordejuela, Captain, 130, 146, 150
Córdoba, Juan Pérez de, 120
Córdova, Diego Fernández de, 145, 155
Coronado, 9
Cortés, 5, 17, 111
Coruña, Agustín de la, 4
Cossin, Bernardo de, 17
Coyovera, 137
Crespo, Alvaro, 126
Cristóbal, Don, 173
Cuencamé, 18, 22, 23, 28, 45, 118, 187
Cueto, Diego Gonzales, 176–182, 187; mission to Sobaibos, 66, 71–73, 135–136, 191
Cuevas, Luis de, 52
Culiacán, province, 162
Culiacán, river. See Río Culiacán
Culiacán, town, 17, 18, 22, 32, 45, 49, 50, 54, 59, 60, 63–67 passim, 70, 72, 73, 142, 174–175, chap. xiv n. 12
Curiel, Juan, 6

Dabertzhofer, Chrysostomo, 190–191. See also notes to chaps. iv, v, viii–x, xii
Daparavopos, tribe, 29
Del Diablo, gorge, 155, 157, 158, 176
Del Río y Losa, Rodrigo, 11, 16, 18–19
Del Valle, Alonso, 156, 157, 159, 161–163, 182, chap. xvii nn. 7, 11, chap. xix nn. 1, 15
Del Valle, Juan, 93, 94, 131, 133, 148, chap. xiv n. 12
Delrío, Martín Antonio, 37
Díaz, Gerónimo, 179, 183
Díaz, Hernando, 154
Díaz, Pedro, 19
Disease, 73, 81, 106, 111. See also Plagues
Domínguez, Tomás, 138

INDEX

Dominicans, 119, 134, 147
Droughts, 73, 116, 180
Duárez, Martín, 52
Dui, Don Francisco, 77
Durango, city (formerly Guadiana), 11, 15–20 *passim*, 34, 45, 143, 146, 151, 153–156 *passim*, 158, 161, 174, 175, 192, chap. xviii n. 8; bishops of, 20, 110, 176, 177, 179, 185; mission center, 19, 21, 24, 26, 27, 32, 33, 39, 45, 51, 59, 75, 87, 88, 93, 94, 96, 105, 118, 128, 129, 143, 145, 149, 152, 153, 178, 185, 187
Durango, state, 165, 190–192

Egurrola, Martín de, 187
El Jaral, 146
El Llanos de Guatimapé, chap. xvii n. 11
Espinareda, Pedro de, 17
Espinosa, Juan Agustín de: birth, 21–22, 80; mission to Laguneros, 27–31, 33, 74–79, 82, 83, 118, chap. v n. 5; mission to Zacatecos, 21–25 *passim*, 45, 74
Estelage, 156
Estrada, Nicolás de, 183, 187
Evía y Valdés, Fray Francisco de Quintanilla, 185
Expeditions: Bartolomé Suárez de Villalta against Hinas, 180–182; Captain Cordejuela against Tepehuanes, 130; Diego Martínez de Hurdaide against Tepehuanes, 136–137; Gaspar de Alvear against Tepehuanes, 140, 153–162; Martín de Olivas against Tepehuanes, 129, 130; Rivera against Acaxées, 59; Urdiñola against Sobaibos, 63; Urdiñola against Xiximes, 100–104
Explorations: Captain Chamuscado, 17; Francisco de Ibarra, 9–16, 32, 45; Cabeza de Vaca, 24

Famines, 39, 88, 180
Ferro, Juan, 10
Floods, 12, 115–116, 169–170
Florencia, Francisco de, 192
Fonte, Juan, 96; martyrdom, 131, 148, 171, chap. xiv n. 12; mission to Tarahumares, 93, 94–96, 118, 131, 186; mission to Tepehuanes, 88, 91–93, 99, 122, 191

Foronda, Juan Ortiz, 119
Franciscans, 3, 13, 165; martyrs, 16, 18, 45, 119, 134, *see also* Azevedo, Pablo; Cossin, Bernardo de; Guttiérez, Juan; Herrera, Father; López, Francisco; Rodríguez, Agustín; missions in Mexico, 9, 10, 14–18 *passim*, 21–22, 24, 25, 45, 46, 50, 143, 144, 151–152, 154, 174, 185, 192
Francisco, spy, 156
Fresnillo, 10, 14
Fuerte, river. *See* Río del Fuerte

García, Tomás, 159, 161
Gascue, Rafael de, 143, 151–152, 155, 174
Gerónimo, cacique, 44
Gigibodari, 91
Gómez, Alonso, 66, 87, 101, 107, chap. xviii n. 8
Gómez, Juan, 152
González, Andrés, 107, 136, 142, 162
Gordo, Juan, 140–141
Gravina, Pedro de, 183–184; mission to Xiximes, 101, 107, 140–142 *passim*, 161, 162, 183–184, 187
Grotto of Santiago, 117
Guadalajara, Bishop of, 18, 60
Guadalajara, 6, 14, 20, 155, 175
Guadalcázar, Marqués de, 145. *See* Córdova, Diego Fernández de
Guadalupe, Sanctuary of Our Lady of, at Parras, 82
Guadiana, diocese and town, 11. *See* Durango
Guadiana, valley. *See* Valle de Guadiana
Guanaceví, 10, 20, 43–44, 87, 88, 89, 118, 120, 131–132, 145–147 *passim*, 170, 171, 187
Guanajuato, 8, 10, 14
Guapexuxe, 54, 101, 103–105 *passim*, 132, 142, 160, 162
Guarisamey, 157, 158, 160, 161, 162, 173, 182, 183, 184, 185
Guasave, pueblo, 50, 122, 124
Guasaves, tribe, 50
Guatimapé, 133, 144, 157, 158
Guazamota, 156, 187
Guixiuita, 169
Gutiérrez, Father Francisco, 54

222 INDEX

Gutiérrez, Francisco Jaques, 172
Guttiérez, Juan, 127
Guzmán, Núño de, 9, 17, 56

Hechiceros, 31, 36–38 passim, 40, 49, 72–73, 83–85, 89–90, 92, 93, 96, 111, 113, 118, 120–125 passim, 135, 138, 139, 155, 163, 164, 169, 174
Hermosillo, Gonzalo de, 20, 110, 175, 176, 177, 179
Herradura, valley, 79
Herrera, Father, 16
Hinas, tribe, 13, 176–182, 184
Hoeras, tribe, 29
Hontiveros, Cristóbal de, 147
Huahuapa, 161
Huaimino, 177
Hucoritame, 94
Humase, pueblo, 94, 160, 162, 183, 184
Humis, tribe, 13, 158–162 passim, 176, 182–184
Hurdaide, Cristóbal Martínez de, 127
Hurdaide, Diego Martínez de, 64, 99, 121, 122, 124, 135–137, chap. xiv n. 4

Ibarra, Diego de, 14, 15
Ibarra, Francisco de, 9, 14–16, 32, 45
Idols, 30, 36–39 passim, 46, 48–49, 50, 53, 68, 69, 71, 75, 89, 90, 92, 104, 113, 122, 123, 139, 142, 150, 153, 163, 169, 174, 181
Ignatio, Pedro, 127
Inavopos, tribe, 29
Indé, 20, 32, 88, 89, 91, 118, 119, 133, 145, 146, 154, 163, 166, 167, 173, 187
Indian tribes. See Acaxées, Ahomemes, Ahomes, Auritilas, Aztecs, Baxameros, Cabezos, Cáhitas, Cahuemetos, Caviseras, Chichimecos, Chicoratos, Chínipas, Conchos, Daparavopos, Guasaves, Hinas, Hoeras, Humis, Inavopos, Irritilas, Jovas, Laguneros, Maiconeras, Mamazorras, Mexicanos, Miopacoas, Naperes, Neguales, Neviras, Nuris, Ocoronis, Ópatas, Pimas, Poagas, Salineros, Sicurabas, Sobaibos, Suaquis, Tahues, Tarahumares, Tarascans, Tepehuanes, Tlaxcaltecos, Tobosos, Ures, Vasapayes, Xiximes, Yaquis, Zacatecos

Indians: Flight of: Guasaves, 50; Serranos, 114; Tepehuanes, 166. Habits and dispositions of, 10, 24, 26, 27, 28–30, 31, 41, 47–49, 76, 81, 83–84, 89–90, 95, 120–124, 128, 165, 182, see also Hechiceros, Idols, Indian tribes, Superstitions. Mistreatment of, 56, 120, 165, chap. vii n. 2. Political organization of, 29–30, 42, 46, 119–120. Rebellions of: at San Juan de Carapoa, 16; in Baja California, 119, see Acaxées, Ocoronis, Sobaibos, Tarahumares, Tepehuanes, Xiximes. Remedies used by, 47, 112–113. Requests of, for baptism or padres, 35, 38, 40, 42, 53, 54, 69, 70–71, 93, 94, 104, 120–121, 179, 183
Irritila, Antón Martín, 77
Irritilas, tribe, 24. See Laguneros
Iztlán, 177

Jesuit: Archives, 189–192. Churches: in Mexico, 6, 22, 25, 43, 53, 66, 82, 105, 116, 118, 145, 148, 174. Generals, see Aquaviva, Claudius; Borgia, Francis; Lainez, Diego; Loyola, Ignatius de; Vitelleschi, Mutius. Martyrs, 1, 3, 7–8, 12, 17, 119, 133–134, 171, 192. Novitiates, 6, 126. Order: founding, 1; first members of, in America, 1–2; golden age of, 7, 17; expulsion of, 172, 190. Provincials, see Ayerve, Floriano de; Cabredo, Rodrigo de; Díaz, Pedro; Díaz, Gerónimo; López, Manuel; Ribas, Andrés Pérez de; Sánchez, Pedro; Váez, Francisco. Schools: in Mexico, 6, 8, 11, 17, 19, 26, 49, 66, 72, 106, 110, 119, 186. Visitors, see Avellaneda, Diego de; Bonifaz, Luis de; Cabredo, Rodrigo de
Jovas, tribe, 186

Kino, Eusebio Francisco, 5, 9, 13, 186

La Tenanchi, 163
Lacateco, Calaraque, 77
Laguna country, 18, 24–25, chap. xvi n. 11. See Laguneros, tribe
Laguna de Mayrán, 25
Laguna de Viesca, 25, chap. ix n. 15
Laguna Grande de San Pedro, 25

INDEX 223

Laguneros, tribe, 24–25, 32, 110–116 *passim*, 134, 138–140, 146, 156, 157, chap. iv n. 31, chap. xvi n. 11; description of, 26–27, 33, 59, 76–77, 78–79, 81, 83; missions to, 25, 27–30, 74–86 *passim*, 109–117 *passim*, 164, 185
Lainez, Diego, 4
Larios, Diego, 80
Larios, Martín, 174, 187
Las Nazas, 139. *See* San Francisco, Mexico
Las Vegas, 71, 72
Las Vírgines, 55, 56, 58, 72, 101
Lautaro, Juan, 121
Llepo, chief, 81, 110
Lomas, José de, 66, 70, 90, 168–170, 187, chap. xviii n. 8
López, Andrés, chief, 149
López, Father Andrés, 133, 163, 166–168, 187, chap. xviii n. 8
López, Diego, 8
López, Francisco, 16–17
López, Manuel, 4
Los Ahoreados, river, 43. *See* Río Tepehuanes
Loyola, Ignatius de, 1, 3–4, 17, 28, 94, chap. xii n. 10
Lucas, Brother, 16
Lucas, Don, 173
Luis, Don, 182

Maicohueta, 160
Maiconera, Don Juan, 77
Maiconeras, tribe, 29
Mainara, 77
Mallen, Juan de, 140, 141, 142, 162, 181, 187
Mamazorras, tribe, chap. iv n. 31
Mangarito, chap. xvi n. 11
Mapimí, 114, 115, 138, 139, 173
Marcos, Don, 144
Martín, Gonzalo, 161, 174
Mayo, river. *See* Río Mayo
Mehigua, 159, 160, 161
Mejía, Pedro, 107
Méndez, Pedro, 49–50, 121
Mendoza, Gerónimo de, 14, 16
Mesquital, 156
Mexicanos, tribe, 34, 35, 81, 91, chap. v n. 9, chap. ix n. 26

Mexico, country, 1, 8; farm produce of, 20, 23, 78, 105, 163, 164; Jesuit missions in, 3–6 *passim*, 7–9, 187, 190; mines of, 9–11 *passim*, 14, 15, 20, 21, 32, 33, 34, 41, 45, 56, 57, 65, 80, 101, 163, 171; topography, 6, 14, 20, 22, 24–25, 41, 66–67, 87–88, 109, 126, 176; travel in, 10–11, 49–50, 54, 66–69 *passim*, 71, 109, 126, 149, 164, 182. *See also* Explorations; Viceroys of; Córdova, Diego Fernández de; Salinas, Count of; Franciscan missions; Durango; Indian tribes; Río del Fuerte, Río Mayo, Río Yaqui, Sinaloa mission, Sonora, Topia
Mexico City, 5, 8, 10, 13, 28
Michoacán, Bishop of, 4
Mihaykuet, 160
Miopacaos, tribe, 29
Mission relics, 3, 26, 82, 106, 148
Missions, historic importance, 164. *See* Franciscan and Jesuit missions
Mitote, 28–29, 114
Mixton War, 56
Montaño, Captain, 147–148, 150, 156
Montaño, Sebastián, 147
Moranta, Gerónimo de, 131, 148, 171, chap. xiv n. 12
Mosquera, Captain, 156
Mota y Escobar, Alonzo de la, 18, 60–62 *passim*, 64

Nájera, Gaspar de, 136
Naperes, tribe, 53
Nayarit, 154, 155, 183
Nazas, river. *See* Río de las Nazas
Neguales, tribe, chap. iv n. 31
Neumann, Joseph, 5, 192, chap. i n. 9
Neviras, tribe, 29
New Spain. *See* Mexico
Nieves, mines, 14
Nieves, river. *See* Río de las Nieves
Nombre de Dios, 16, 17, 32, 45
Nuestra Señora del Zape, 88. *See* Zape
Nueva Galicia, 15, 56, 155
Nueva Vizcaya, 12, 15–18 *passim*, 22, 26, 28, 31, 80, 86, 117, 156, 163, 168, 171, 191
Numanán, 10
Nuris, tribe, 137

224 INDEX

Oaxaca, 6, chap. xiv n. 12
Obregón, 15, 45, 48
Ocoronis, tribe, 121
Ocotitlán, 52
Ocotlán, 91, 92, 93, 137, chap. xvi n. 11
Olivas, Martín de, 129, 130
Oñate, Cristóbal de, 9, 14
Ópatas, tribe, 12, 99, 186
Orisame, 94
Orozco, Diego de, 127, 129–130, 145, 149, chap. xiv n. 12
Orozco y Berra, 24, chap. v n. 1, chap. ix n. 26
Ortigosa, Pedro de, 49
Osa, Francisco de la, 177
Otatitlán, 66, 67, 71, 73, 105, 178, 185
Oyarzabal, Sebastián de, 154

Pablo, chief, 144–145, 149
Pacho, Martín, 77
Pachos, nation, 84
Pangua, Diego Díaz de, 80–81, 114–115, 191
Papasquiaro, 42, 87, 88, 118–119, 120, 123–124, 146, 173, 174; mission in, 42, 91, 94, 120, 166, 168–169, 170, 173, 183; siege at, 127–131, 139, 149, 150, 153, 154, 169, 174
Paquimé, 16
Parral, 32, 171, 186
Parras, pueblo, 10. *See* Santa María de las Parras
Parras, Sierra de las, 109
Pátzcuaro, 6, 9, 11
Peláez, Martín, 18–19, chap. x n. 21
Peñol de Pospa, 60
Pérez, Martín, 11–12, 16, 18, 24, 111, chap. iii n. 15
Pérez de Ribas, Andrés. *See* Ribas, Andrés Pérez de
Piaxtla, province, 162, chap. xvi n. 11
Piaxtla, river. *See* Río Piaxtla
Pimas, tribe, 12, 32, 99
Plagues, 12, 23–24, 73, 106, 107, 110–117 *passim*, 138
Poagas, tribe, 29
Presidio, river. *See* Río del Presidio
Puebla, 6, 49
Purbandiro, 10

Quatro Ciénegas, 79
Quautlatas, 123–125 *passim*, 135, 163, 169
Quebos, pueblo, 178. *See* Quilitlán and Santiago (on Río Piaxtla)
Quebrada de Topia, 67
Quellar, Diego de, 187
Quequejal, Juan, 162
Quesada, Alonso de, 174
Quilitlán, 178, 180. *See* Quebos and Santiago (on Río Piaxtla)
Quiroga, Don Vasco de, 4

Rafael, cacique, 173
Ramírez, Gerónimo, Indian, 41
Ramírez, Father Gerónimo, 21–24 *passim*, 33–34, 36, 38–39, 46, 74, 87, chap. iv n. 7, chap. v n. 5; mission to Tepehuanes, 33–44 *passim*, 74, 87–89 *passim*, 118, 122, chap. v n. 5
Ramírez, Guillermo, 51, 54
Ramos, river. *See* Río de Ramos
Relics. *See* Mission relics
Remedios, river. *See* Río de los Remedios
Rendón, Pedro, 147
Ribas, Andrés Pérez de, 84, 107, 145, 153–154, 190; reference to writings of, 25, 27, 28, 37, 47, 53–54, 72, 73, 82, 85–86, 90, 107–108, 109, 111, 112, 123–124, 133, 144, 170–172 *passim*, 190–192 *passim*. *See also* notes to chaps. iii–xix
Río Aguanaval. *See* Río de las Nieves
Río Balvarte, 155
Río Culiacán, 68, 176
Río de las Nazas, 23–25 *passim*, 32, 75, 78–79, 88, 115, 120, chap. ix n. 26
Río de las Nieves, 22, 24, 25, 26, 75, chap. ix n. 15
Río de los Ahoreados, 43. *See* Río Tepehuanes
Río de los Remedios, 52, 66, 97
Río de Ramos, 39
Río de San Pedro, 20
Río de Santiago, 39, 41, 42, 87, 127, 150
Río de Zape, 88, 148
Río del Fuerte, 12, 16, 37, 106, 107, 108, 121, 123, 135, 145, 164
Río del Presidio, 155, 184
Río Mayo, 12, 106, 121, 145
Río Ocoroni, 135

INDEX 225

Río Petachán, 135
Río Piaxtla, 155, 157, 158, 176, 181, chap. xvii n. 11
Río San Lorenzo, 66, 97, 176
Río Sinaloa, 12, 45, 71, 107, 119, 122, 135–136, 137
Río Sonora, 12
Río Tepehuanes, 39, 42, 88, 126, 127
Río y Losa, Rodrigo del, 11, 16, 18–19, 20
Río Yaqui, 12, 37, 99, 108, 145, 164
Rivera, Rodrigo de, 59–60, 62, 63
Robles, Diego de, 27
Robles, Vito Alessio, 99, chap. vii nn. 18, 20, chap. ix n. 22, chap. xi n. 5
Rodríguez, Agustín, 16
Rosales, Gerónimo de, 152
Ruiz, Alonzo: 58, 100, 191; mission to Acaxées, 53, 54, 55, 58–59, 65–68, 87, 191
Ruiz, Juan, 57
Ruiz, Father Juan, 139

Saeta, Francisco Xavier, 119
St. Mary of the Grapevines, 25. *See* Santa María de las Parras
Salinas, Count of, 101
Salineros, tribe, 156, chap. iv n. 31
Salvatierra, Juan María, 9, 28
Saltillo, 10, 28, 80, 117, 154, 163
San Andrés, 10, 18, 32, 46–47, 49–55 *passim*, 56–59 *passim*, 64, 65, 66, 87, 92, 105, 107, 111, 118, 126, 140, 162, 179–181 *passim*, 185, 187, 191, chap. xviii n. 8
San Antonio, 174
San Bartolomé, pueblo, 49, 53, 184
San Bartolomé, valley, 187
San Benito, 14
San Bernabé, 14
San Clemente, Gerónimo de, 66, 191
San Clemente, Guillermo de, 187
San Felipe, 10
San Francisco, Jacinto de, 17
San Francisco, Mexico, 79, 139
San Francisco de Mezquital, 187
San Francisco Javier, pueblo, 177
San Gerónimo, 80, 115–116, chap. ix n. 17, chap. xii n. 1
San Gregorio, 55, 56, 66, 67, 176

San Hipólito, 10, 49, 55, 56, 57, 100, 102, 107, 140, 142, 160, 162, 177, 181, 187
San Ignacio, Coahuila, 78, 80, 155, chap. ix n. 17
San Ignacio, Durango, 120
San Ignacio, Sinaloa, 106, 136
San Ignacio del Zape, 149. *See* Zape
San Ildefonso de Tocorito, 71
San José, 69
San Juan Bautista de Carapoa, 16
San Juan del Río, 16, 21, 32, 146, 185, 187
San Lorenzo, river. *See* Río San Lorenzo
San Luis de la Paz, 11
San Luis Potosí, 10
San Martín, mines, 14–15
San Martín, pueblo, 53
San Miguel, Mexico, 53, 58, 106
San Nicolás, pueblo, 80
San Pablo, pueblo, 184
San Pablo, valley of. *See* Valle de San Pablo
San Pedro, Coahuila, 80, 168, chap. ix nn. 16, 17
San Pedro, Durango, 53
San Pedro, lagoon, 74, 78
San Pedro, pueblo (on Río Piaxtla), 184
San Pedro, river, 20
San Pedro y San Pablo, college, 6
San Pedro y San Pablo de Bacapa, 71
San Pedro y San Pablo del Valle de Topia, 45, chap. vi n. 5
San Sebastián, pueblo (on Río del Presidio), 153, 154, 155
San Sebastián de Huaimino, 180. *See* Huaimino
San Simón, 71, 170. *See* Yamorinoa
Sánchez, Juan, 6
Sánchez, Manuel, 119
Sánchez, Pedro, 4–5
Sanguesa, Juan de, 174
Santa Ana, pueblo, 52, 78, 80, chap. ix nn. 15, 17
Santa Bárbara, 10, 16, 32, 93, 96, chap. ix n. 17
Santa Catalina (now Tepehuanes), 43, 87–88, 118–119, 126, 146; attacks at, 126, 127–128, 143, 147–149 *passim*, 166, 173; mission of, 43–44, 118–119, 121, 122, 149, 169–170, 187, chap. v n. 42

Santa Cruz, mission, 118
Santa Cruz, pueblo, 92, 93
Santa Cruz del Valle, 46, 49
Santa María, Juan de, 16–17
Santa María, shrine, 171
Santa María, Sinaloa, 71. *See* Tecuciapa
Santa María de las Parras, 25–26, 28, 29–30, 74, 109; mission of, 25, 27–28, 75–83 *passim*, 87, 106, 109–110, 114, 126, 139, 175, 185–186, 187, 191, 192, chap. iv nn. 11, 20, chap. ix n. 17, chap. xvi n. 11, chap. xviii n. 8, *see also* Laguneros
Santa María de Otaés, 183–184, 185
Santarén, Hernando de, 49–50, 62–64, 92, 113, 137, 140, 149, 183, chap. xiv n. 12; mission to Acaxées, 16, 46–55 *passim*, 60–63 *passim*, 65–68 *passim*, 70–71, 73, 87, 90–91 *passim*, 118, 135; mission to Xiximes, 107, 131, 132, 142, 160–161
Santiago, Grotto of, 117
Santiago (in Laguna country), 80
Santiago (on Río Piaxtla), 178, 180, 183. *See* Quilitlán and Quebos
Santiago Papasquiaro, 42. *See* Papasquiaro
Sariana, 158, 159
Sauceda (now Canatlán), 34, 130, 146, 151, 153, 157; missions at, 35, 36, 39, 40, 41, 87, 118, 170, 187
Sedeño, Antonio, 5
Serra, Junípero, 9, 28
Serrano, Francisco, 184
Sicurabas, tribe, 71
Sierra de Carantapa, 54, 65, 66, 68, 70
Sierra de las Parras, 109
Sierra Madre, 12, 15, 20, 24, 32, 43, 44, 74, 97, 118, 176, 185, 186, 189
Sierras de las Cruces, 15
Sinaloa, mission, 11, 12, 16, 18, 24, 27, 50, 64, 111, 135–137 *passim*, 145, 153, 154, 179, 186
Sinaloa, province, 11, 176
Sinaloa, river. *See* Río Sinaloa
Sinaloa, town, 46, 49, 99
Sobaibos, tribe, 56, 58, 62, 66, 191
Solier, Guillermo de, 187
Sombrerete, 10, 14, 32
Sonora, mission, 16, 153
Sores, Jacques de. *See* Soria, Jacques de
Soria, Jacques de, 7, chap. ii n. 1

Spirits, 27, 36–39 *passim*, 48–49, 72–73, 89–91, 111, 113, 116–117, 120, 121–124 *passim*, 139, 174. *See also* Idols, Superstitions
Suaquis, tribe, 121, 164
Suárez, Captain. *See* Villalta, Bartolomé Suárez de
Suárez, Juan, 141
Superstitions, 27, 36, 46, 48–49 *passim*, 72–73, 81, 83–85, 89–91, 95, 105, 112–115, 118, 123–124, 140–141, 169–170

Tahues, tribe, 18, 176
Tamaral, Nicolás, 119
Tamarón, Pedro, 172
Tamazula, 66, 185, 191, chap. viii n. 18
Tanner, Mathias, 192, chap. xiv nn. 5, 12
Tapia, Gonzalo de, 8–11, 18, 45–47, 49–50, 75, chap. iii n. 15; at Sinaloa, 11, 16, 18–19 *passim*, 21, 24, 28, 45–46, 186; death of, 27, 46, 50, 119
Tarahumar, mission, 5
Tarahumara, 119
Tarahumares, tribe, 32, 91–93 *passim*, 95–96, 99, 118–119, 147–148, 173–174, chap. ix n. 41, chap. xvi n. 11; missions to, 5, 12, 93–96 *passim*, 118, 170, 184
Tarascans, tribe, 9, 20–21, 22, 34, 91; missions to, 9, 10, 34, 35, 46, 49
Taxicora, 37, 121
Tecuciapa (called Santa María), 66, 68, 70–71, 90, 135, 137, 142, 156, 169
Tenerape, 123–124, 132, 140, 146, 149–150, 166, 168–169
Tepehuanes, river. *See* Río Tepehuanes
Tepehuanes, town (formerly Santa Catalina), 15, 43, 126. *See* Santa Catalina
Tepehuanes, tribe, 19, 32–33, 90, 92–93, 99, 118, 135, 137, 153–154, 167–170 *passim*, 183; attempt to corrupt other tribes, 124, 134, 135–139, 141–142, 179–180, 183, 184; description of, 32–35, 42–43, 83–84, 89–92 *passim*, 118–119, 122; missions to, 12, 19, 33–44 *passim*, 74, 87–96, 99, 118–123, 163, 166–175 *passim*, 176, 183, 185–186, 191; revolt of, 12, 33, 43, 49, 90, 93–94, 118–125, 126–134, 135–142, 143–152, 153–165, 173, 183, 185, 191

INDEX

Tepotzotlán, 6, 126
Tepuxtla, 180
Tesia, 106
Teuchius, 161
Texame, 157, 158, 162
Tlaxcaltecos, tribe, 20, 28, 81, chap. ix n. 26, chap. xvi n. 22
Tobosos, tribe, 156, 173
Toledano, Bartolomé, 187
Tomás, Juan, 52
Topia, 10, 15–18 *passim*, 20, 32, 43, 45–47, 49–51, 54, 55, 56–58 *passim*, 60–63 *passim*, 65–67 *passim*, 70, 87, 105, 111, 118, 126, 140, 141, 162, 183, 185, 187, 191, chap. iii n. 15, chap. xviii n. 8
Topia, San Pedro y San Pablo del Valle de, 67, chap. vi n. 5
Topia, Valle de. *See* Valle de Topia
Torillo, Juan, 173
Torres, Pedro de, 136
Tovar, Hernando de, 126–128 *passim*, 133, 143, 149, chap. xiv n. 12
Tovoropa, 46
Tunal, 123, 143–144 *passim*, 148, 153, 173, 180
Tupac Amarú, 56
Tutino, Andrés, 54, 65, 66, 132, 140–142
Tutuqui, Luis, 136

Ubamari, 92
Urdiñola, Francisco, 9, 63–64, 66, 80, 94, 99–104, 122, 124, 154
Ure, pueblo, 50
Ures, tribe, 134
Uria, Alfonso de, 156

Vadiravato, 72
Váez, Francisco, 54, 74–75
Valenzuela, Hernandilla de, 155, 158
Valle, Alonso del. *See* Del Valle, Alonso
Valle, Juan del. *See* Del Valle, Juan
Valle de Guadiana, 15, 16, 20
Valle de Parras, 25
Valle de San Bartolomé, 187
Valle de San Pablo, 93–96 *passim*, 170, chap. xvi n. 11
Valle de Topia, 15, 45–47 *passim*, 50
Valle del Águila, 92

Vasapayes, tribe, 29
Velasco, Pedro de, 122, 135, 136
Vera, Francisco de, 101, 103
Vera Cruz, 5, 6, 9
Vernon, Miguel, 187
Vesga, Mateo de, 173, 191, chap. xviii n. 20
Villalta, Bartolomé Suárez de, 100, 102, 140–142 *passim*, 154, 156, 163, 168, 177, 180–182
Villalta, Cristóbal de, 28
Villaseca, Alonso de, 4
Vinagre y Cuscusillo, Juan, 161
Vírgines, Las, 55, 56, 58, 72, 101
Vitelleschi, Mutius, 7, chap. xvi n. 23

Wizards. *See* Hechiceros

Xavier, Francis, 1, 17, 106
Ximenes, Diego, 184
Ximenes, Pedro, 180–181
Xiximes, tribe, 32, 66, 97–104, 124, 134, 153–154, 156–157 *passim*, 158, 160, 162, 176–177, 182, chap. xvi n. 11; missions to, 12, 46–47, 73, 94, 103–108, 118, 131, 140, 176–177, 183–184, 185; rebellion of, 94, 100–102, 141–142, 156–157, 185
Xoxotilma, 54, 101, 103

Yamoriba, 156, 160, 162, 181, 185
Yamorinoa, 71
Yaqui, river. *See* Río Yaqui
Yaquis, tribe, 37, 121, 134, 137, chap. ix n. 41; missions to, 12, 37, 108, 121–122, 153, 164
Yerepuato, 10
Yotoca, Pedro, 136

Zacatecas, 6, 11, 14, 15, 18, 21–22, 26, 32, 59, 74, 75, 145
Zacatecos, tribe, 21–25, 32, 74, 80
Zapata, Antón Martín, 28
Zape, pueblo, 88–89, 91, 92, 94, 118, 123, 125, 126, 131–132, 146, 147, 154, 166, 170–171, 173–175 *passim*
Zape, river. *See* Río de Zape
Zapiuris, 159–162 *passim*

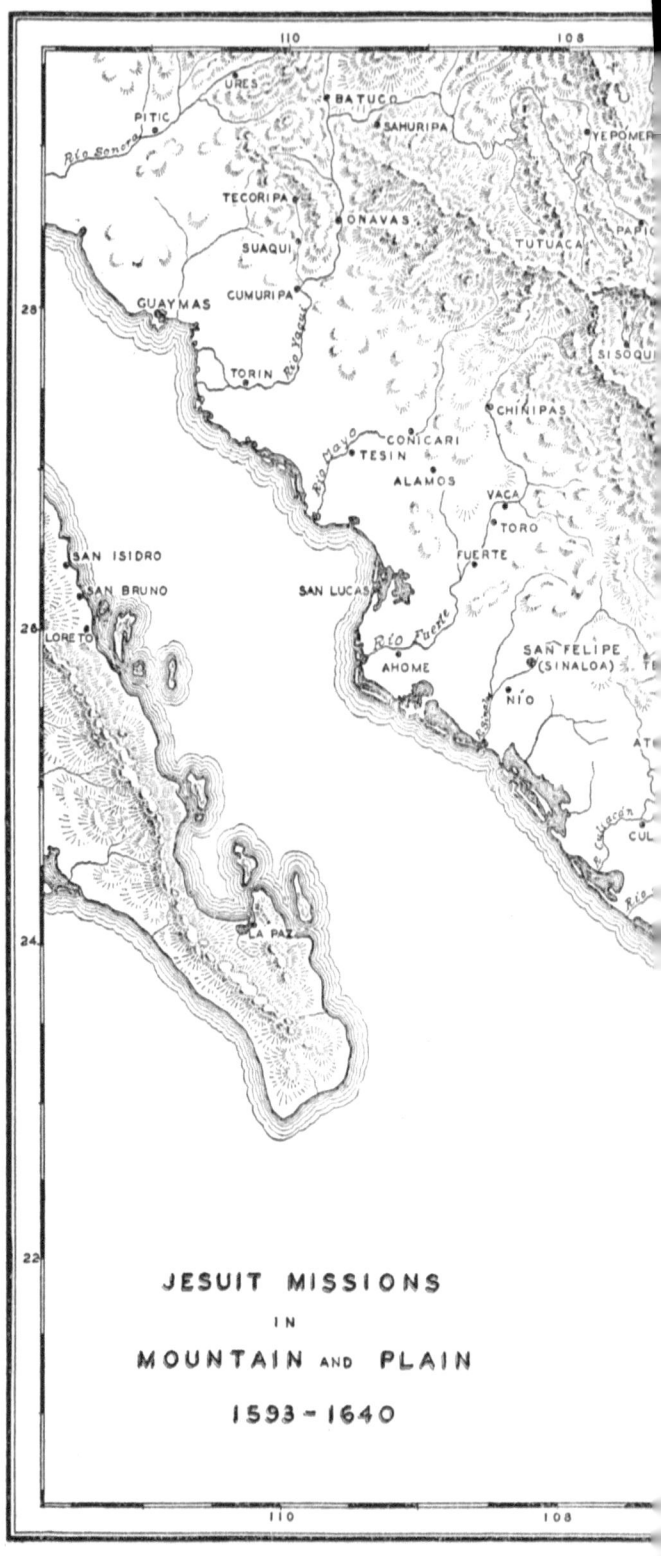

Map to accompany *Pioneer Jesuits in Northern Mexico*, by Peter Masten

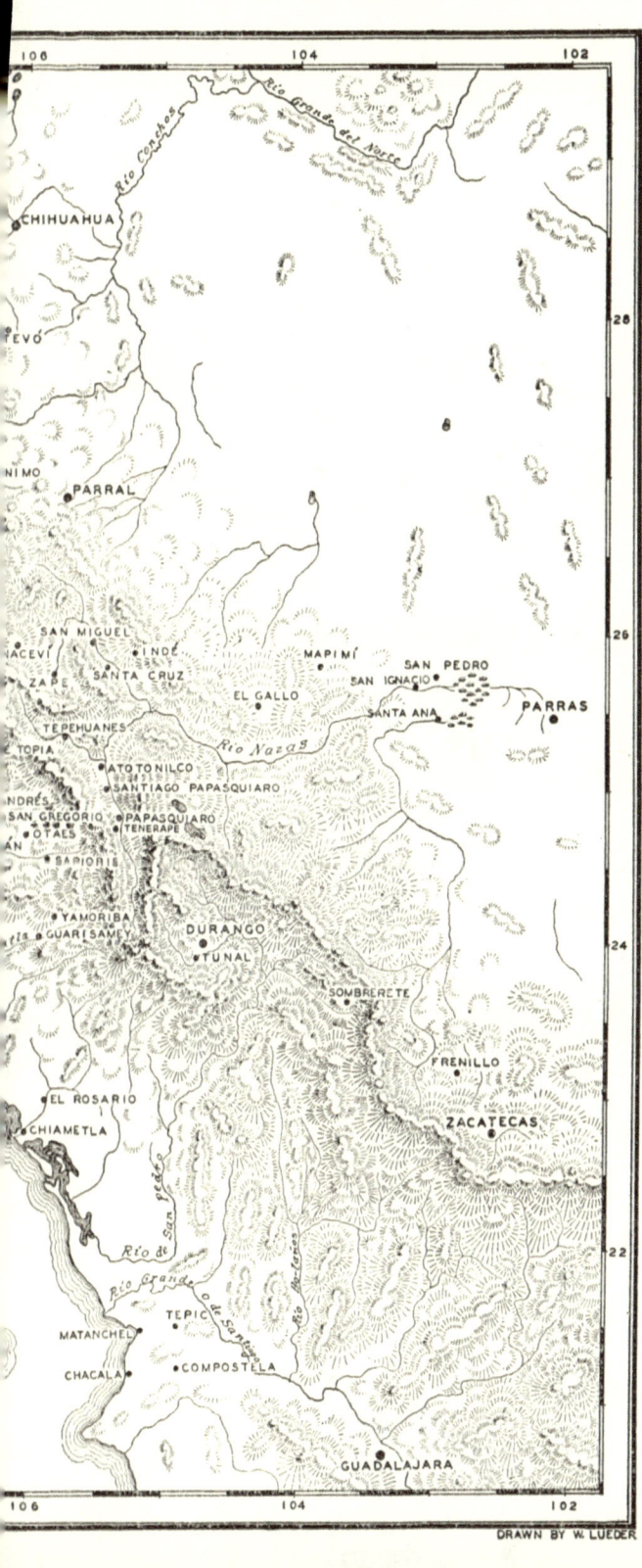

www.ingramcontent.com/pod-product-compliance
Lightning Source LLC
Chambersburg PA
CBHW021702230426
43668CB00008B/704